written by ALES **KOT**

drawn by MORGAN **JESKE**

colored by SLOANE **LEONG**

lettered by ED **BRISSON**

With a special thank you to

Jordie **Bellaire**

for coloring the covers

image

IMAGE COMICS, INC.
Robert Kirkman - chief operating officer
Erik Larsen - chief financial officer
Todd McFarlane - president
Marc Silvestri - chief executive officer
Jim Valentino - vice-president

Eric Stephenson - publisher
Ron Richards - director of business development
Jennifer de Guzman - pr & marketing director
Branwyn Bigglestone - accounts manager
Emily Miller - accounting assistant
Jamie Parreno - marketing assistant
Jenna Savage - administrative assistant
Kevin Yuen - digital rights coordinator
Jonathan Chan - production manager
Drew Gill - art director
Tyler Shainline - print manager
Monica Garcia - production artist
Vincent Kukua - production artist
Jana Cook - production artist
www.imagecomics.com

CHANGE TP
ISBN: 978-1-160706-682-8
First Printing

THE GREAT OLD TRUTH IS RISING

People ask me all the time, "Why on earth do you don that thick, itchy, black hooded robe on a perfectly good Saturday night and hang out beachside chanting at the inky, undulating sea with all those totally weird cult dudes who are unwaveringly devoted to the catalyzing of the Great Old One?"

Hey... fair question.

My reply goes something like this, "How can you not be in this cult?"

Now that may seem flippant. And let's not forget, I am a murdering cultist asshole mindlessly in service to something greater than myself, so being a flippant dick is the least of my sins. But my response actually goes deeper than you might think.

To understand those of us who worship the "vast shape with prime real-estate on the sunken city of R'lyeh", as "he" is known in the o.g. underground scene (dig?), you have to first know that over the years the master to which we pledge servitude has gotten a bit of a bum rap. Up until now it's all been "loathsome" this and "corpse city" that and "man's insignificance before the expansive cosmic horror" blah dee blah dee blah.

But that's getting it all wrong, see.

Put simply, The Great Old One isn't a "One" at all... it's just a truth writ large. THE TRUTH, really. The Great Old Truth of all things. The truth that, for better or for worse, all there is in any moment... in every moment, from the micro to the macro, is change.

Now my fellow cult members Ales Kot, Morgan Jeske, Sloane Leong and Ed Brisson have created this lovely manifesto that you hold in your brave hands. They've come to correct the record. It is not a horrible monster, they say, but instead, The Great Old Truth that sleeps at the bottom of the quantum ocean, down at the very substrate of all things, holding the whole universe forever in its dreaming sway.

Their book is ambitious. It seeks to illustrate, or at the very least trace around the infinite, eternal edges of the obscure idea of change. Because change is all there is. Its lessons are the only ones that keep on coming long after you've already learned them. The idea of change is, in fact, so boundless, so central to the human – and inhuman and non-human – experience, that Kot and crew have employed the aesthetics of maximalism here, in the hopes of catching as complete a glimpse of The Great Old Truth as possible. They cast a wide net of ideas, events and characters (all portrayed in brilliant page layouts perfectly splashed with a palette of muted pastels). The book is packed with poetry, pulp references, personal reflections, cultural allusions, and a deep commitment to the creators' own internal experiences. It's an incantation. Our creators are standing on the shore in their itchy, atavistic robes alongside us all. Calling out to the mystery that is constantly ending and beginning everything everywhere.

So really, you don't have to join our cult... because you're already in it. Change is coming. It's inevitable. Everything else is a lie. You can fight it, but The Great Old Truth always wins and fighting will only make it hurt more in the end. Better to embrace impermanence than to struggle against the way of things.

I know this is all a little scary, this rising ancient creature of a truth. Of course it is. But it's also beautiful. Because when things are at their darkest, when you think that you're losing everything that was important to you, when all you loved and know of love is transmuting into something you have no real understanding of and you find yourself burning, roaring, in the crucible of change, Kot and crew say, "do not fear"...

Instead expect rebirth.

- Joshua Dysart, Venice Beach, Ca. 5/13

Post Script: The first thing Ales does when he walks through my door, delivering physical copies of his comic for me to consider, is ask for a Sharpie. I dig one up. Comic creators are rarely far from a new, finely-tipped permanent marker. He opens the last page of the last issue and proceeds to precisely redact the final lines in the back of the book. "We changed this bit here for the trade," he says. Then he writes, with a natural letterer's touch, the new line by hand. Before I've even had a chance to read it in its original form (is there ever an original form?) he has altered the artifact right in front of me. Do I have to say it? I can't resist. He has changed it. "Huh," he says, tilting at the thin, stacked black lines he's made, "looks like one of the trigrams of the I Ching." Outside, from the depths of the ocean, The Great Old Truth rises again and again and again and again and again... always and forever.

Joshua Dysart has been writing comic books to one degree of success or another since 1996. He has worked with giants in the industry on such titles as Swamp Thing, Conan the Barbarian, Hellboy and others. In 2007 he spent time in Northern Uganda interviewing child soldiers and war-affected civilians for Vertigo's multiple Eisner nominated series, "The Unknown Soldier". He currently writes "Harbinger" for Valiant.

Take me outta context.
Take me outta here.
Put the windows down.
Swing it down.
Really tune it out.

Holy Ghost!
'Do It Again'

If the moon smiled, she would
resemble you. You leave the
same impression of something
beautiful, but annihilating.

Sylvia Plath
'The Rival'

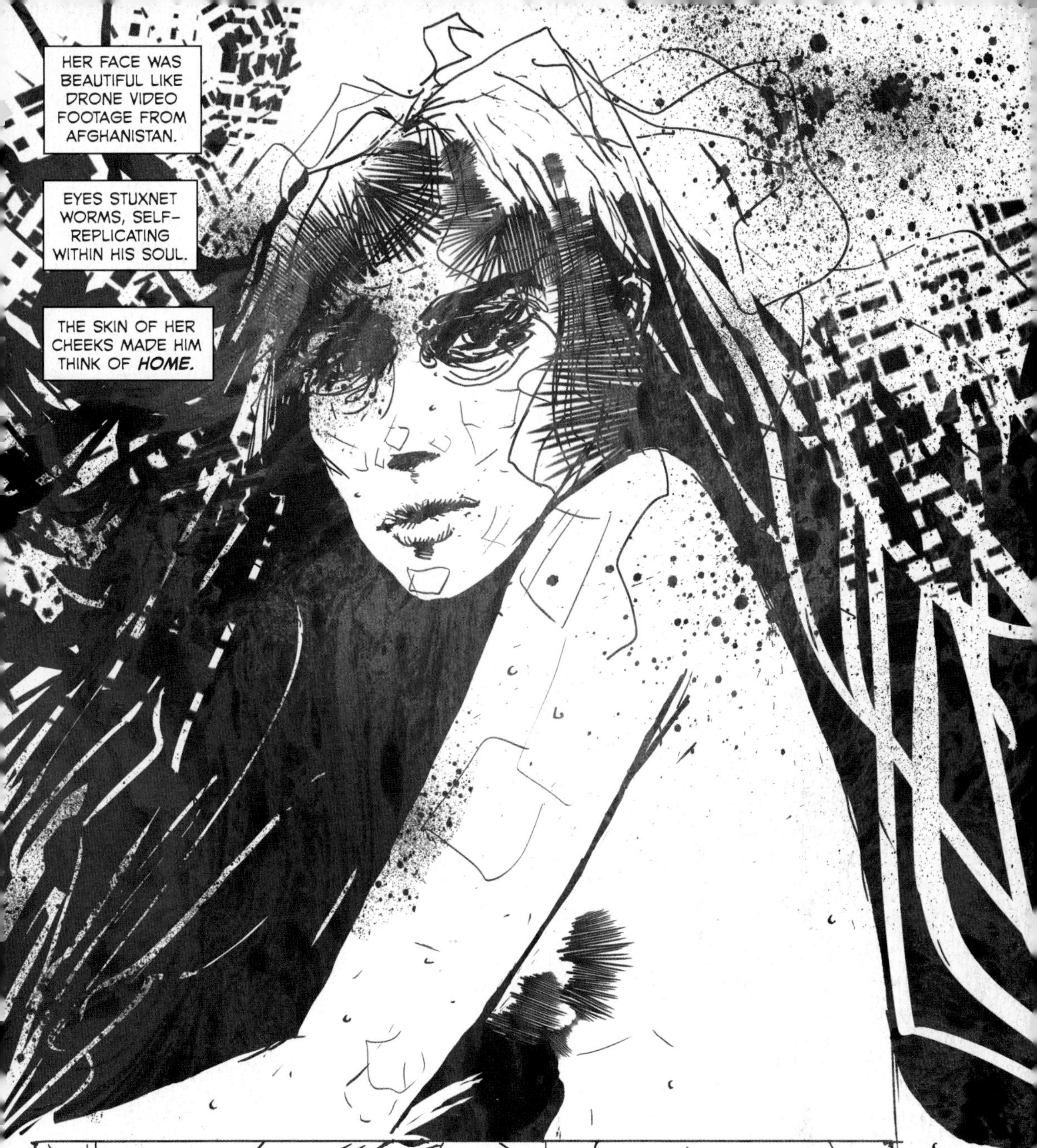
HER FACE WAS BEAUTIFUL LIKE DRONE VIDEO FOOTAGE FROM AFGHANISTAN.
EYES STUXNET WORMS, SELF-REPLICATING WITHIN HIS SOUL.
THE SKIN OF HER CHEEKS MADE HIM THINK OF *HOME.*

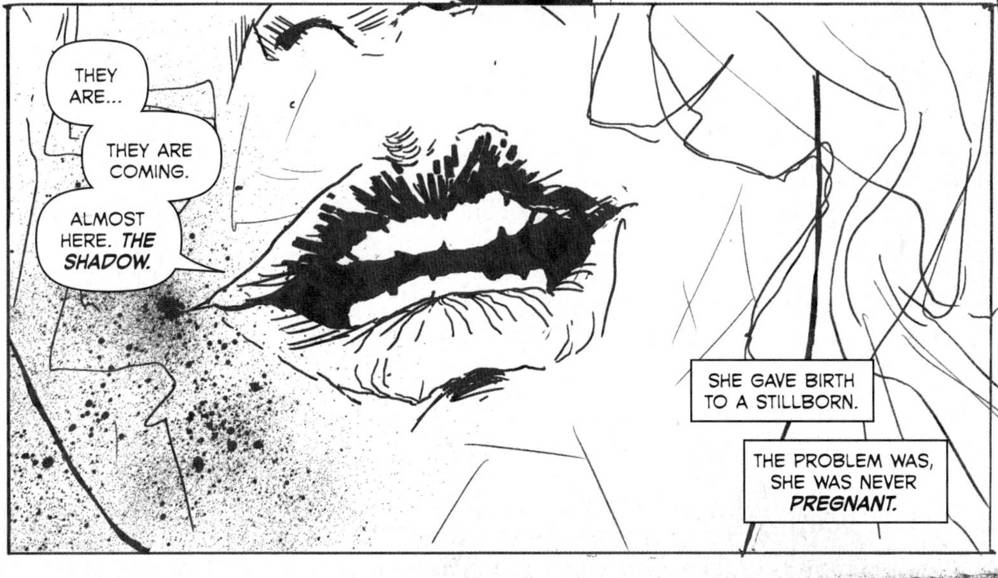
THEY ARE...
THEY ARE COMING.
ALMOST HERE. *THE SHADOW.*
SHE GAVE BIRTH TO A STILLBORN.
THE PROBLEM WAS, SHE WAS NEVER *PREGNANT.*

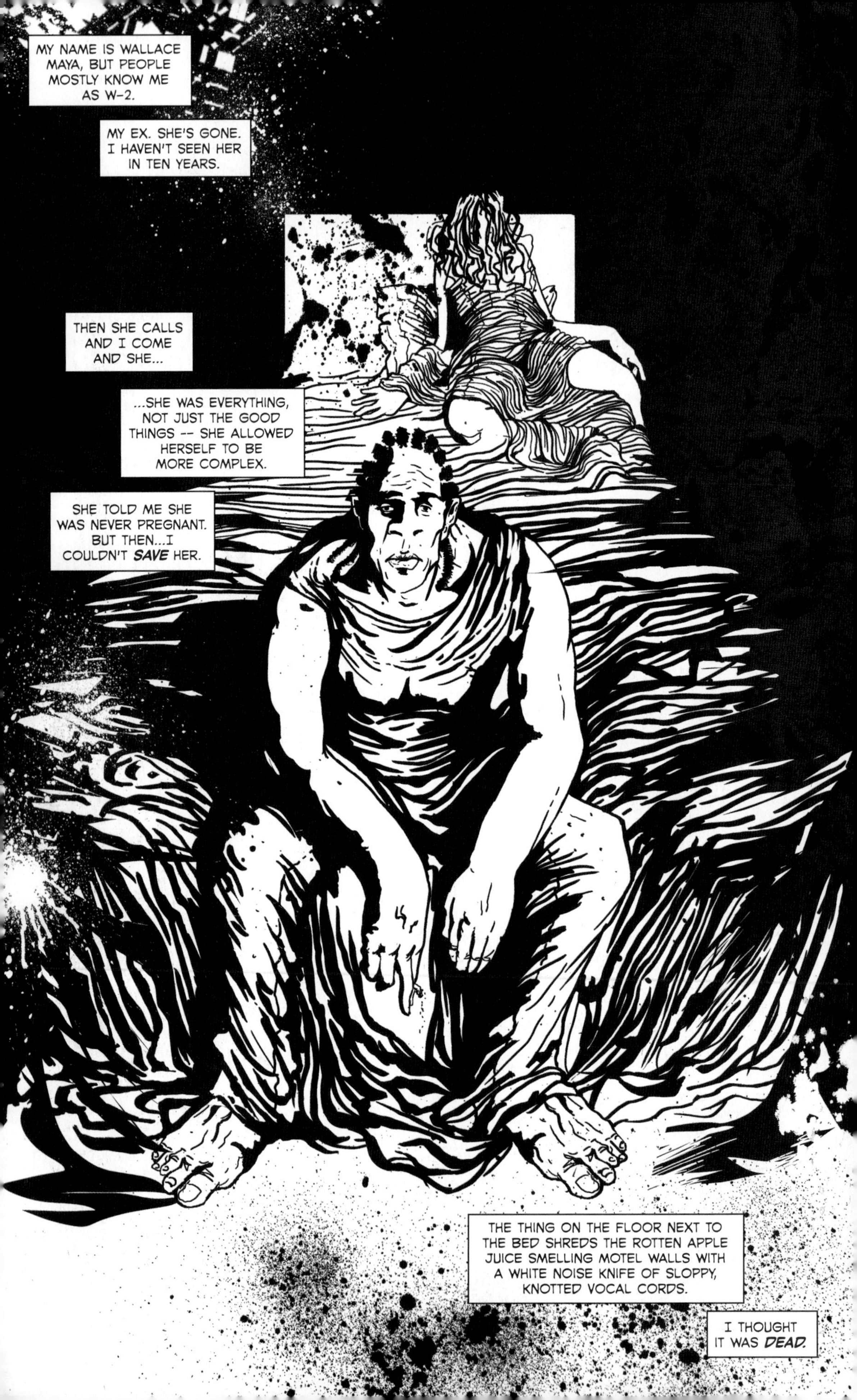
MY NAME IS WALLACE MAYA, BUT PEOPLE MOSTLY KNOW ME AS W-2.
MY EX. SHE'S GONE. I HAVEN'T SEEN HER IN TEN YEARS.
THEN SHE CALLS AND I COME AND SHE...
...SHE WAS EVERYTHING, NOT JUST THE GOOD THINGS -- SHE ALLOWED HERSELF TO BE MORE COMPLEX.
SHE TOLD ME SHE WAS NEVER PREGNANT. BUT THEN...I COULDN'T *SAVE* HER.
THE THING ON THE FLOOR NEXT TO THE BED SHREDS THE ROTTEN APPLE JUICE SMELLING MOTEL WALLS WITH A WHITE NOISE KNIFE OF SLOPPY, KNOTTED VOCAL CORDS.
I THOUGHT IT WAS *DEAD.*

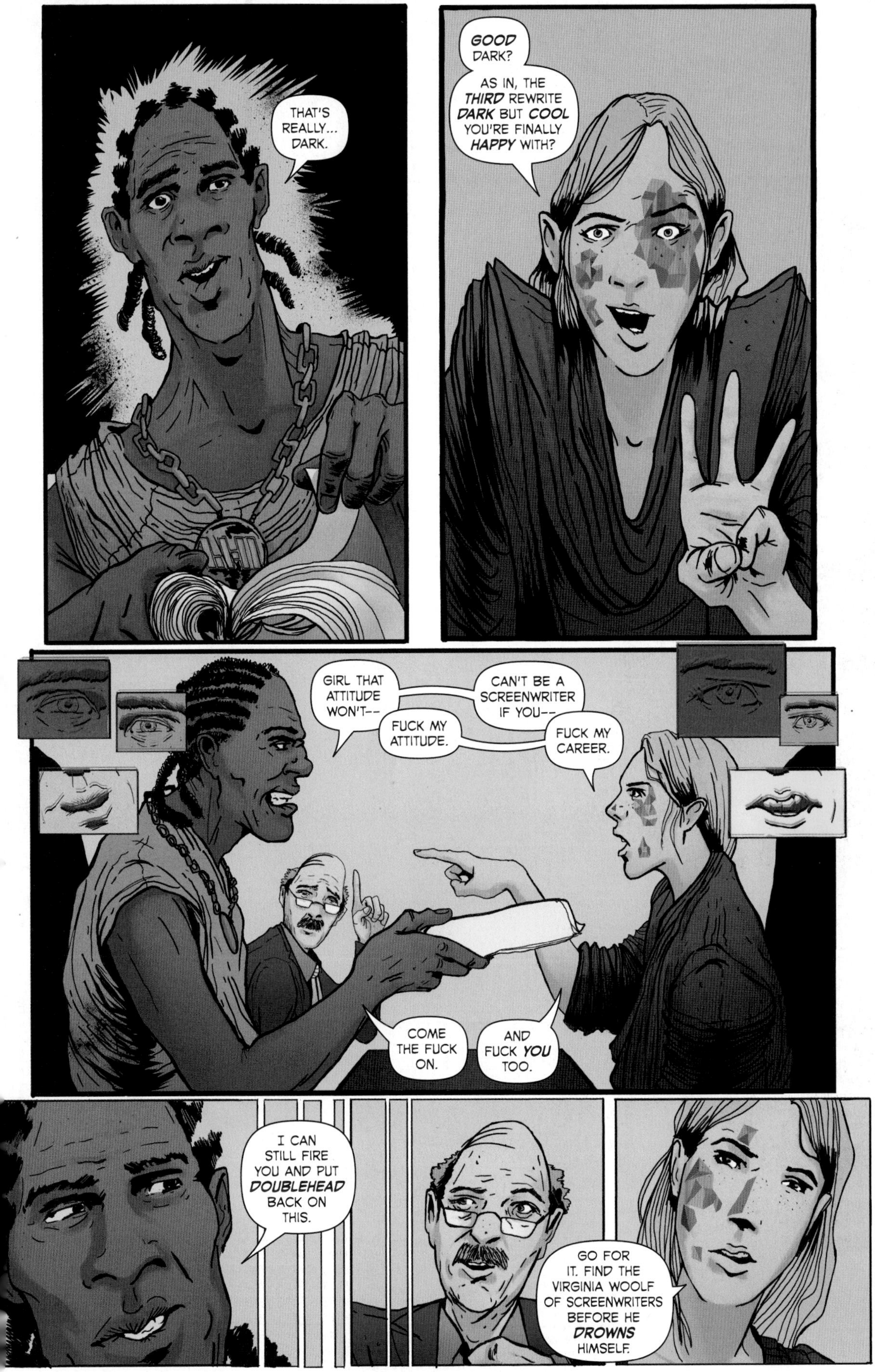
THAT'S REALLY... DARK.
GOOD DARK?
AS IN, THE THIRD REWRITE DARK BUT COOL YOU'RE FINALLY HAPPY WITH?
GIRL THAT ATTITUDE WON'T--
CAN'T BE A SCREENWRITER IF YOU--
FUCK MY ATTITUDE.
FUCK MY CAREER.
COME THE FUCK ON.
AND FUCK YOU TOO.
I CAN STILL FIRE YOU AND PUT DOUBLEHEAD BACK ON THIS.
GO FOR IT. FIND THE VIRGINIA WOOLF OF SCREENWRITERS BEFORE HE DROWNS HIMSELF.

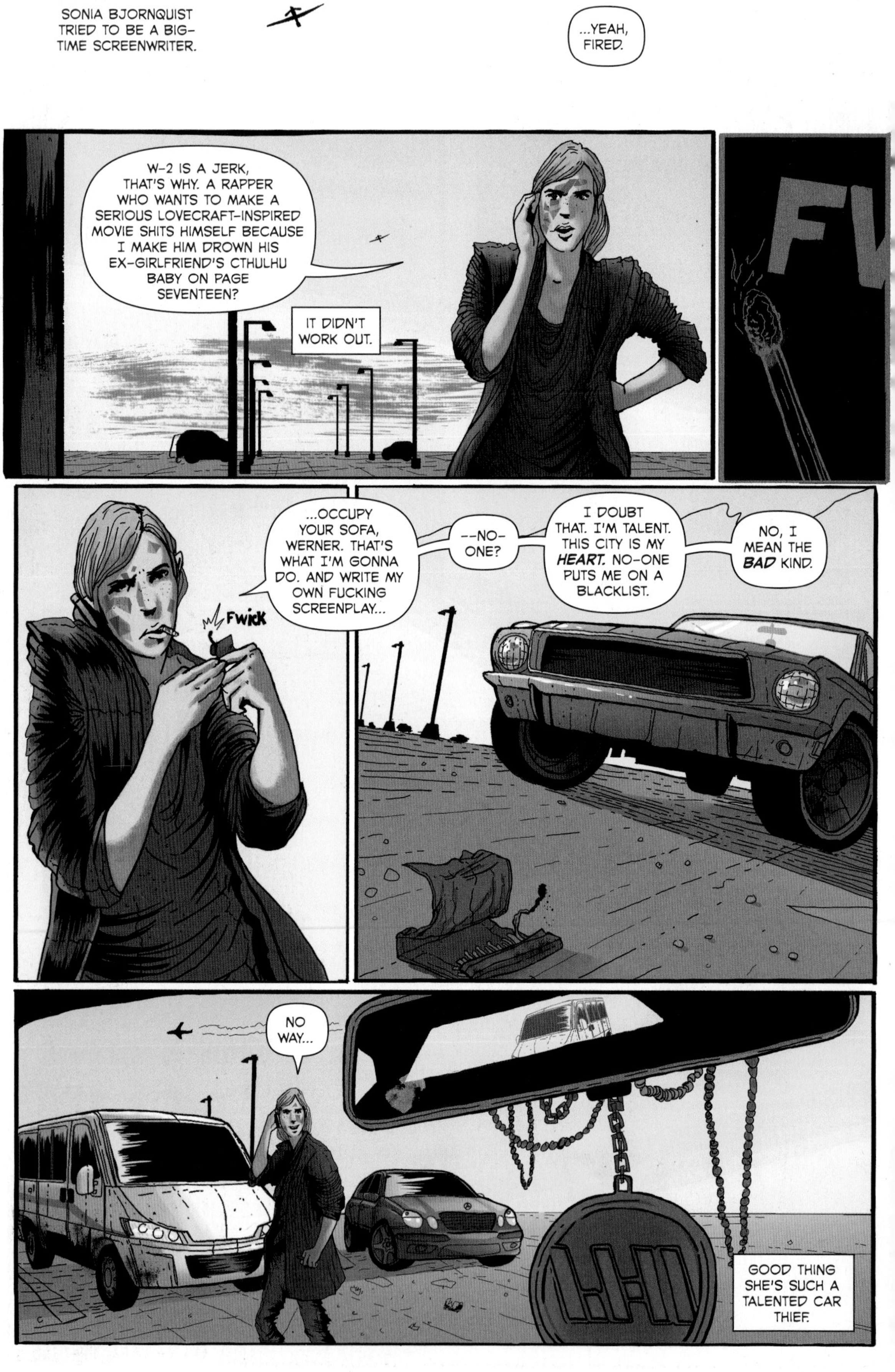
SONIA BJORNQUIST TRIED TO BE A BIG-TIME SCREENWRITER.
...YEAH, FIRED.
W-2 IS A JERK, THAT'S WHY. A RAPPER WHO WANTS TO MAKE A SERIOUS LOVECRAFT-INSPIRED MOVIE SHITS HIMSELF BECAUSE I MAKE HIM DROWN HIS EX-GIRLFRIEND'S CTHULHU BABY ON PAGE SEVENTEEN?
IT DIDN'T WORK OUT.
FWICK
...OCCUPY YOUR SOFA, WERNER. THAT'S WHAT I'M GONNA DO. AND WRITE MY OWN FUCKING SCREENPLAY...
--NO-ONE?
I DOUBT THAT. I'M TALENT. THIS CITY IS MY HEART. NO-ONE PUTS ME ON A BLACKLIST.
NO, I MEAN THE BAD KIND.
NO WAY...
GOOD THING SHE'S SUCH A TALENTED CAR THIEF.

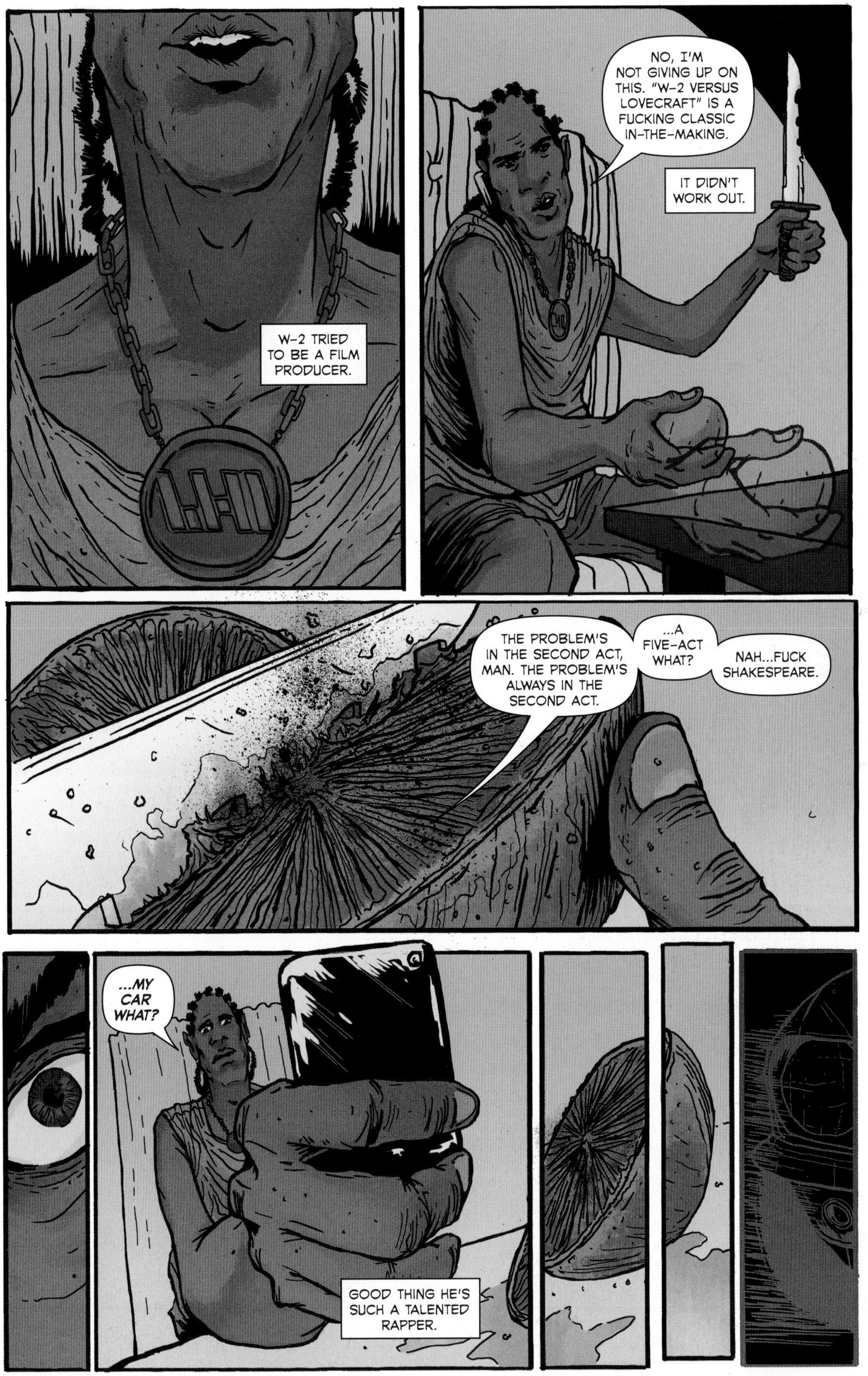
W–2 TRIED TO BE A FILM PRODUCER.
NO, I'M NOT GIVING UP ON THIS. "W–2 VERSUS LOVECRAFT" IS A FUCKING CLASSIC IN–THE–MAKING.
IT DIDN'T WORK OUT.
THE PROBLEM'S IN THE SECOND ACT, MAN. THE PROBLEM'S ALWAYS IN THE SECOND ACT.
...A FIVE–ACT WHAT?
NAH...FUCK SHAKESPEARE.
...MY CAR WHAT?
GOOD THING HE'S SUCH A TALENTED RAPPER.

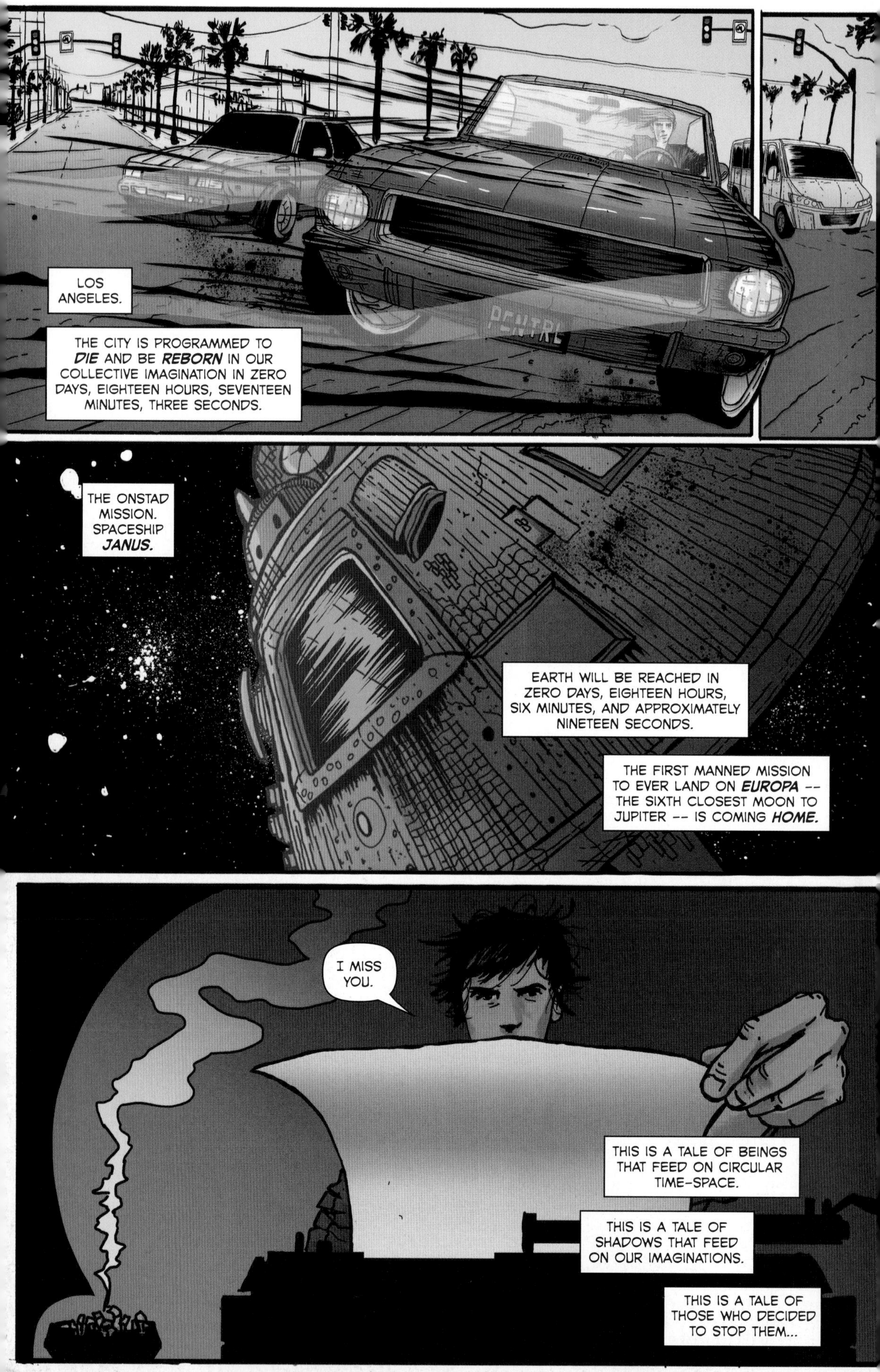
LOS ANGELES.
THE CITY IS PROGRAMMED TO DIE AND BE REBORN IN OUR COLLECTIVE IMAGINATION IN ZERO DAYS, EIGHTEEN HOURS, SEVENTEEN MINUTES, THREE SECONDS.
THE ONSTAD MISSION. SPACESHIP JANUS.
EARTH WILL BE REACHED IN ZERO DAYS, EIGHTEEN HOURS, SIX MINUTES, AND APPROXIMATELY NINETEEN SECONDS.
THE FIRST MANNED MISSION TO EVER LAND ON EUROPA -- THE SIXTH CLOSEST MOON TO JUPITER -- IS COMING HOME.
I MISS YOU.
THIS IS A TALE OF BEINGS THAT FEED ON CIRCULAR TIME-SPACE.
THIS IS A TALE OF SHADOWS THAT FEED ON OUR IMAGINATIONS.
THIS IS A TALE OF THOSE WHO DECIDED TO STOP THEM...

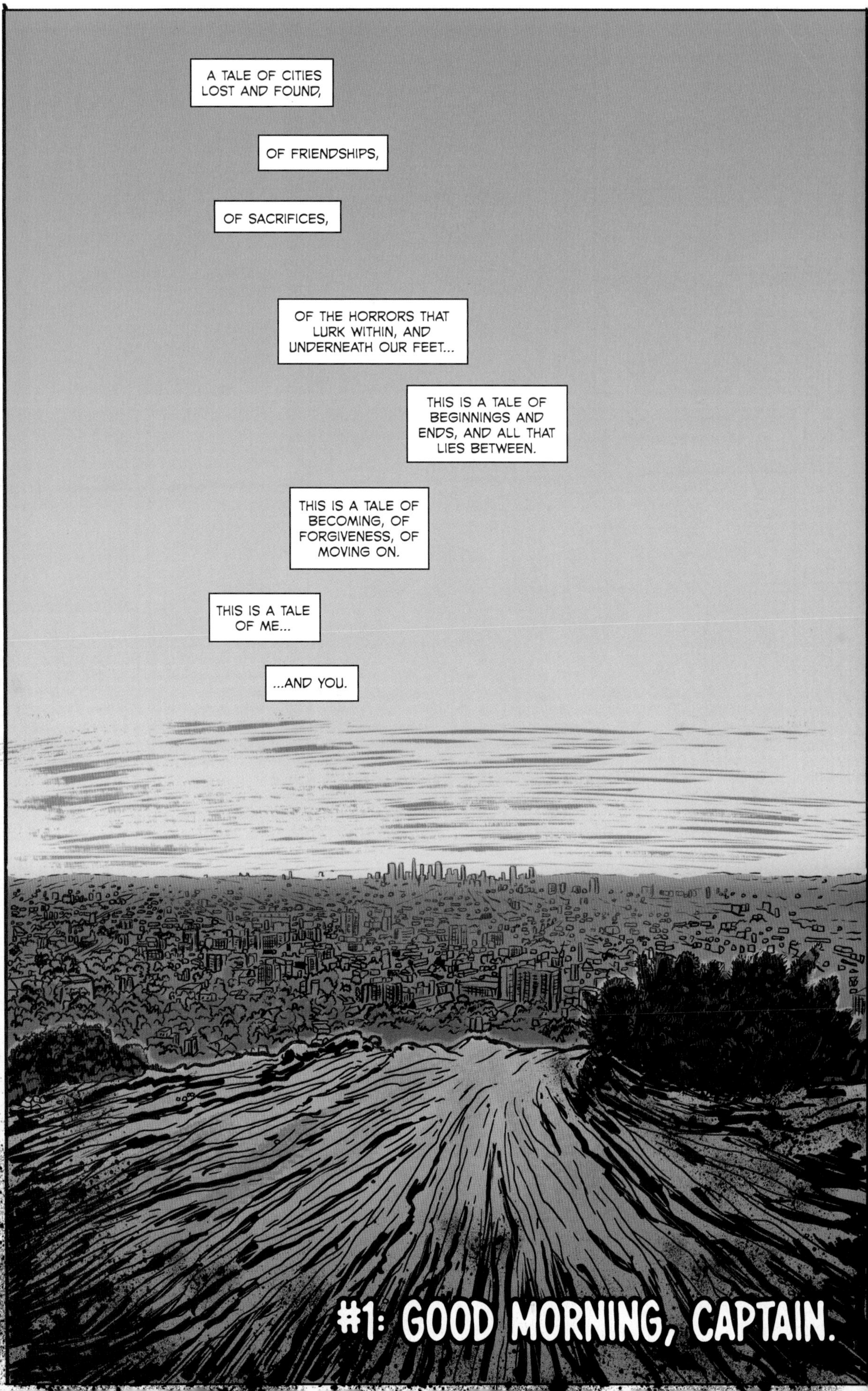
A TALE OF CITIES LOST AND FOUND,
OF FRIENDSHIPS,
OF SACRIFICES,
OF THE HORRORS THAT LURK WITHIN, AND UNDERNEATH OUR FEET...
THIS IS A TALE OF BEGINNINGS AND ENDS, AND ALL THAT LIES BETWEEN.
THIS IS A TALE OF BECOMING, OF FORGIVENESS, OF MOVING ON.
THIS IS A TALE OF ME...
...AND YOU.
#1: GOOD MORNING, CAPTAIN.

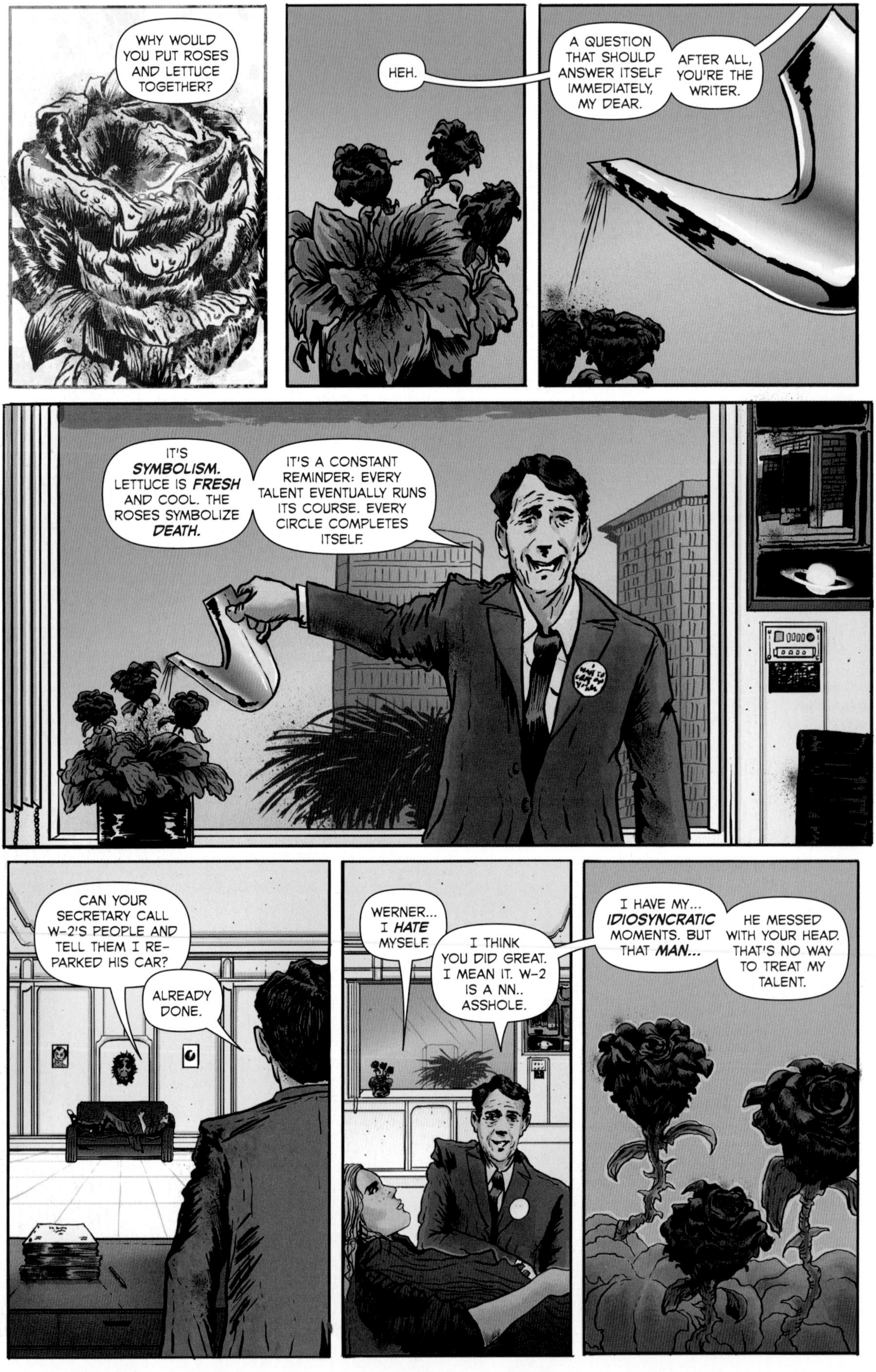
WHY WOULD YOU PUT ROSES AND LETTUCE TOGETHER?
HEH.
A QUESTION THAT SHOULD ANSWER ITSELF IMMEDIATELY, MY DEAR.
AFTER ALL, YOU'RE THE WRITER.
IT'S **SYMBOLISM.** LETTUCE IS **FRESH** AND COOL. THE ROSES SYMBOLIZE **DEATH.**
IT'S A CONSTANT REMINDER: EVERY TALENT EVENTUALLY RUNS ITS COURSE. EVERY CIRCLE COMPLETES ITSELF.
CAN YOUR SECRETARY CALL W-2'S PEOPLE AND TELL THEM I RE-PARKED HIS CAR?
ALREADY DONE.
WERNER... I **HATE** MYSELF.
I THINK YOU DID GREAT. I MEAN IT. W-2 IS A NN.. ASSHOLE.
I HAVE MY... **IDIOSYNCRATIC** MOMENTS. BUT THAT **MAN...**
HE MESSED WITH YOUR HEAD. THAT'S NO WAY TO TREAT MY TALENT.

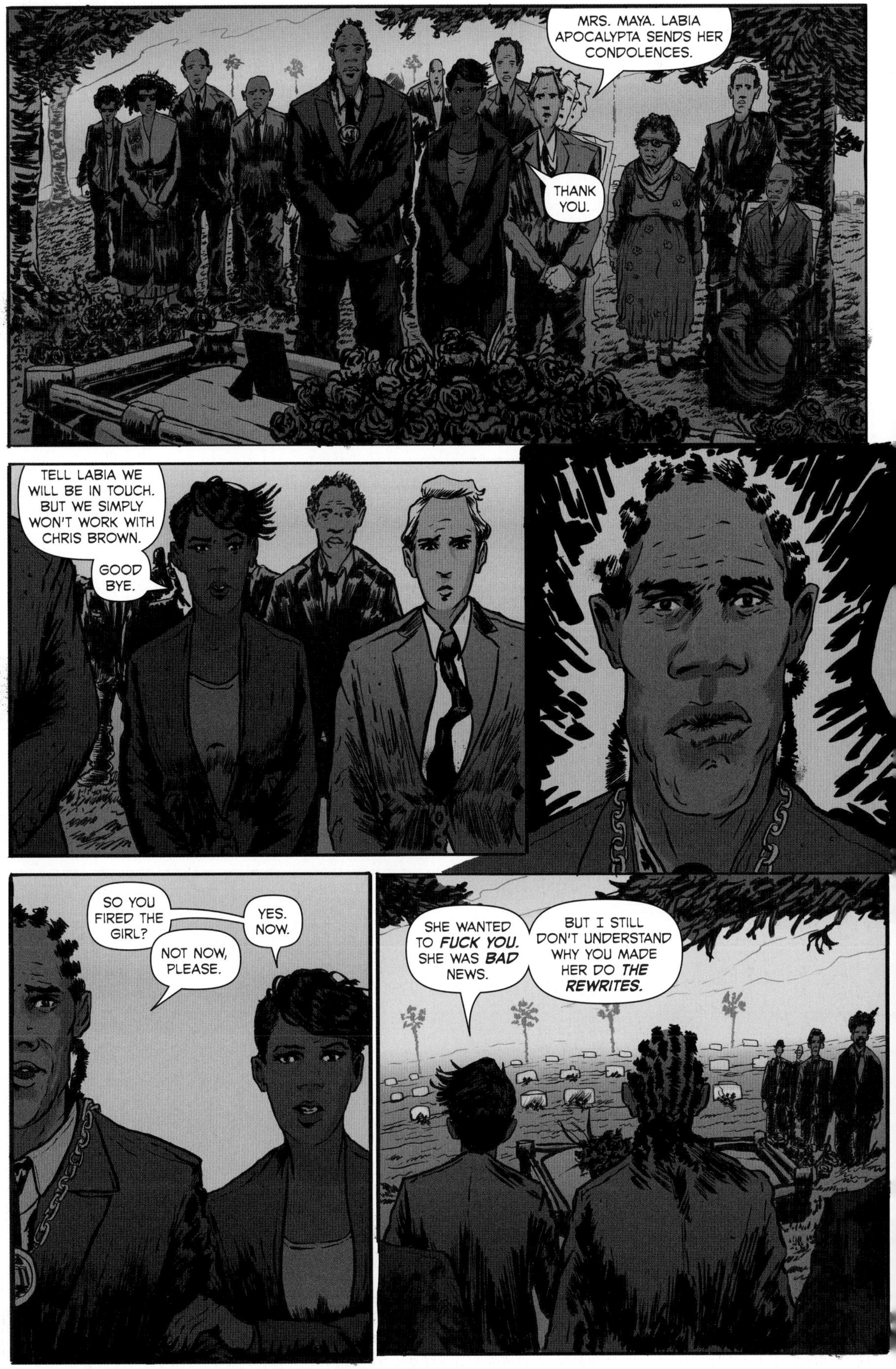
MRS. MAYA. LABIA APOCALYPTA SENDS HER CONDOLENCES.
THANK YOU.
TELL LABIA WE WILL BE IN TOUCH. BUT WE SIMPLY WON'T WORK WITH CHRIS BROWN.
GOOD BYE.
SO YOU FIRED THE GIRL?
YES. NOW.
NOT NOW, PLEASE.
SHE WANTED TO FUCK YOU. SHE WAS BAD NEWS.
BUT I STILL DON'T UNDERSTAND WHY YOU MADE HER DO THE REWRITES.

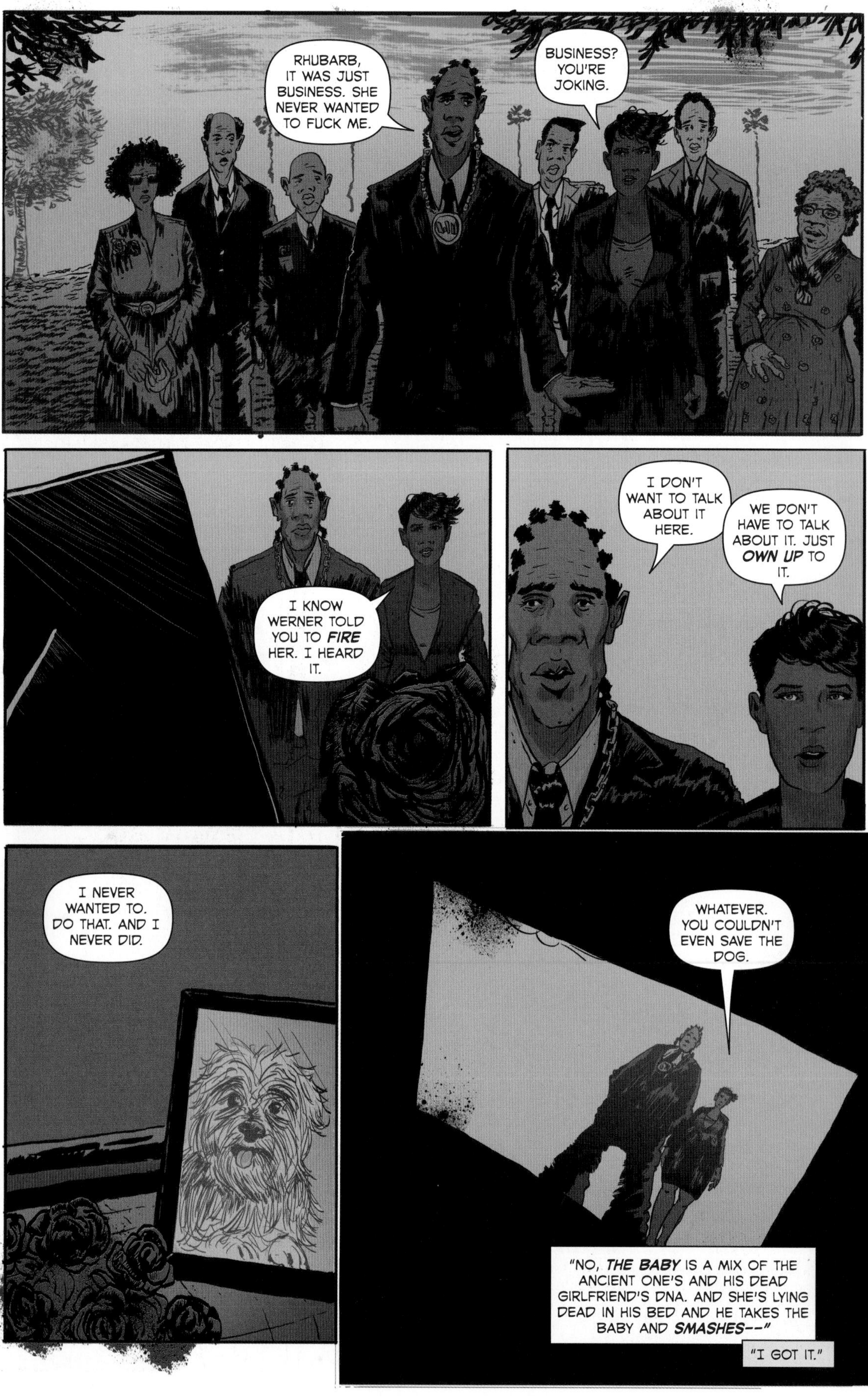
RHUBARB, IT WAS JUST BUSINESS. SHE NEVER WANTED TO FUCK ME.
BUSINESS? YOU'RE JOKING.
I KNOW WERNER TOLD YOU TO FIRE HER. I HEARD IT.
I DON'T WANT TO TALK ABOUT IT HERE.
WE DON'T HAVE TO TALK ABOUT IT. JUST OWN UP TO IT.
I NEVER WANTED TO. DO THAT. AND I NEVER DID.
WHATEVER. YOU COULDN'T EVEN SAVE THE DOG.
"NO, THE BABY IS A MIX OF THE ANCIENT ONE'S AND HIS DEAD GIRLFRIEND'S DNA. AND SHE'S LYING DEAD IN HIS BED AND HE TAKES THE BABY AND SMASHES--"
"I GOT IT."

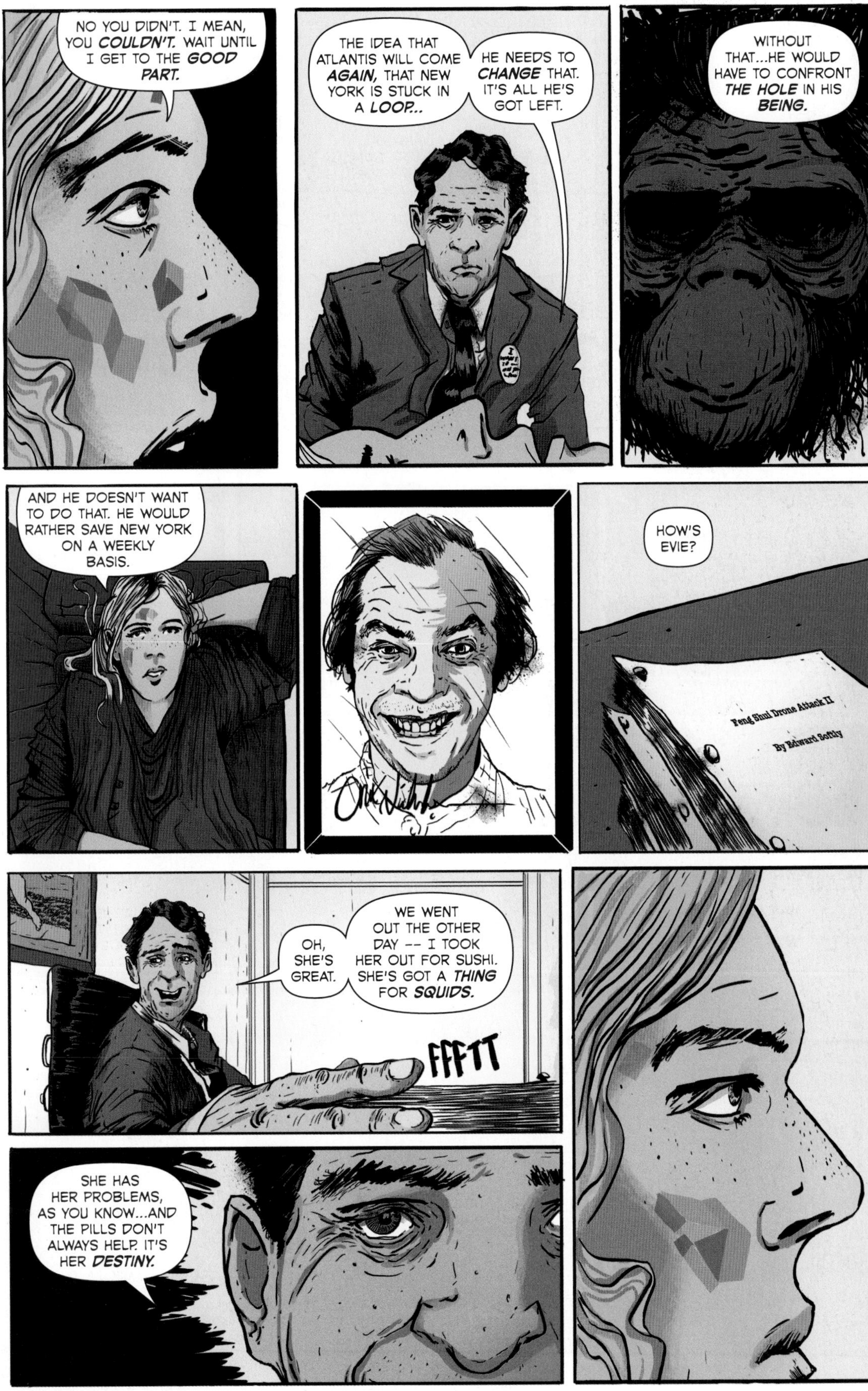
NO YOU DIDN'T. I MEAN, YOU COULDN'T. WAIT UNTIL I GET TO THE GOOD PART.
THE IDEA THAT ATLANTIS WILL COME AGAIN, THAT NEW YORK IS STUCK IN A LOOP...
HE NEEDS TO CHANGE THAT. IT'S ALL HE'S GOT LEFT.
WITHOUT THAT...HE WOULD HAVE TO CONFRONT THE HOLE IN HIS BEING.
AND HE DOESN'T WANT TO DO THAT. HE WOULD RATHER SAVE NEW YORK ON A WEEKLY BASIS.
HOW'S EVIE?
Feng Shui Drone Attack II
By Edward Softly
OH, SHE'S GREAT.
WE WENT OUT THE OTHER DAY -- I TOOK HER OUT FOR SUSHI. SHE'S GOT A THING FOR SQUIDS.
FFFTT
SHE HAS HER PROBLEMS, AS YOU KNOW...AND THE PILLS DON'T ALWAYS HELP. IT'S HER DESTINY.

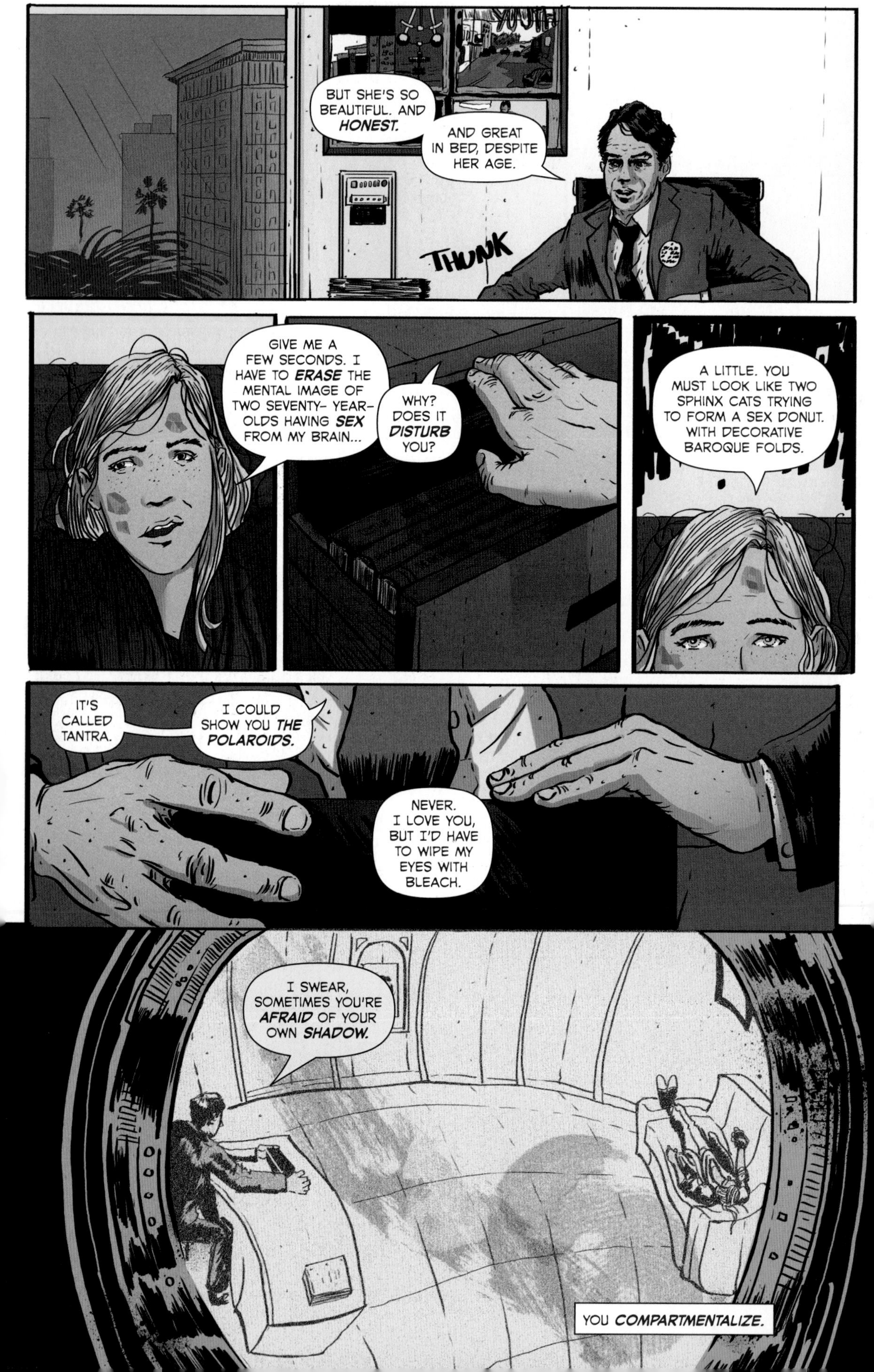

BUT SHE'S SO BEAUTIFUL. AND HONEST.
AND GREAT IN BED, DESPITE HER AGE.
THUNK
GIVE ME A FEW SECONDS. I HAVE TO ERASE THE MENTAL IMAGE OF TWO SEVENTY- YEAR-OLDS HAVING SEX FROM MY BRAIN...
WHY? DOES IT DISTURB YOU?
A LITTLE. YOU MUST LOOK LIKE TWO SPHINX CATS TRYING TO FORM A SEX DONUT. WITH DECORATIVE BAROQUE FOLDS.
IT'S CALLED TANTRA.
I COULD SHOW YOU THE POLAROIDS.
NEVER. I LOVE YOU, BUT I'D HAVE TO WIPE MY EYES WITH BLEACH.
I SWEAR, SOMETIMES YOU'RE AFRAID OF YOUR OWN SHADOW.
YOU COMPARTMENTALIZE.

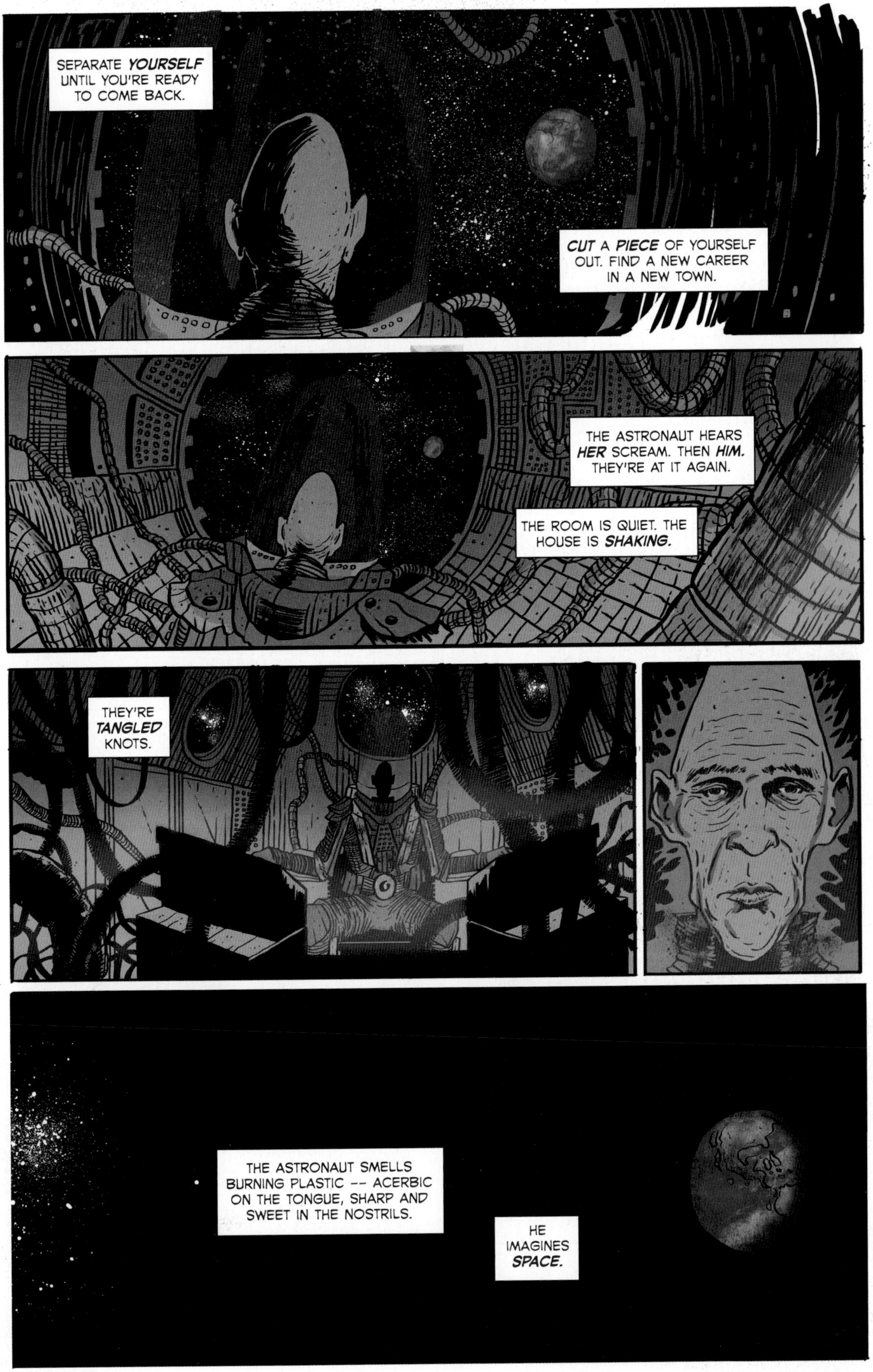
SEPARATE YOURSELF UNTIL YOU'RE READY TO COME BACK.
CUT A PIECE OF YOURSELF OUT. FIND A NEW CAREER IN A NEW TOWN.
THE ASTRONAUT HEARS HER SCREAM. THEN HIM. THEY'RE AT IT AGAIN.
THE ROOM IS QUIET. THE HOUSE IS SHAKING.
THEY'RE TANGLED KNOTS.
THE ASTRONAUT SMELLS BURNING PLASTIC -- ACERBIC ON THE TONGUE, SHARP AND SWEET IN THE NOSTRILS.
HE IMAGINES SPACE.

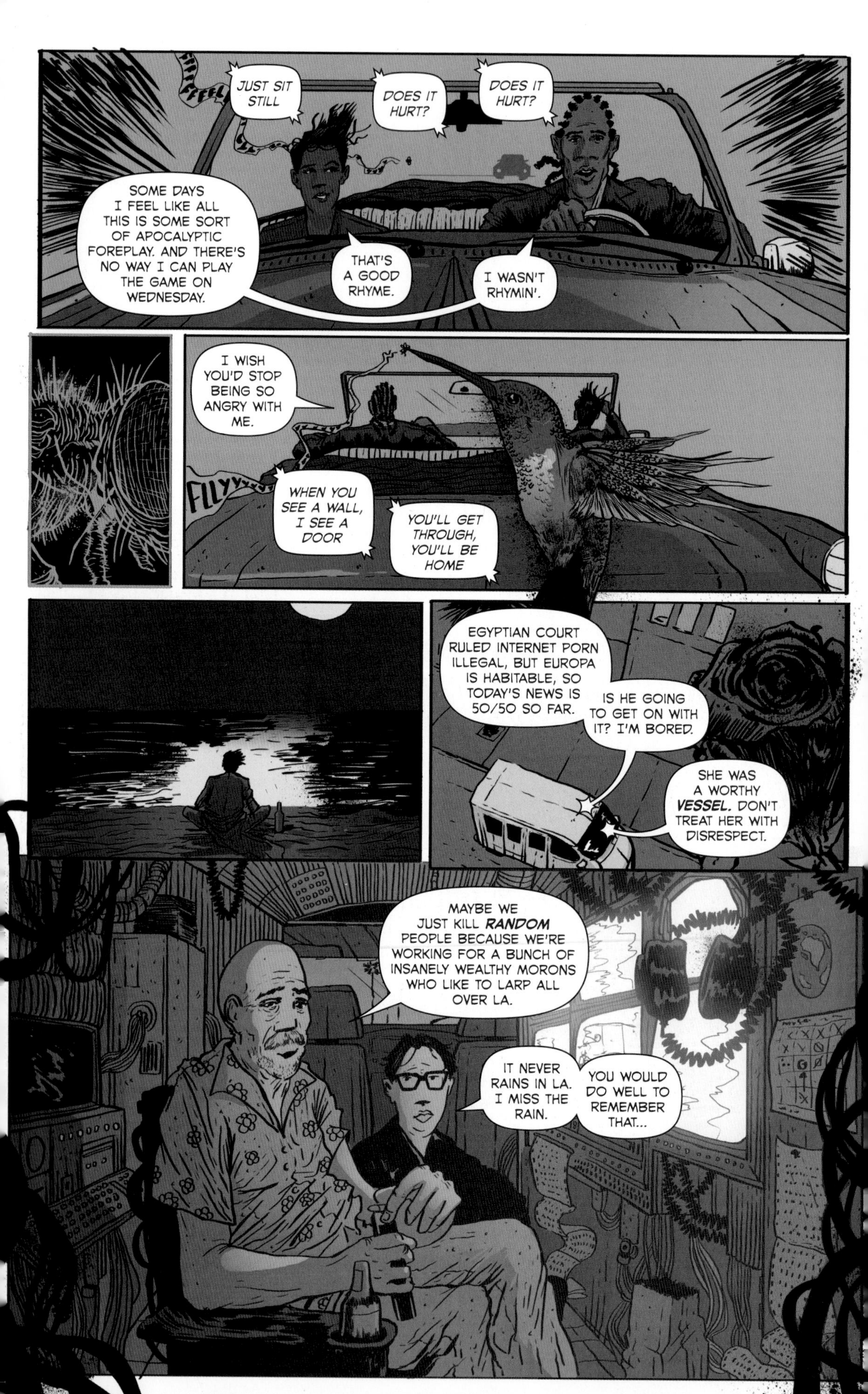
FEEL
JUST SIT STILL
DOES IT HURT?
DOES IT HURT?
SOME DAYS I FEEL LIKE ALL THIS IS SOME SORT OF APOCALYPTIC FOREPLAY. AND THERE'S NO WAY I CAN PLAY THE GAME ON WEDNESDAY.
THAT'S A GOOD RHYME.
I WASN'T RHYMIN'.
I WISH YOU'D STOP BEING SO ANGRY WITH ME.
FLLYYYY
WHEN YOU SEE A WALL, I SEE A DOOR
YOU'LL GET THROUGH, YOU'LL BE HOME
EGYPTIAN COURT RULED INTERNET PORN ILLEGAL, BUT EUROPA IS HABITABLE, SO TODAY'S NEWS IS 50/50 SO FAR.
IS HE GOING TO GET ON WITH IT? I'M BORED.
SHE WAS A WORTHY **VESSEL.** DON'T TREAT HER WITH DISRESPECT.
MAYBE WE JUST KILL ***RANDOM*** PEOPLE BECAUSE WE'RE WORKING FOR A BUNCH OF INSANELY WEALTHY MORONS WHO LIKE TO LARP ALL OVER LA.
IT NEVER RAINS IN LA. I MISS THE RAIN.
YOU WOULD DO WELL TO REMEMBER THAT...

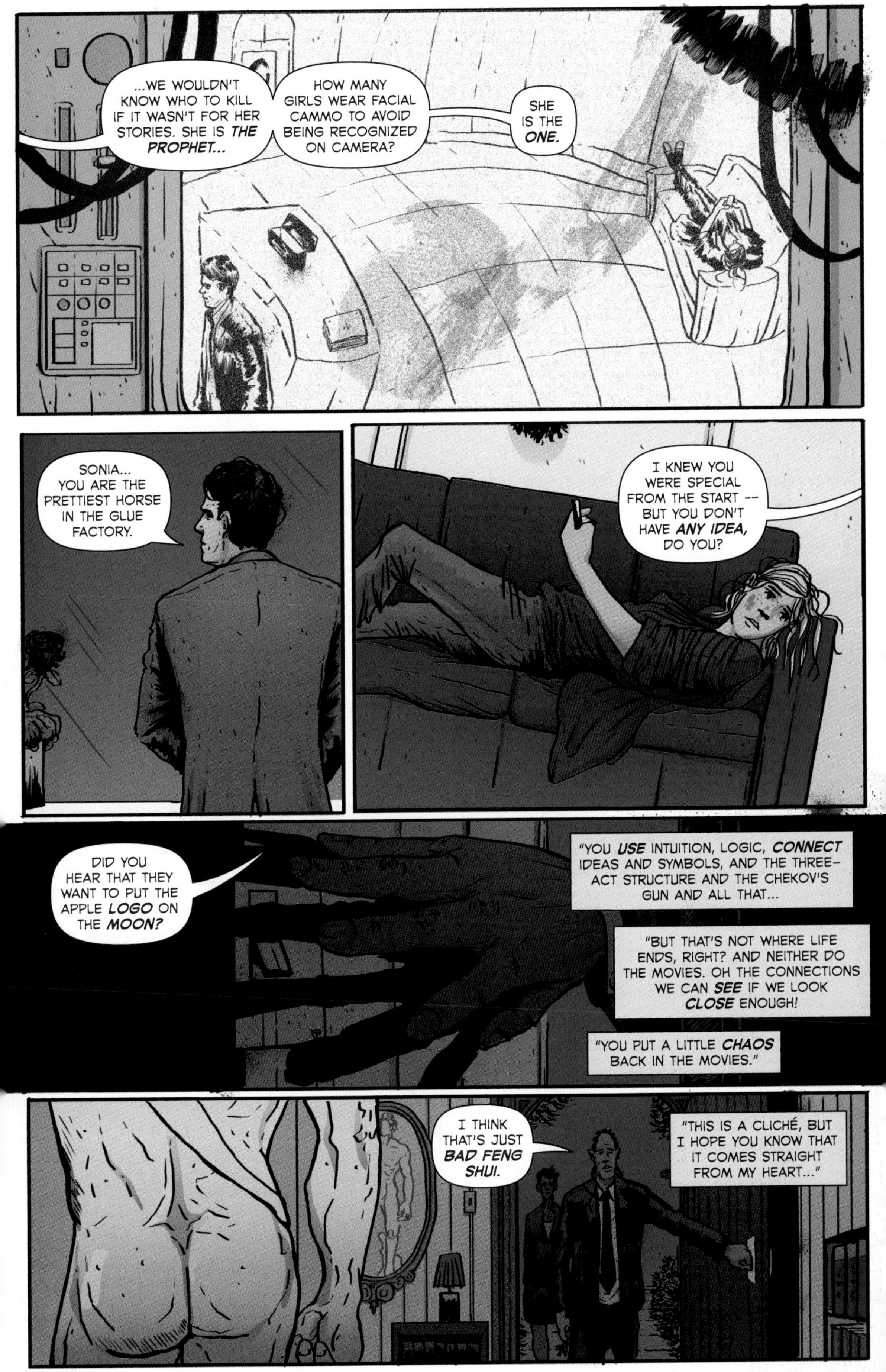
...WE WOULDN'T KNOW WHO TO KILL IF IT WASN'T FOR HER STORIES. SHE IS *THE PROPHET...*
HOW MANY GIRLS WEAR FACIAL CAMMO TO AVOID BEING RECOGNIZED ON CAMERA?
SHE IS THE *ONE.*
SONIA... YOU ARE THE PRETTIEST HORSE IN THE GLUE FACTORY.
I KNEW YOU WERE SPECIAL FROM THE START -- BUT YOU DON'T HAVE *ANY IDEA,* DO YOU?
DID YOU HEAR THAT THEY WANT TO PUT THE APPLE *LOGO* ON THE *MOON?*
"YOU *USE* INTUITION, LOGIC, *CONNECT* IDEAS AND SYMBOLS, AND THE THREE-ACT STRUCTURE AND THE CHEKOV'S GUN AND ALL THAT...
"BUT THAT'S NOT WHERE LIFE ENDS, RIGHT? AND NEITHER DO THE MOVIES. OH THE CONNECTIONS WE CAN *SEE* IF WE LOOK *CLOSE* ENOUGH!
"YOU PUT A LITTLE *CHAOS* BACK IN THE MOVIES."
I THINK THAT'S JUST *BAD FENG SHUI.*
"THIS IS A CLICHÉ, BUT I HOPE YOU KNOW THAT IT COMES STRAIGHT FROM MY HEART..."

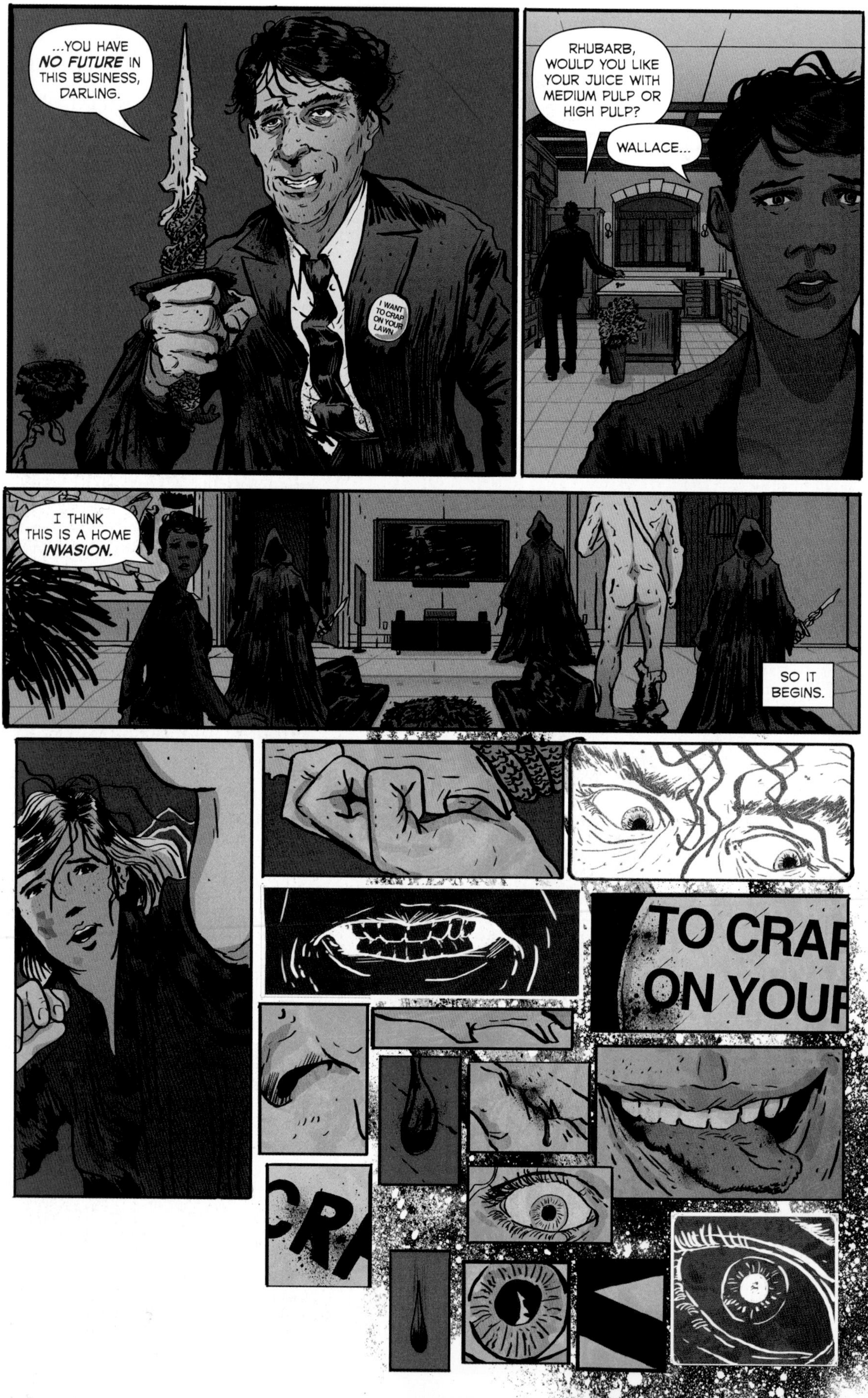
...YOU HAVE NO FUTURE IN THIS BUSINESS, DARLING.
I WANT TO CRAP ON YOUR LAWN
RHUBARB, WOULD YOU LIKE YOUR JUICE WITH MEDIUM PULP OR HIGH PULP?
WALLACE...
I THINK THIS IS A HOME INVASION.
SO IT BEGINS.
TO CRAP ON YOUR
CRA

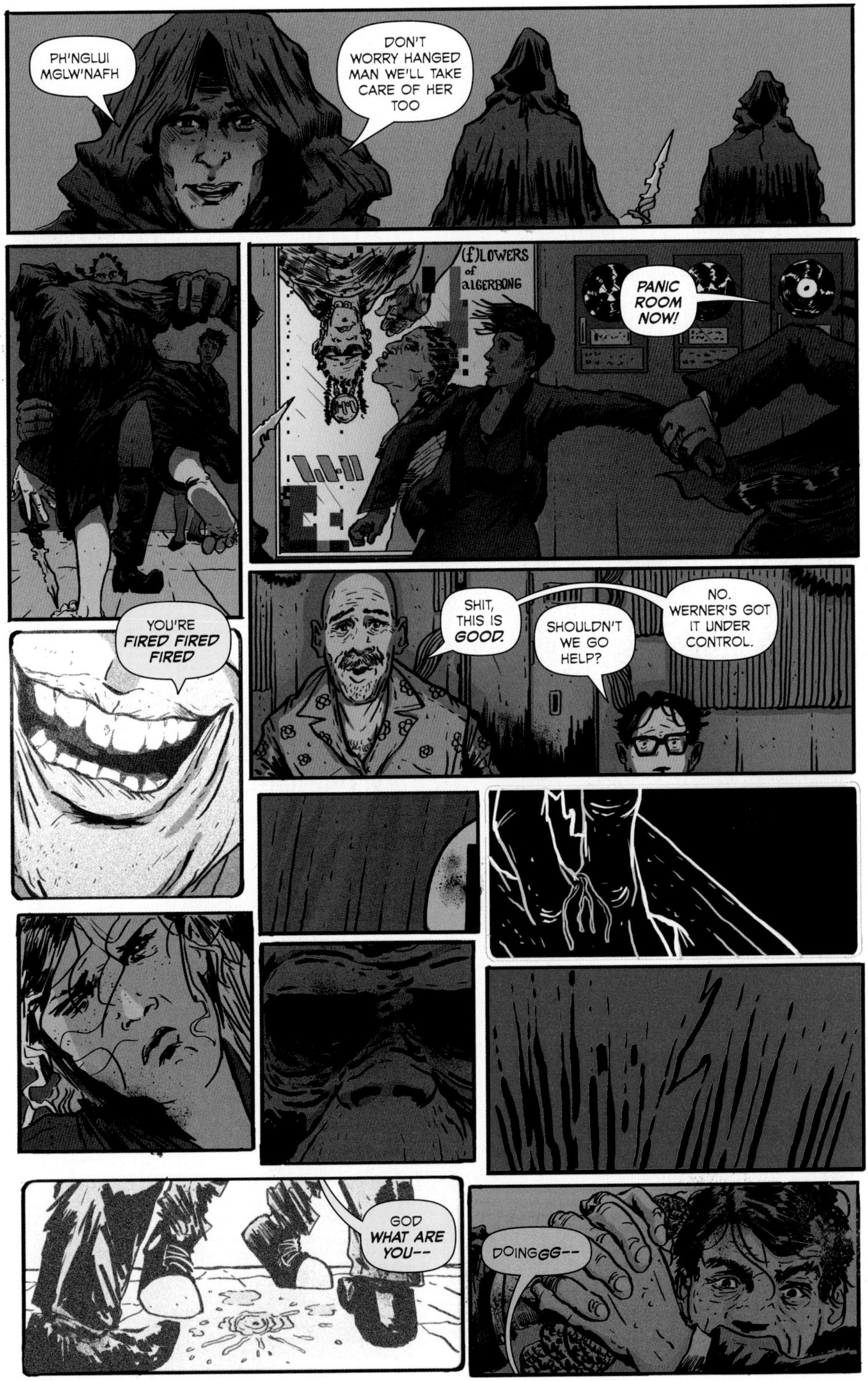
PH'NGLUI MGLW'NAFH
DON'T WORRY HANGED MAN WE'LL TAKE CARE OF HER TOO
(f)LOWERS of aLGERBONG
PANIC ROOM NOW!
YOU'RE FIRED FIRED FIRED
SHIT, THIS IS GOOD.
SHOULDN'T WE GO HELP?
NO. WERNER'S GOT IT UNDER CONTROL.
GOD WHAT ARE YOU--
DOINGGG--

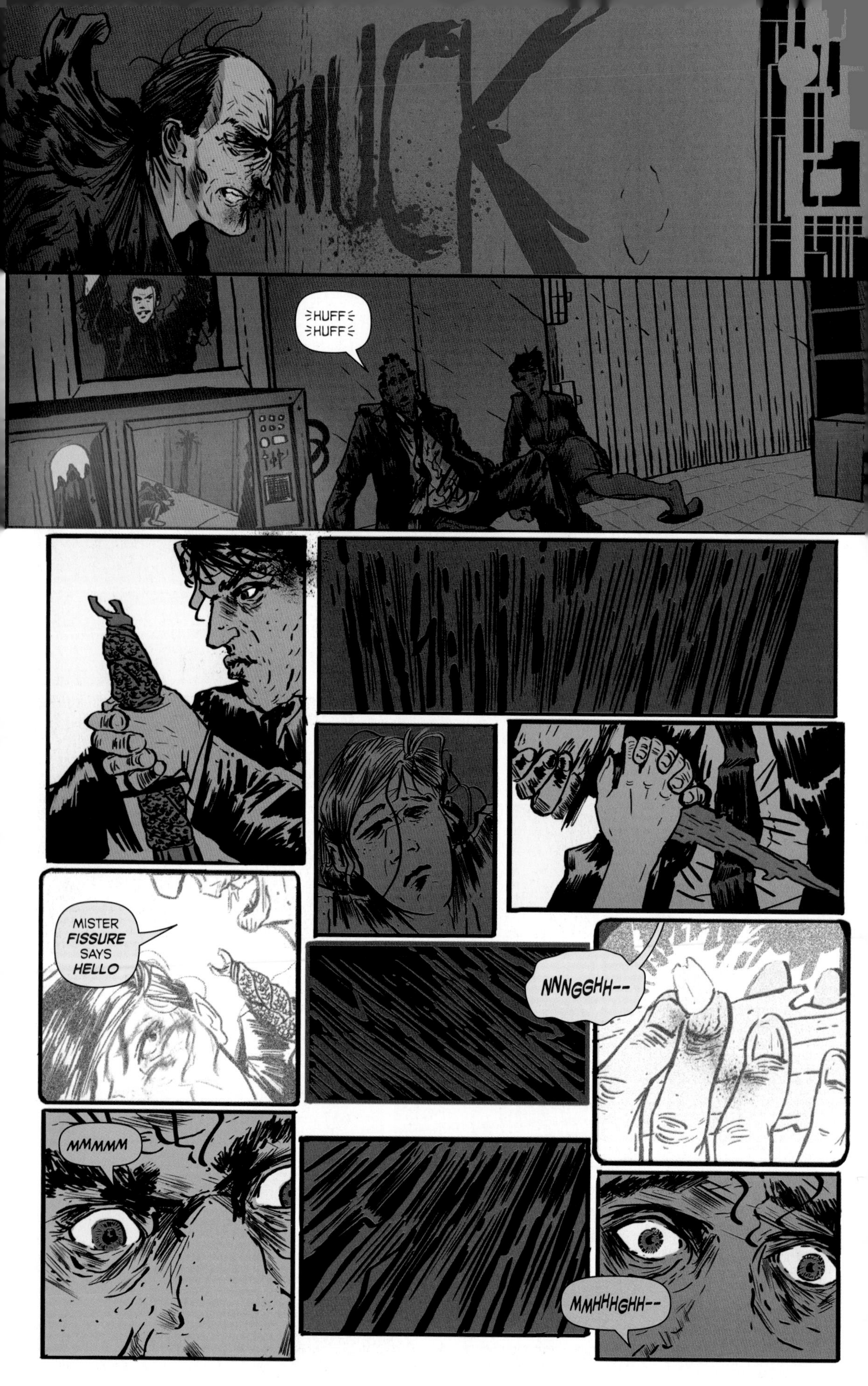
THUCK
HUFF HUFF
MISTER FISSURE SAYS HELLO
NNNGGHH--
MMMMM
MMHHHGHH--

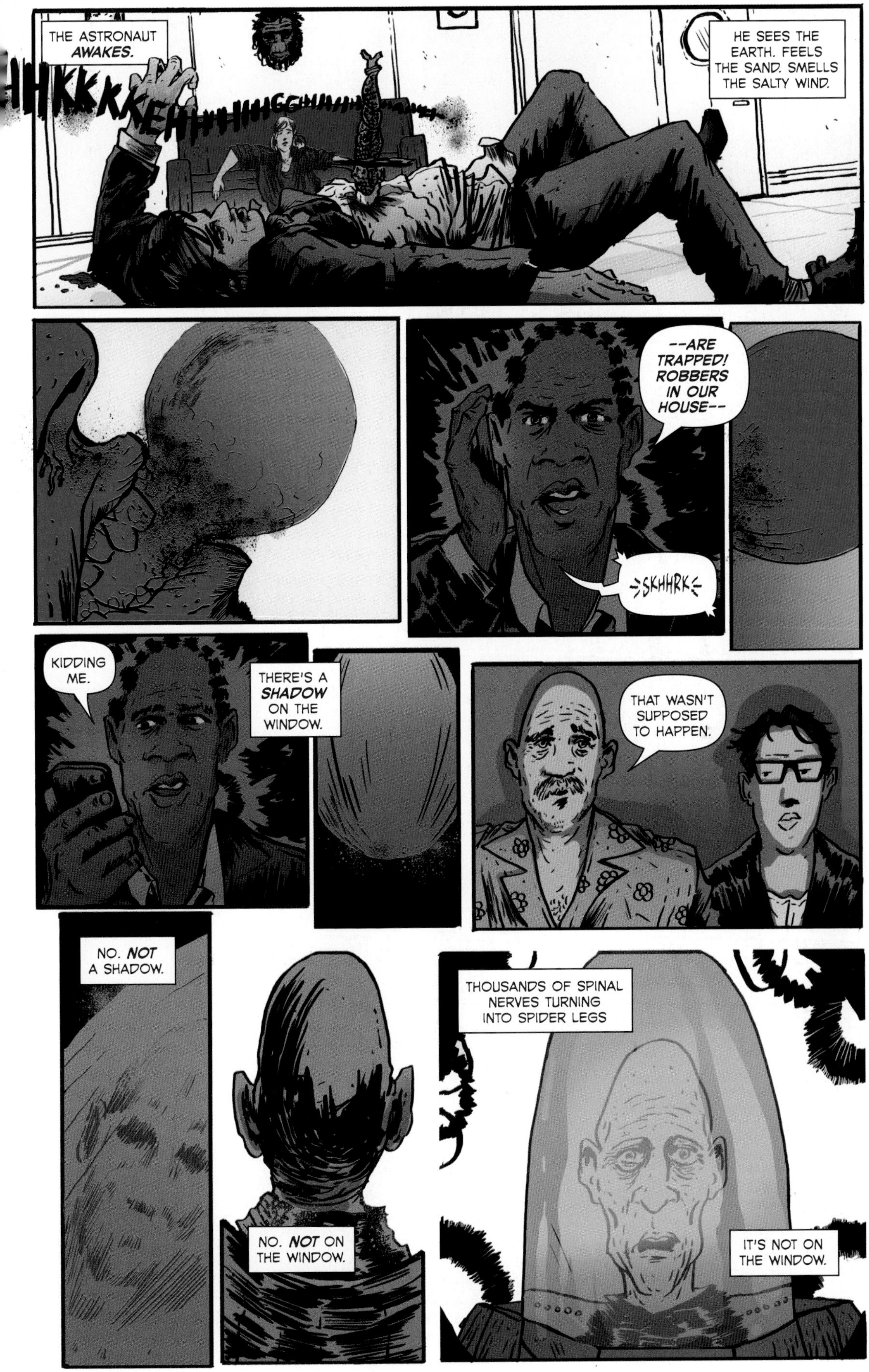
THE ASTRONAUT AWAKES.
HHKKKKKEHHHHHHHGGHHHH
HE SEES THE EARTH. FEELS THE SAND. SMELLS THE SALTY WIND.
--ARE TRAPPED! ROBBERS IN OUR HOUSE--
SKHHRK
KIDDING ME.
THERE'S A SHADOW ON THE WINDOW.
THAT WASN'T SUPPOSED TO HAPPEN.
NO. NOT A SHADOW.
NO. NOT ON THE WINDOW.
THOUSANDS OF SPINAL NERVES TURNING INTO SPIDER LEGS
IT'S NOT ON THE WINDOW.

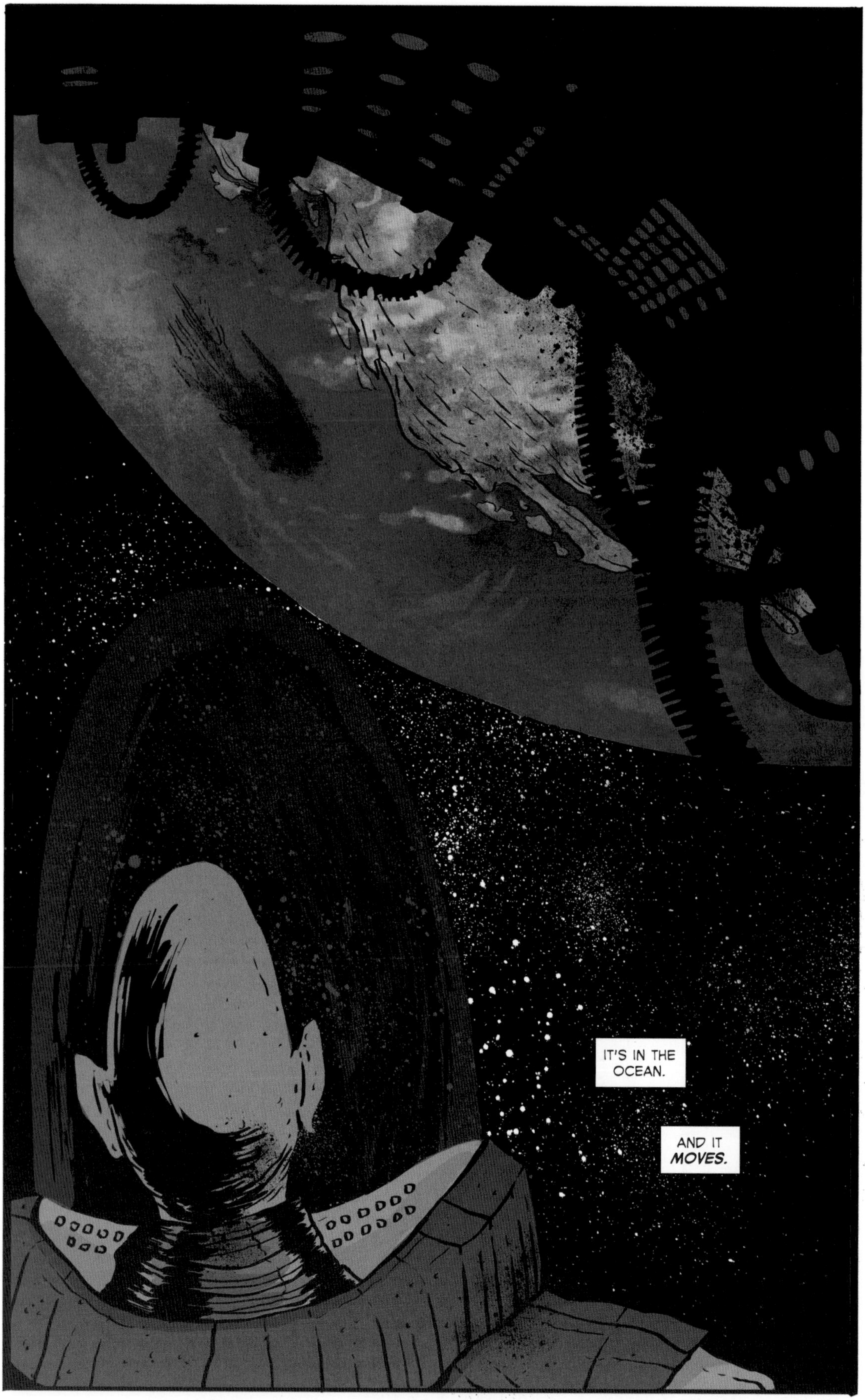
IT'S IN THE OCEAN.
AND IT *MOVES.*

Who said that time heals all wounds?
It would be better to say that time heals
everything - except wounds. With time,
the hurt of separation loses its real limits.
With time, the desired body will soon
disappear, and if the desiring body has
already ceased to exist for the other,
then what remains is a wound,
disembodied.

Chris Marker
'Sans-Soleil'

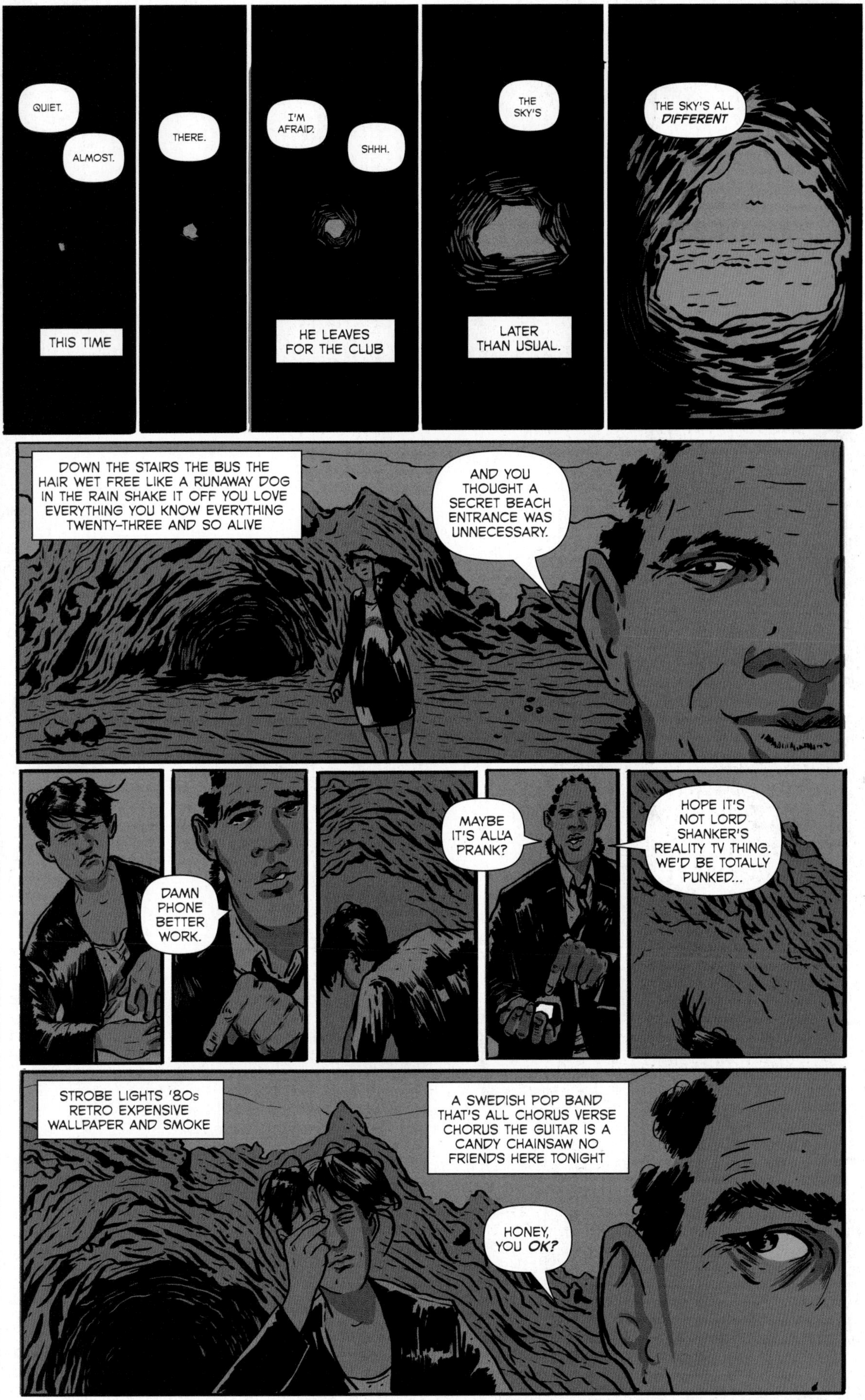
QUIET.
ALMOST.
THIS TIME
THERE.
I'M AFRAID.
SHHH.
HE LEAVES FOR THE CLUB
THE SKY'S
LATER THAN USUAL.
THE SKY'S ALL DIFFERENT
DOWN THE STAIRS THE BUS THE HAIR WET FREE LIKE A RUNAWAY DOG IN THE RAIN SHAKE IT OFF YOU LOVE EVERYTHING YOU KNOW EVERYTHING TWENTY-THREE AND SO ALIVE
AND YOU THOUGHT A SECRET BEACH ENTRANCE WAS UNNECESSARY.
DAMN PHONE BETTER WORK.
MAYBE IT'S ALL'A PRANK?
HOPE IT'S NOT LORD SHANKER'S REALITY TV THING. WE'D BE TOTALLY PUNKED...
STROBE LIGHTS '80s RETRO EXPENSIVE WALLPAPER AND SMOKE
A SWEDISH POP BAND THAT'S ALL CHORUS VERSE CHORUS THE GUITAR IS A CANDY CHAINSAW NO FRIENDS HERE TONIGHT
HONEY, YOU OK?

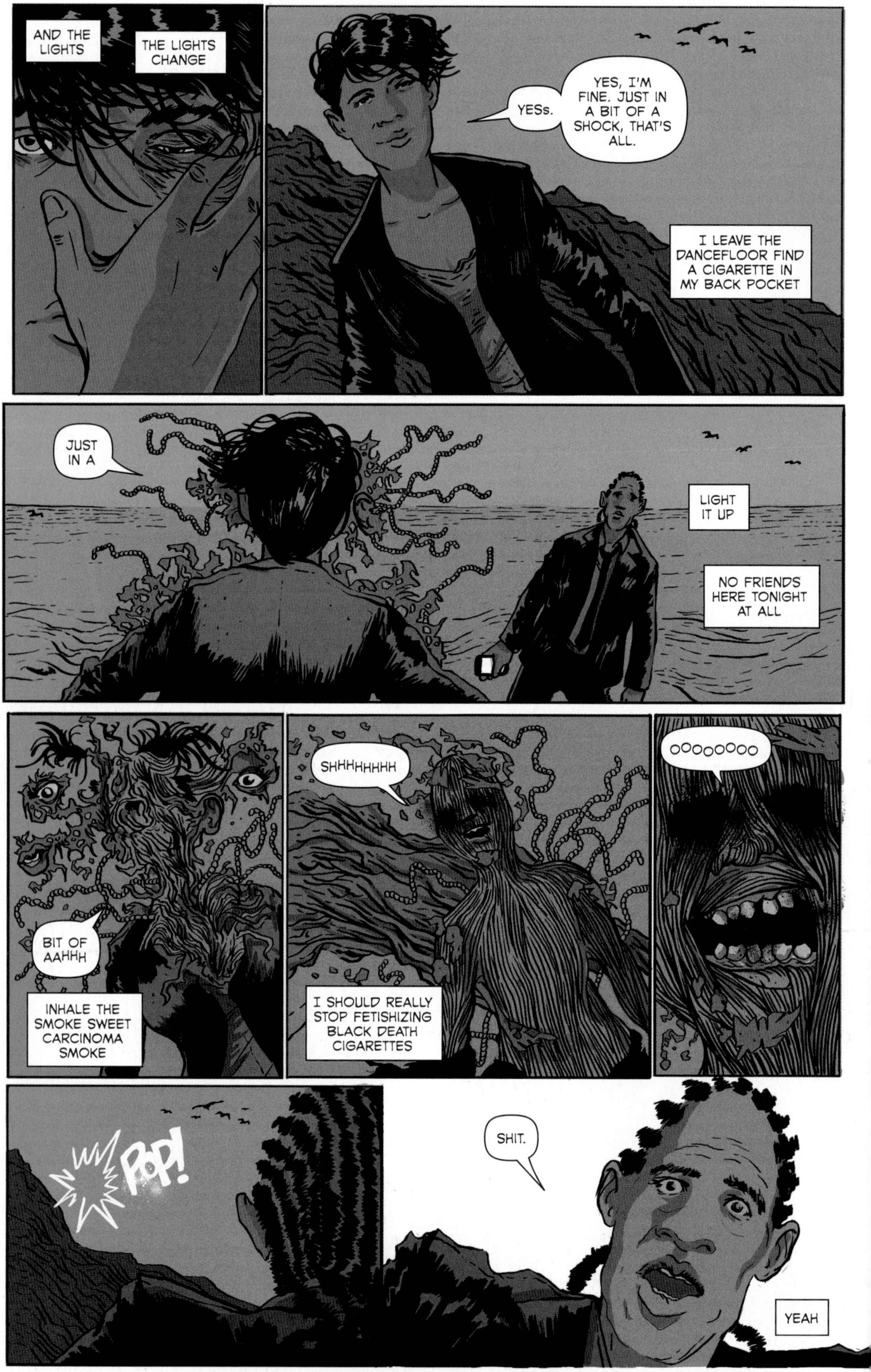
AND THE LIGHTS
THE LIGHTS CHANGE
YESs.
YES, I'M FINE. JUST IN A BIT OF A SHOCK, THAT'S ALL.
I LEAVE THE DANCEFLOOR FIND A CIGARETTE IN MY BACK POCKET
JUST IN A
LIGHT IT UP
NO FRIENDS HERE TONIGHT AT ALL
BIT OF AAHHH
INHALE THE SMOKE SWEET CARCINOMA SMOKE
SHHHHHHHH
I SHOULD REALLY STOP FETISHIZING BLACK DEATH CIGARETTES
OOOOOOOO
POP!
SHIT.
YEAH

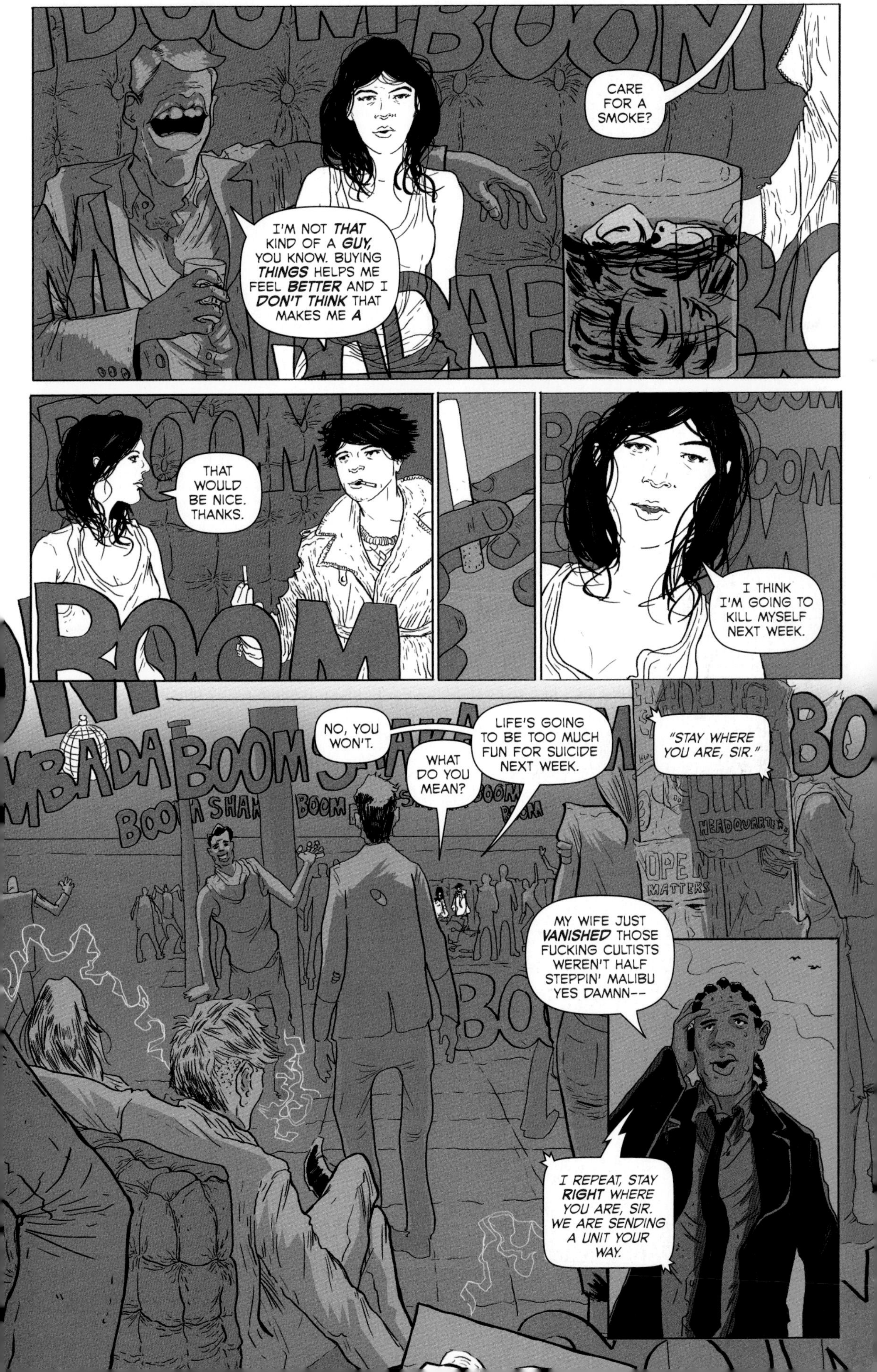
CARE FOR A SMOKE?
I'M NOT *THAT* KIND OF A *GUY,* YOU KNOW. BUYING *THINGS* HELPS ME FEEL *BETTER* AND I *DON'T THINK* THAT MAKES ME *A*
THAT WOULD BE NICE. THANKS.
I THINK I'M GOING TO KILL MYSELF NEXT WEEK.
NO, YOU WON'T.
WHAT DO YOU MEAN?
LIFE'S GOING TO BE TOO MUCH FUN FOR SUICIDE NEXT WEEK.
"STAY WHERE YOU ARE, SIR."
MY WIFE JUST *VANISHED* THOSE FUCKING CULTISTS WEREN'T HALF STEPPIN' MALIBU YES DAMNN--
I REPEAT, STAY ***RIGHT*** *WHERE YOU ARE, SIR. WE ARE SENDING A UNIT YOUR WAY.*

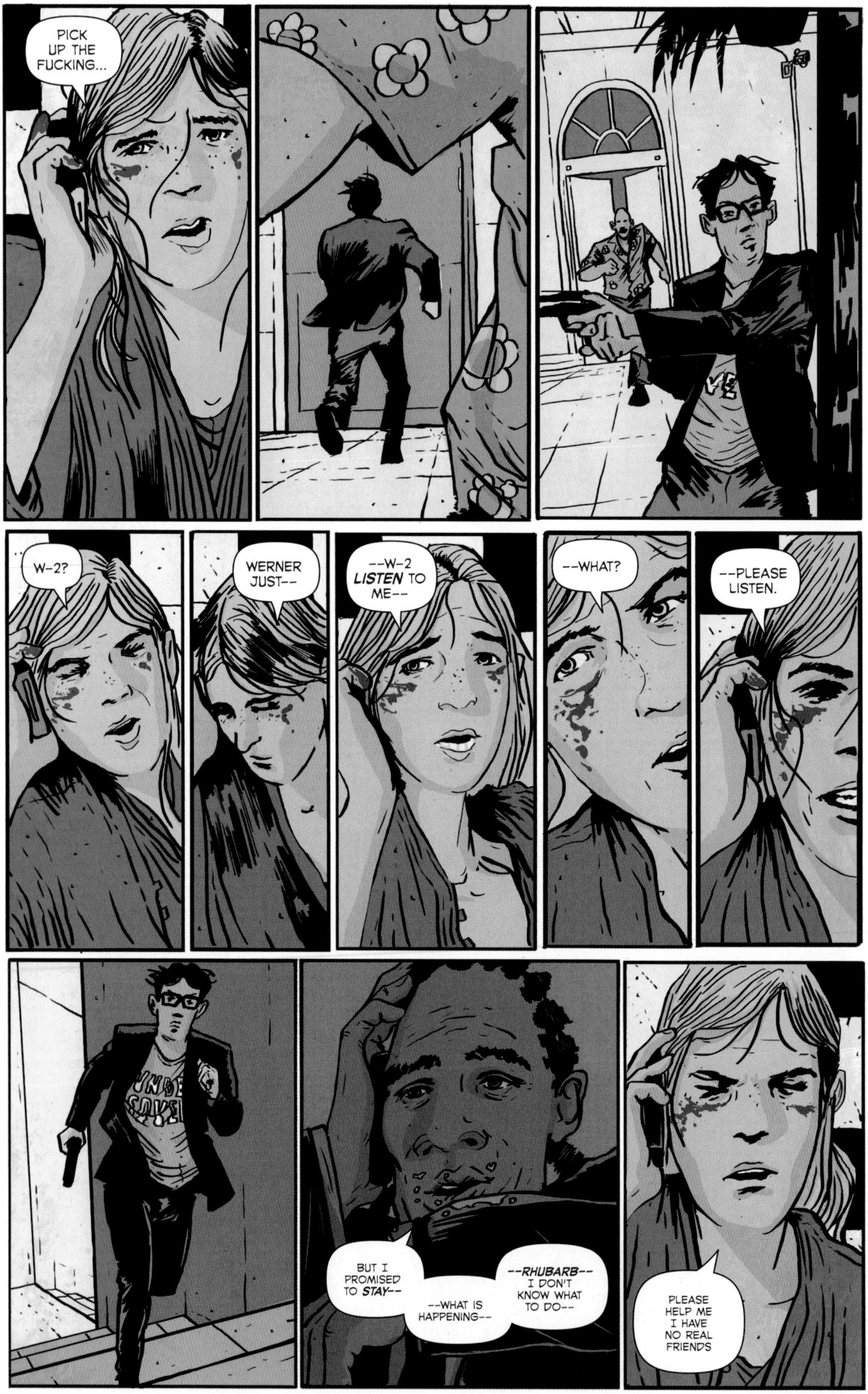
PICK UP THE FUCKING...
W-2?
WERNER JUST--
--W-2 LISTEN TO ME--
--WHAT?
--PLEASE LISTEN.
BUT I PROMISED TO STAY--
--WHAT IS HAPPENING--
--RHUBARB-- I DON'T KNOW WHAT TO DO--
PLEASE HELP ME I HAVE NO REAL FRIENDS

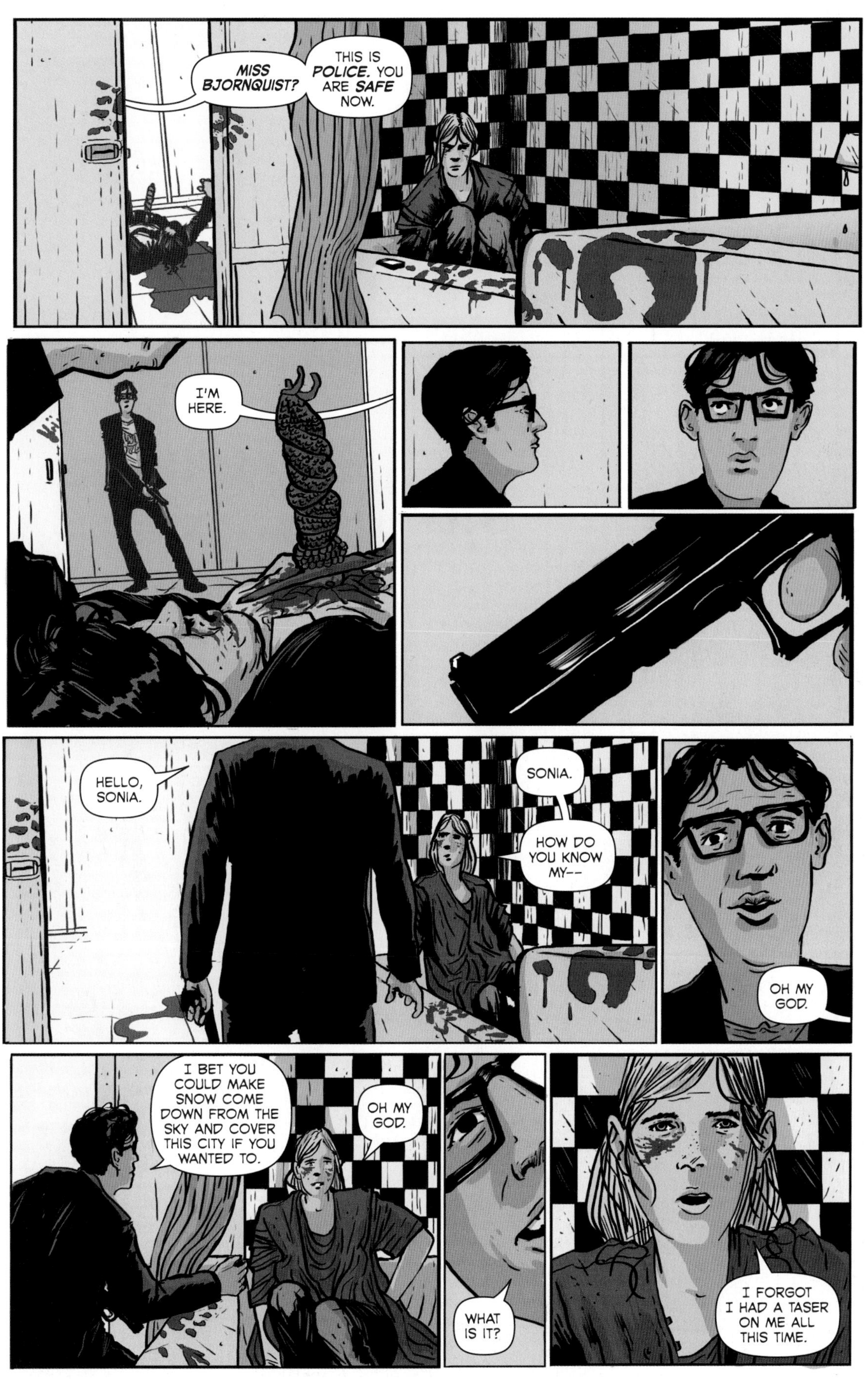
MISS BJORNQUIST?
THIS IS POLICE. YOU ARE SAFE NOW.
I'M HERE.
HELLO, SONIA.
SONIA.
HOW DO YOU KNOW MY--
OH MY GOD.
I BET YOU COULD MAKE SNOW COME DOWN FROM THE SKY AND COVER THIS CITY IF YOU WANTED TO.
OH MY GOD.
WHAT IS IT?
I FORGOT I HAD A TASER ON ME ALL THIS TIME.

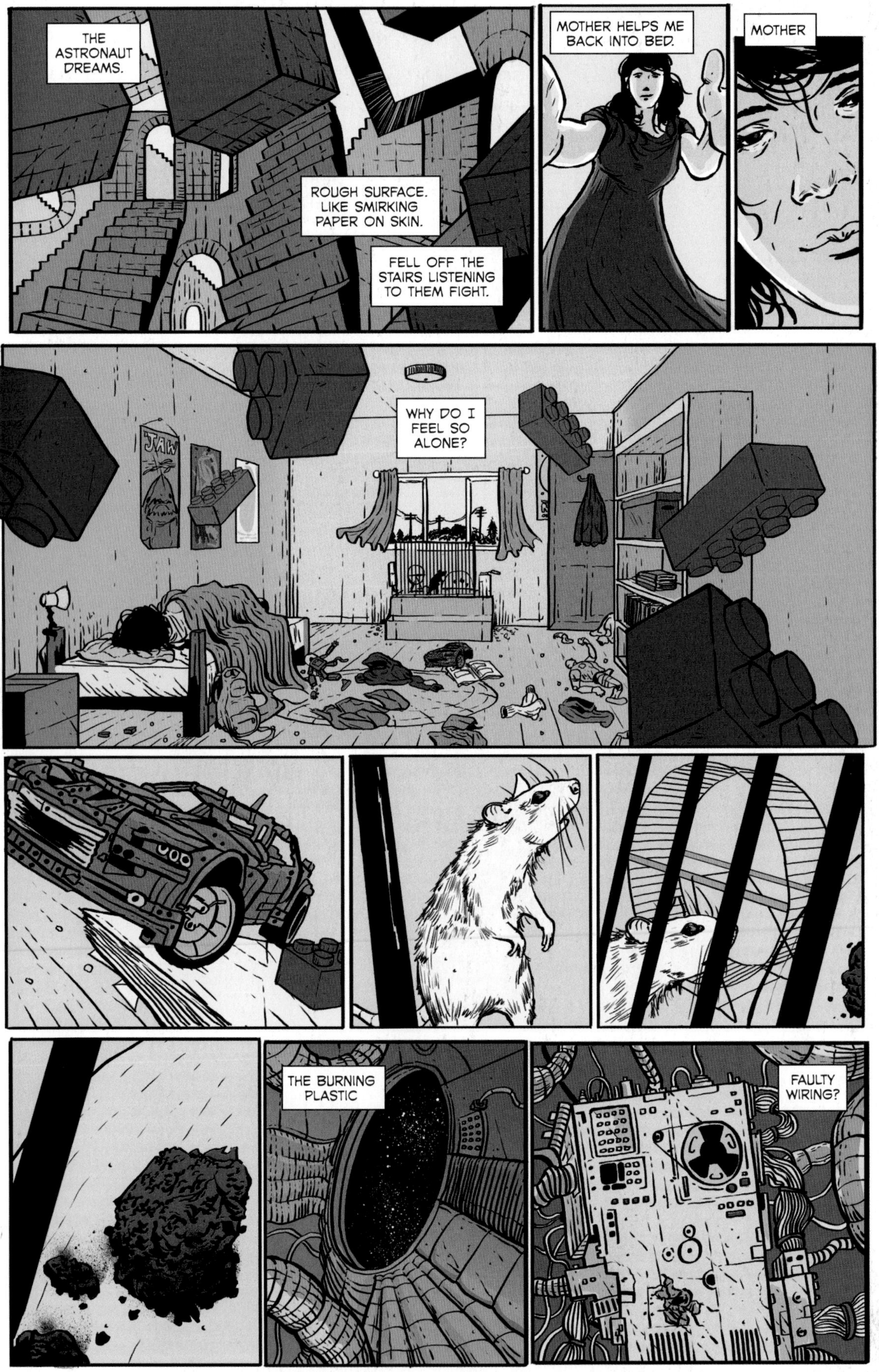
THE ASTRONAUT DREAMS.
ROUGH SURFACE. LIKE SMIRKING PAPER ON SKIN.
FELL OFF THE STAIRS LISTENING TO THEM FIGHT.
MOTHER HELPS ME BACK INTO BED.
MOTHER
WHY DO I FEEL SO ALONE?
JAW
THE BURNING PLASTIC
FAULTY WIRING?

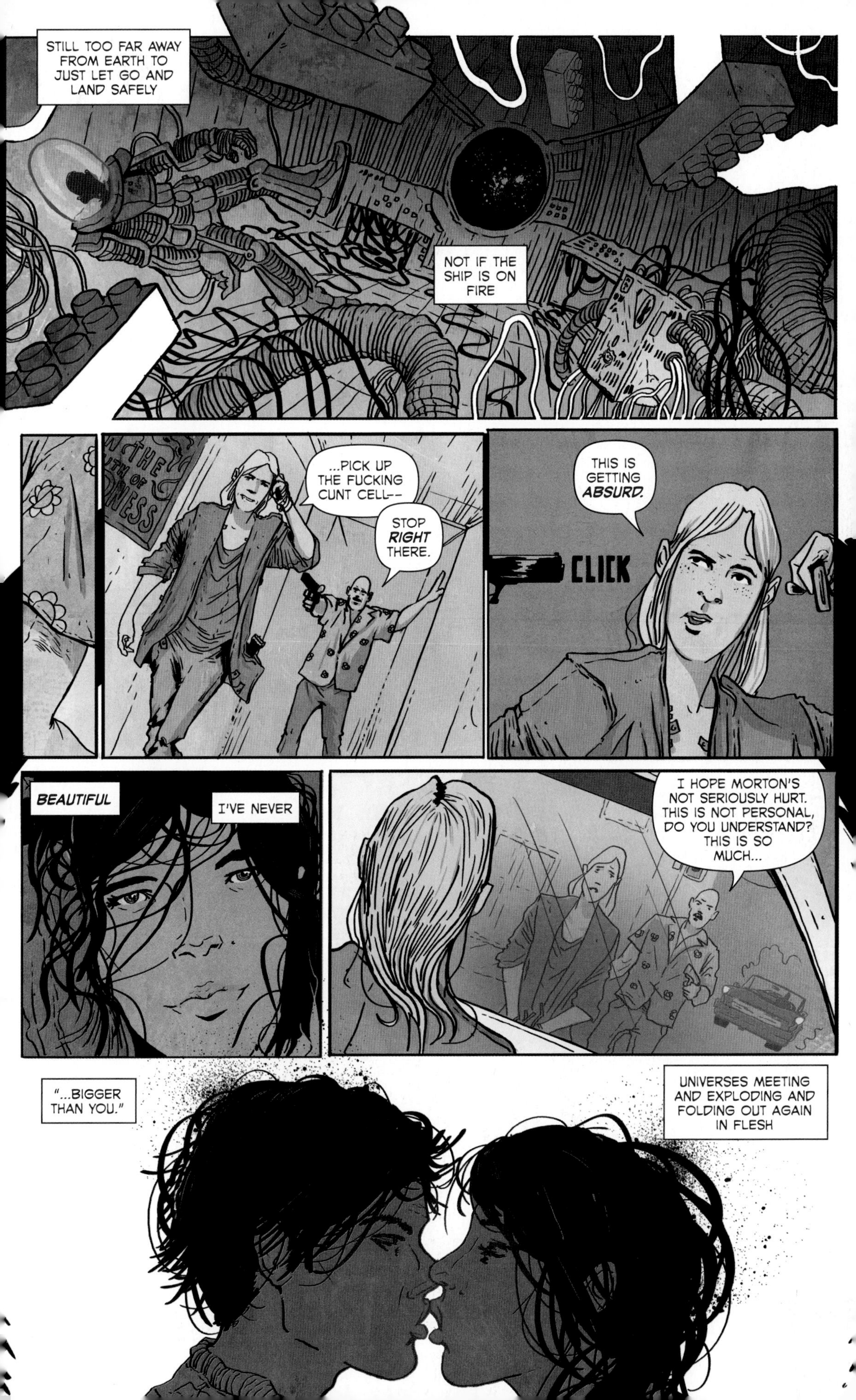

STILL TOO FAR AWAY FROM EARTH TO JUST LET GO AND LAND SAFELY
NOT IF THE SHIP IS ON FIRE
...PICK UP THE FUCKING CUNT CELL--
STOP RIGHT THERE.
THIS IS GETTING ABSURD.
CLICK
BEAUTIFUL
I'VE NEVER
I HOPE MORTON'S NOT SERIOUSLY HURT. THIS IS NOT PERSONAL, DO YOU UNDERSTAND? THIS IS SO MUCH...
"...BIGGER THAN YOU."
UNIVERSES MEETING AND EXPLODING AND FOLDING OUT AGAIN IN FLESH

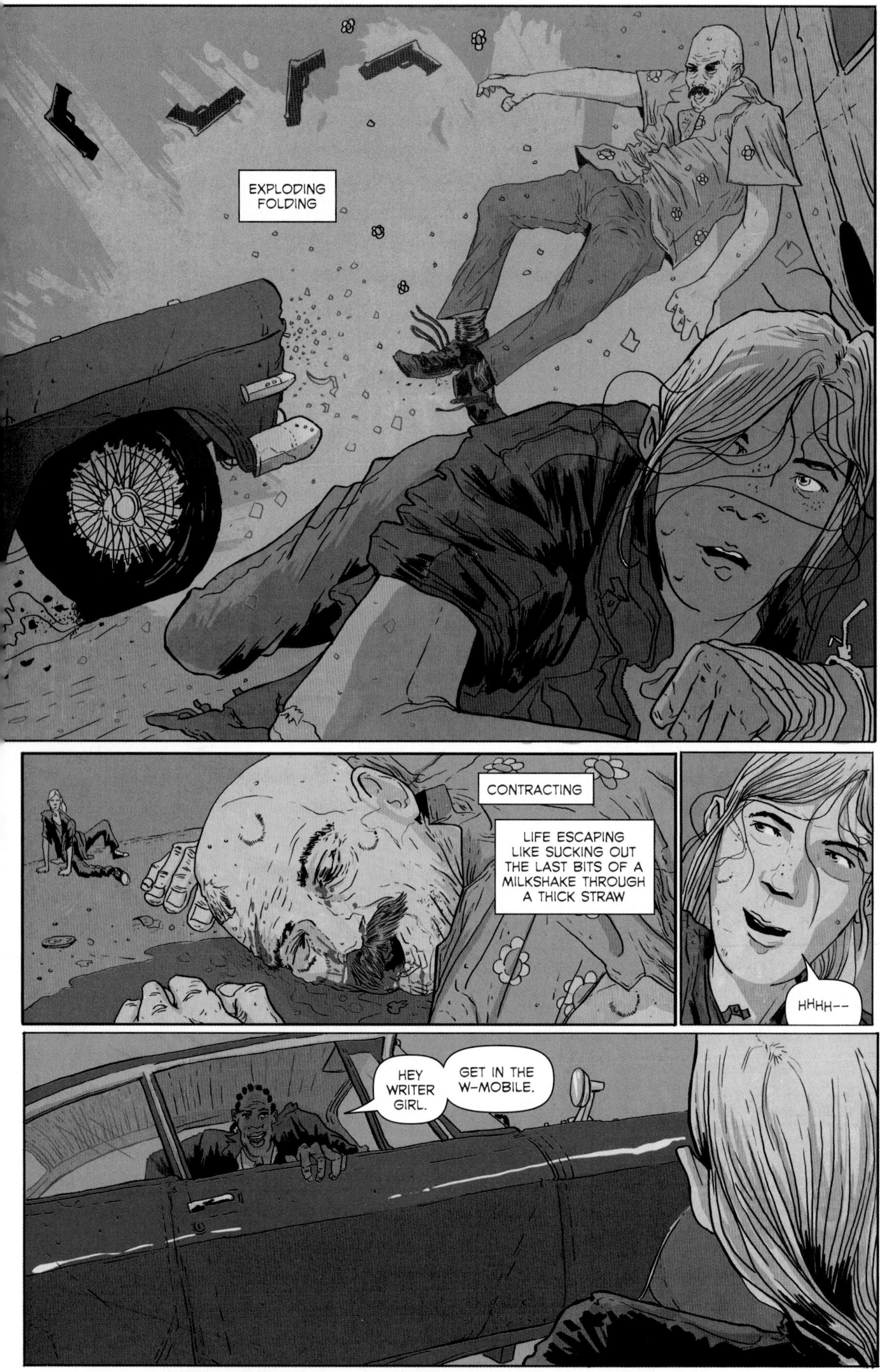
EXPLODING FOLDING
CONTRACTING
LIFE ESCAPING LIKE SUCKING OUT THE LAST BITS OF A MILKSHAKE THROUGH A THICK STRAW
HHHH--
HEY WRITER GIRL.
GET IN THE W-MOBILE.

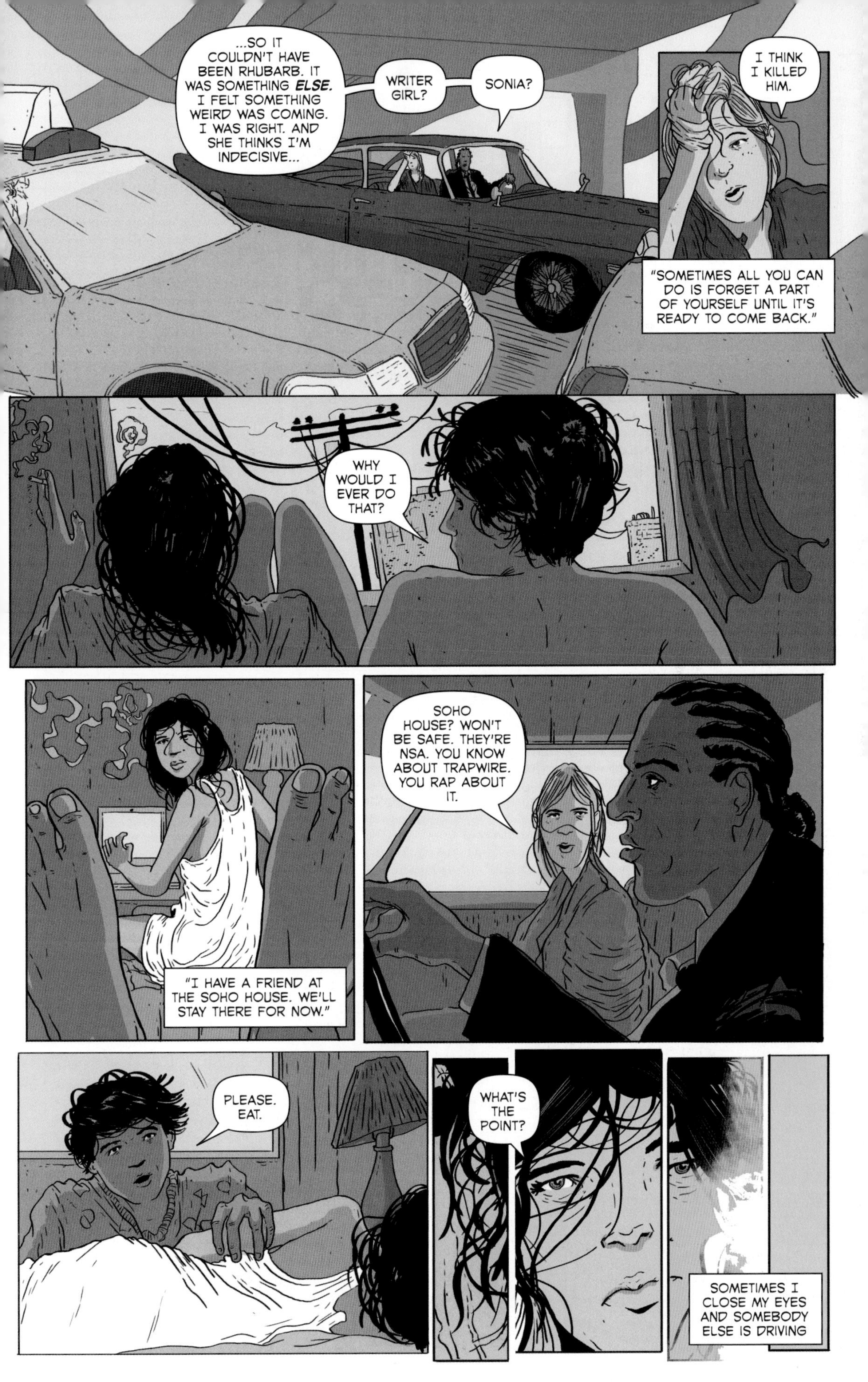
...SO IT COULDN'T HAVE BEEN RHUBARB. IT WAS SOMETHING **ELSE.** I FELT SOMETHING WEIRD WAS COMING. I WAS RIGHT. AND SHE THINKS I'M INDECISIVE...
WRITER GIRL?
SONIA?
I THINK I KILLED HIM.
"SOMETIMES ALL YOU CAN DO IS FORGET A PART OF YOURSELF UNTIL IT'S READY TO COME BACK."
WHY WOULD I EVER DO THAT?
"I HAVE A FRIEND AT THE SOHO HOUSE. WE'LL STAY THERE FOR NOW."
SOHO HOUSE? WON'T BE SAFE. THEY'RE NSA. YOU KNOW ABOUT TRAPWIRE. YOU RAP ABOUT IT.
PLEASE. EAT.
WHAT'S THE POINT?
SOMETIMES I CLOSE MY EYES AND SOMEBODY ELSE IS DRIVING

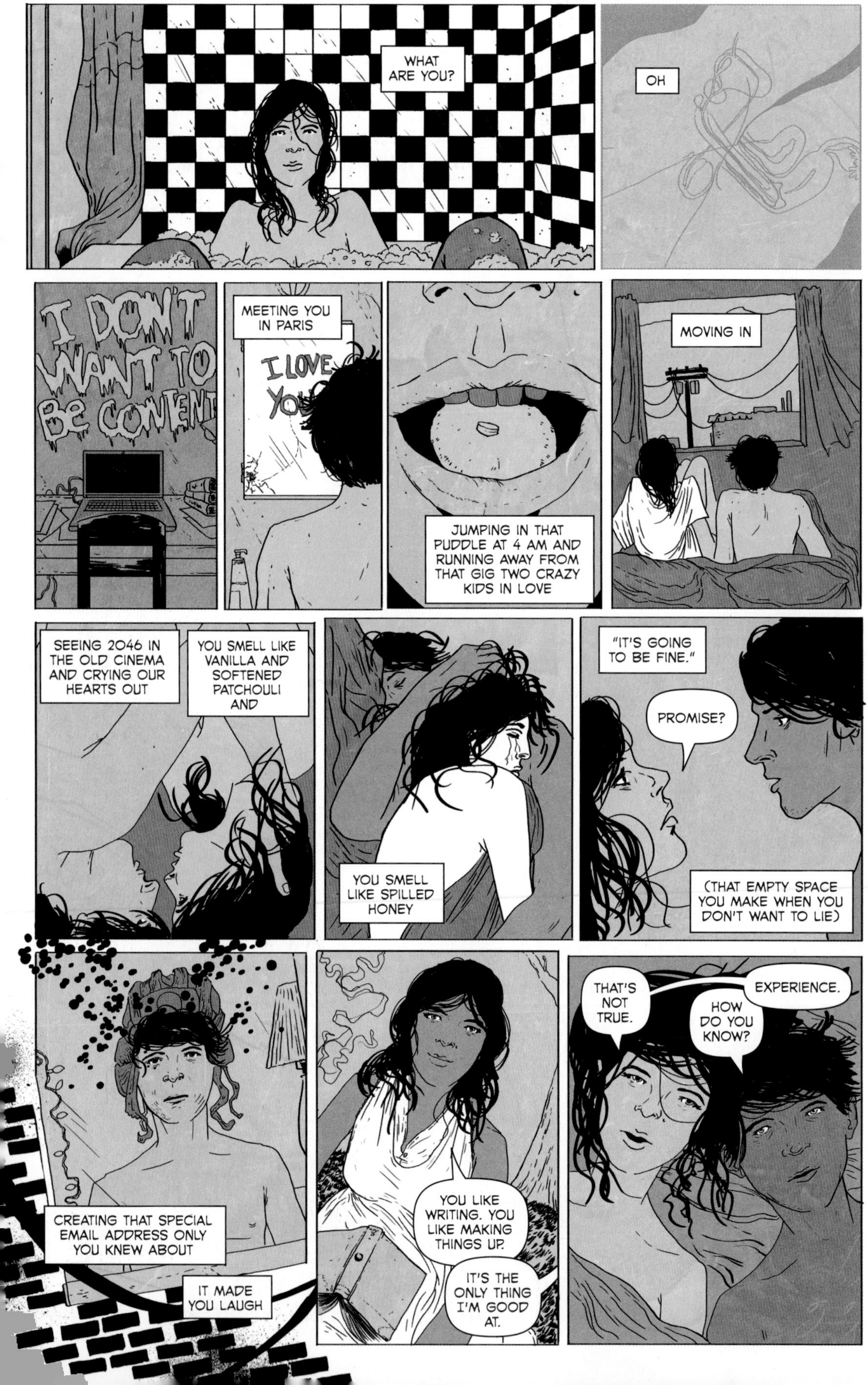
WHAT ARE YOU?
OH
I DON'T WANT TO BE CONTENT
MEETING YOU IN PARIS
I LOVE YOU
JUMPING IN THAT PUDDLE AT 4 AM AND RUNNING AWAY FROM THAT GIG TWO CRAZY KIDS IN LOVE
MOVING IN
SEEING 2046 IN THE OLD CINEMA AND CRYING OUR HEARTS OUT
YOU SMELL LIKE VANILLA AND SOFTENED PATCHOULI AND
YOU SMELL LIKE SPILLED HONEY
"IT'S GOING TO BE FINE."
PROMISE?
(THAT EMPTY SPACE YOU MAKE WHEN YOU DON'T WANT TO LIE)
CREATING THAT SPECIAL EMAIL ADDRESS ONLY YOU KNEW ABOUT
IT MADE YOU LAUGH
YOU LIKE WRITING. YOU LIKE MAKING THINGS UP.
IT'S THE ONLY THING I'M GOOD AT.
THAT'S NOT TRUE.
EXPERIENCE.
HOW DO YOU KNOW?

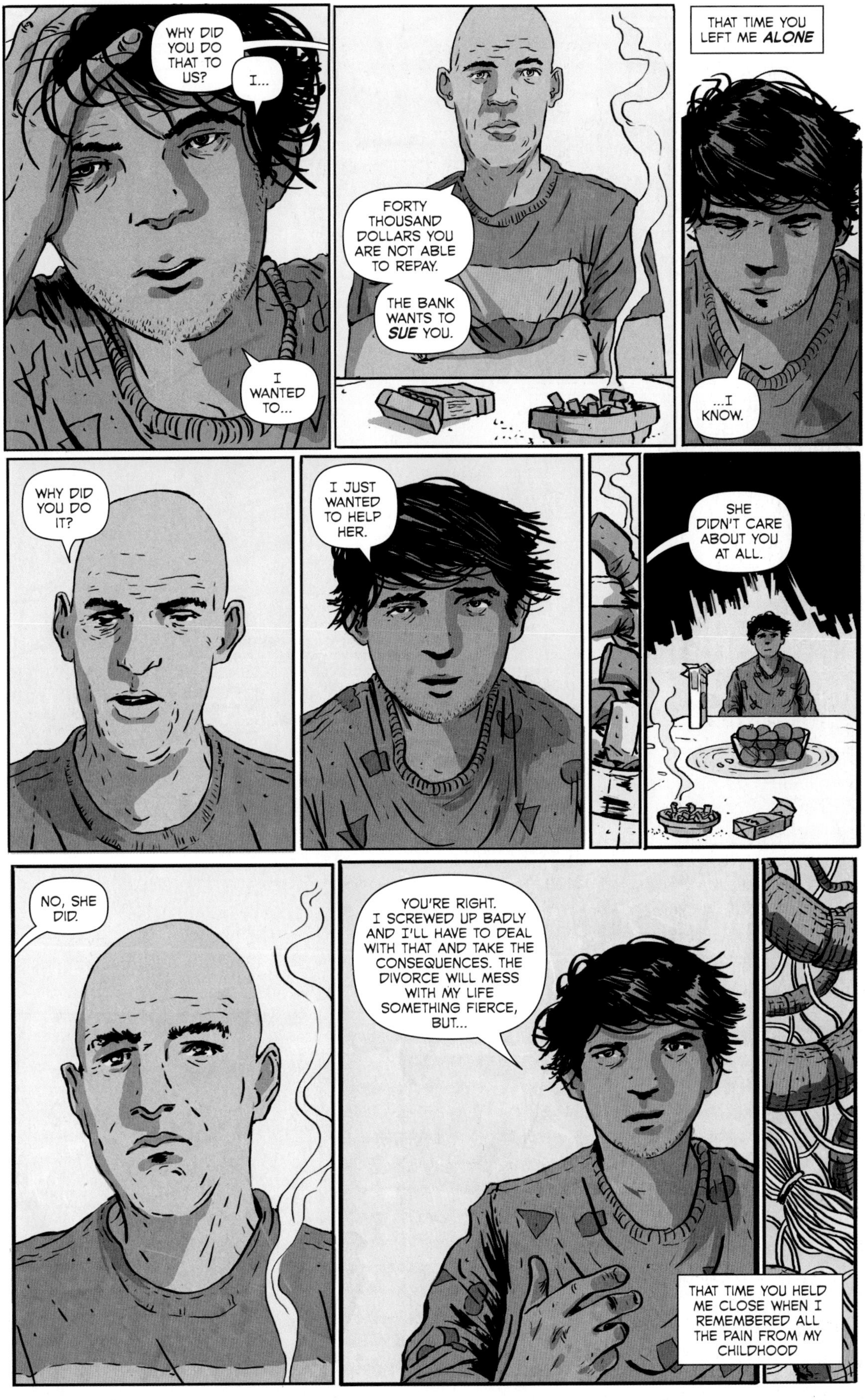
WHY DID YOU DO THAT TO US?
I...
I WANTED TO...
FORTY THOUSAND DOLLARS YOU ARE NOT ABLE TO REPAY.
THE BANK WANTS TO *SUE* YOU.
THAT TIME YOU LEFT ME *ALONE*
...I KNOW.
WHY DID YOU DO IT?
I JUST WANTED TO HELP HER.
SHE DIDN'T CARE ABOUT YOU AT ALL.
NO, SHE DID.
YOU'RE RIGHT. I SCREWED UP BADLY AND I'LL HAVE TO DEAL WITH THAT AND TAKE THE CONSEQUENCES. THE DIVORCE WILL MESS WITH MY LIFE SOMETHING FIERCE, BUT...
THAT TIME YOU HELD ME CLOSE WHEN I REMEMBERED ALL THE PAIN FROM MY CHILDHOOD

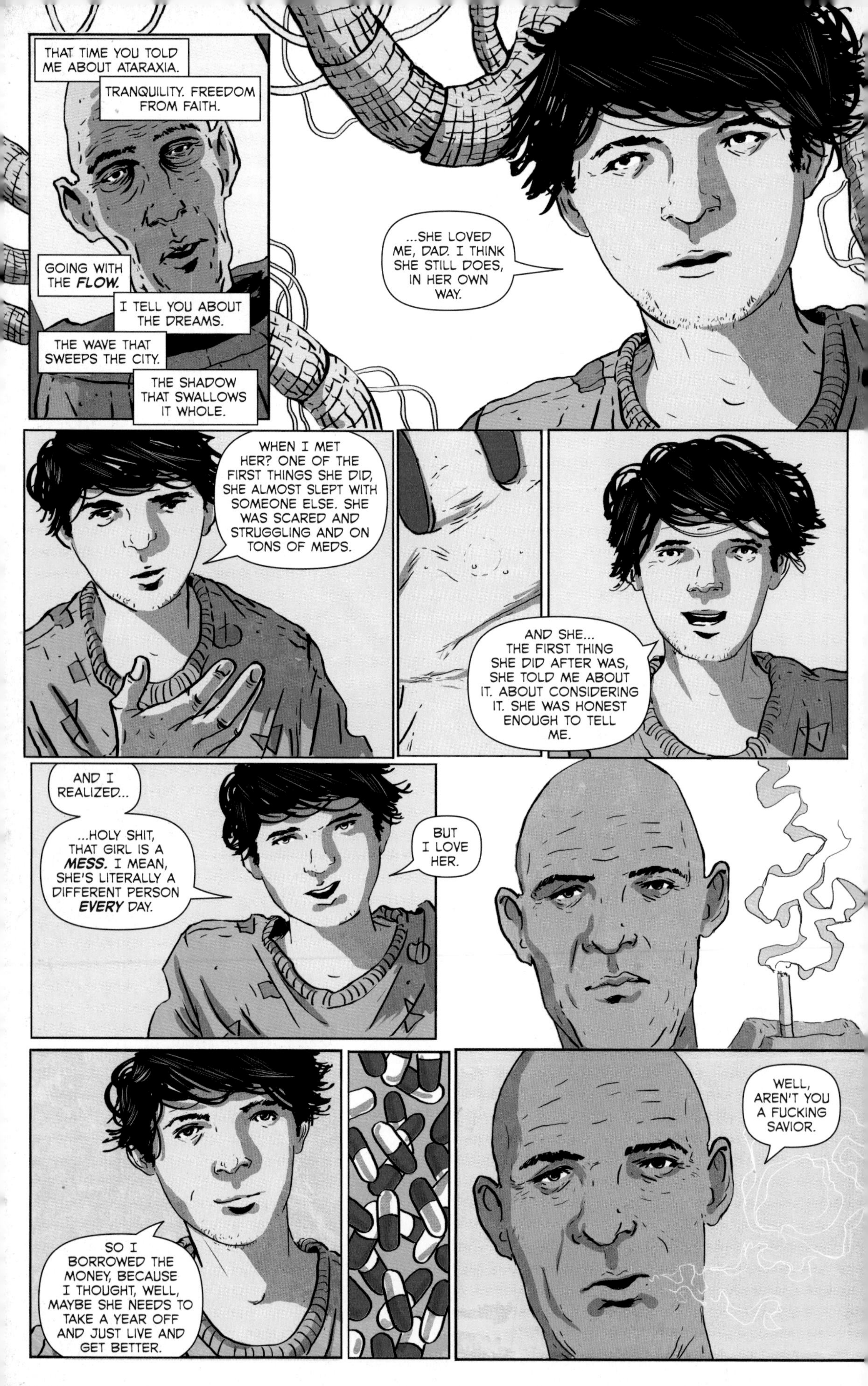
THAT TIME YOU TOLD ME ABOUT ATARAXIA.
TRANQUILITY. FREEDOM FROM FAITH.
GOING WITH THE *FLOW.*
I TELL YOU ABOUT THE DREAMS.
THE WAVE THAT SWEEPS THE CITY.
THE SHADOW THAT SWALLOWS IT WHOLE.
...SHE LOVED ME, DAD. I THINK SHE STILL DOES, IN HER OWN WAY.
WHEN I MET HER? ONE OF THE FIRST THINGS SHE DID, SHE ALMOST SLEPT WITH SOMEONE ELSE. SHE WAS SCARED AND STRUGGLING AND ON TONS OF MEDS.
AND SHE... THE FIRST THING SHE DID AFTER WAS, SHE TOLD ME ABOUT IT. ABOUT CONSIDERING IT. SHE WAS HONEST ENOUGH TO TELL ME.
AND I REALIZED...
...HOLY SHIT, THAT GIRL IS A *MESS.* I MEAN, SHE'S LITERALLY A DIFFERENT PERSON *EVERY* DAY.
BUT I LOVE HER.
SO I BORROWED THE MONEY, BECAUSE I THOUGHT, WELL, MAYBE SHE NEEDS TO TAKE A YEAR OFF AND JUST LIVE AND GET BETTER.
WELL, AREN'T YOU A FUCKING SAVIOR.

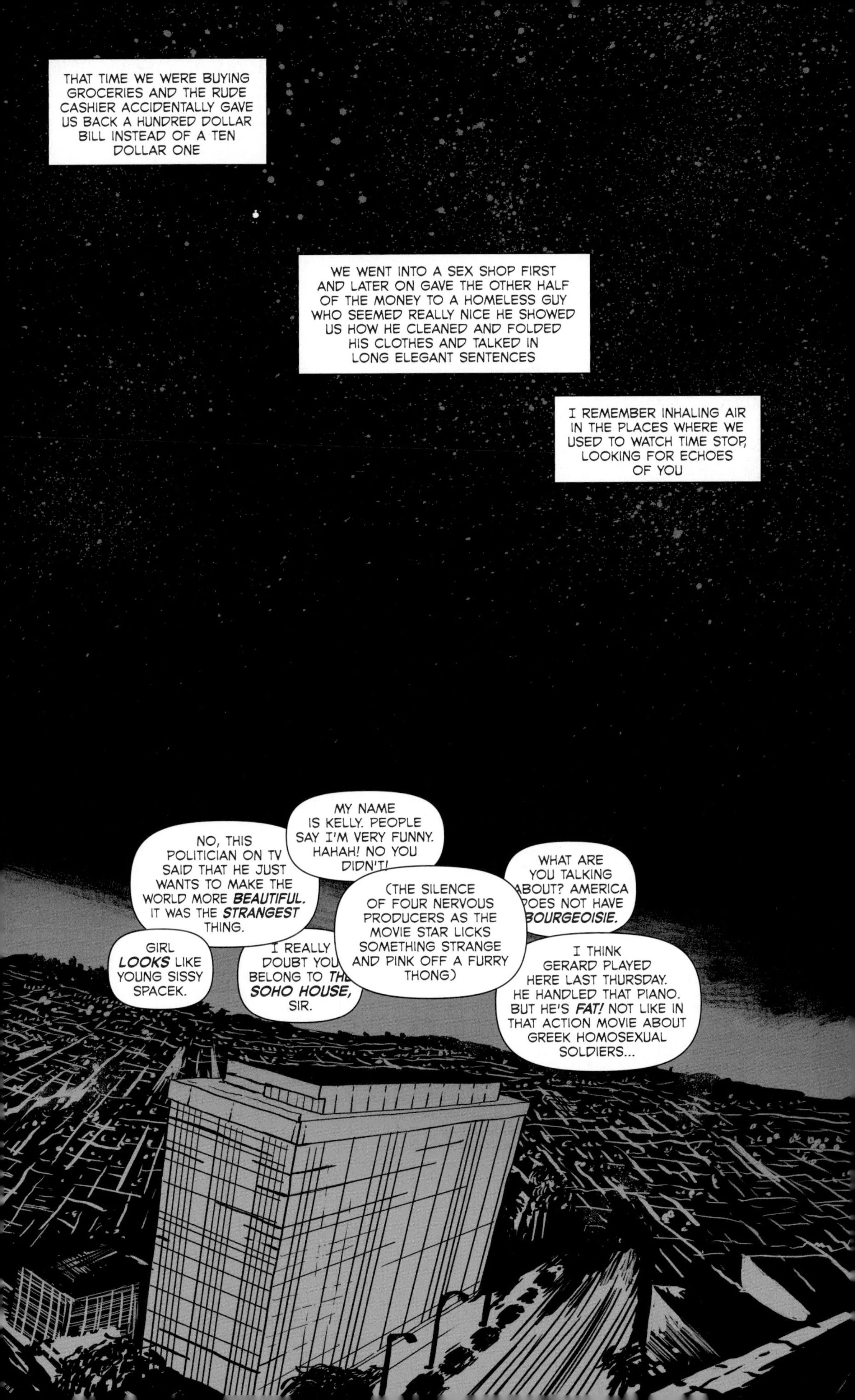

THAT TIME WE WERE BUYING GROCERIES AND THE RUDE CASHIER ACCIDENTALLY GAVE US BACK A HUNDRED DOLLAR BILL INSTEAD OF A TEN DOLLAR ONE
WE WENT INTO A SEX SHOP FIRST AND LATER ON GAVE THE OTHER HALF OF THE MONEY TO A HOMELESS GUY WHO SEEMED REALLY NICE HE SHOWED US HOW HE CLEANED AND FOLDED HIS CLOTHES AND TALKED IN LONG ELEGANT SENTENCES
I REMEMBER INHALING AIR IN THE PLACES WHERE WE USED TO WATCH TIME STOP, LOOKING FOR ECHOES OF YOU
NO, THIS POLITICIAN ON TV SAID THAT HE JUST WANTS TO MAKE THE WORLD MORE ***BEAUTIFUL.*** IT WAS THE ***STRANGEST*** THING.
MY NAME IS KELLY. PEOPLE SAY I'M VERY FUNNY. HAHAH! NO YOU DIDN'T!
WHAT ARE YOU TALKING ABOUT? AMERICA DOES NOT HAVE ***BOURGEOISIE.***
(THE SILENCE OF FOUR NERVOUS PRODUCERS AS THE MOVIE STAR LICKS SOMETHING STRANGE AND PINK OFF A FURRY THONG)
GIRL ***LOOKS*** LIKE YOUNG SISSY SPACEK.
I REALLY DOUBT YOU BELONG TO ***THE SOHO HOUSE,*** SIR.
I THINK GERARD PLAYED HERE LAST THURSDAY. HE HANDLED THAT PIANO. BUT HE'S ***FAT!*** NOT LIKE IN THAT ACTION MOVIE ABOUT GREEK HOMOSEXUAL SOLDIERS...

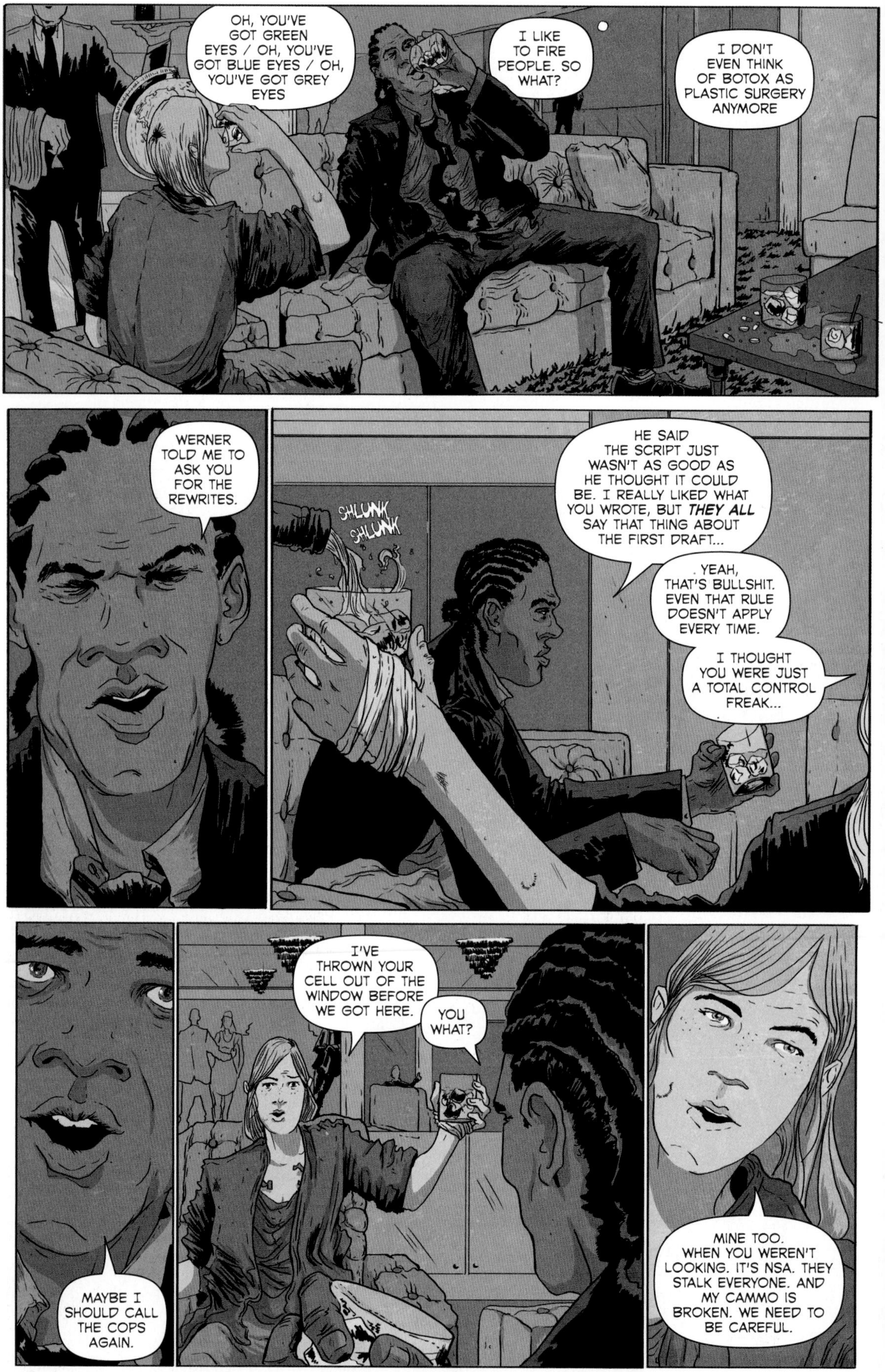
OH, YOU'VE GOT GREEN EYES / OH, YOU'VE GOT BLUE EYES / OH, YOU'VE GOT GREY EYES
I LIKE TO FIRE PEOPLE. SO WHAT?
I DON'T EVEN THINK OF BOTOX AS PLASTIC SURGERY ANYMORE
WERNER TOLD ME TO ASK YOU FOR THE REWRITES.
SHLUNK SHLUNK
HE SAID THE SCRIPT JUST WASN'T AS GOOD AS HE THOUGHT IT COULD BE. I REALLY LIKED WHAT YOU WROTE, BUT *THEY ALL* SAY THAT THING ABOUT THE FIRST DRAFT...
. YEAH, THAT'S BULLSHIT. EVEN THAT RULE DOESN'T APPLY EVERY TIME.
I THOUGHT YOU WERE JUST A TOTAL CONTROL FREAK...
MAYBE I SHOULD CALL THE COPS AGAIN.
I'VE THROWN YOUR CELL OUT OF THE WINDOW BEFORE WE GOT HERE.
YOU WHAT?
MINE TOO. WHEN YOU WEREN'T LOOKING. IT'S NSA. THEY STALK EVERYONE. AND MY CAMMO IS BROKEN. WE NEED TO BE CAREFUL.

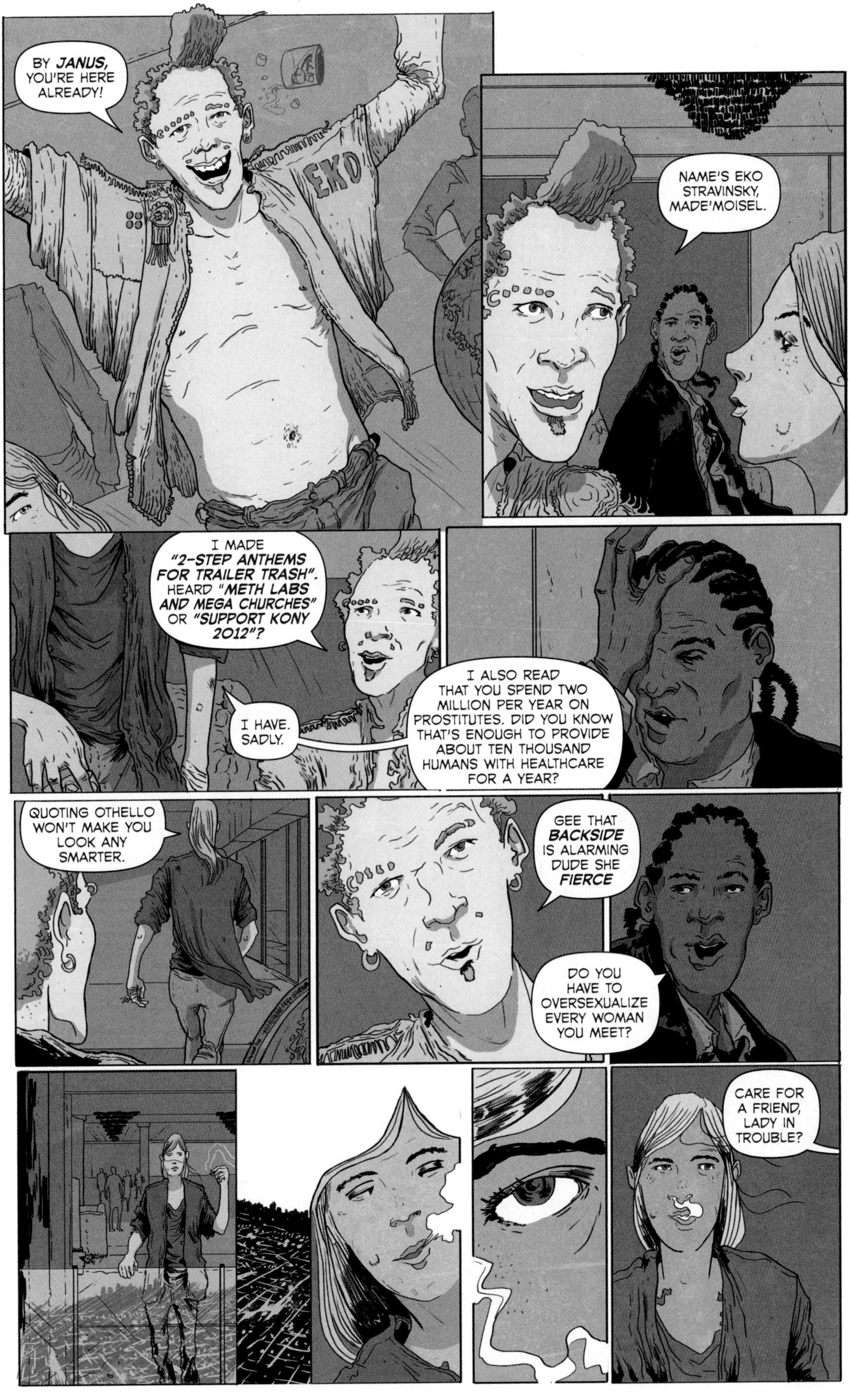
BY *JANUS,* YOU'RE HERE ALREADY!
NAME'S EKO STRAVINSKY, MADE'MOISEL.
I MADE ***"2-STEP ANTHEMS FOR TRAILER TRASH".*** HEARD ***"METH LABS AND MEGA CHURCHES"*** OR ***"SUPPORT KONY 2012"?***
I HAVE. SADLY.
I ALSO READ THAT YOU SPEND TWO MILLION PER YEAR ON PROSTITUTES. DID YOU KNOW THAT'S ENOUGH TO PROVIDE ABOUT TEN THOUSAND HUMANS WITH HEALTHCARE FOR A YEAR?
QUOTING OTHELLO WON'T MAKE YOU LOOK ANY SMARTER.
GEE THAT ***BACKSIDE*** IS ALARMING DUDE SHE ***FIERCE***
DO YOU HAVE TO OVERSEXUALIZE EVERY WOMAN YOU MEET?
CARE FOR A FRIEND, LADY IN TROUBLE?

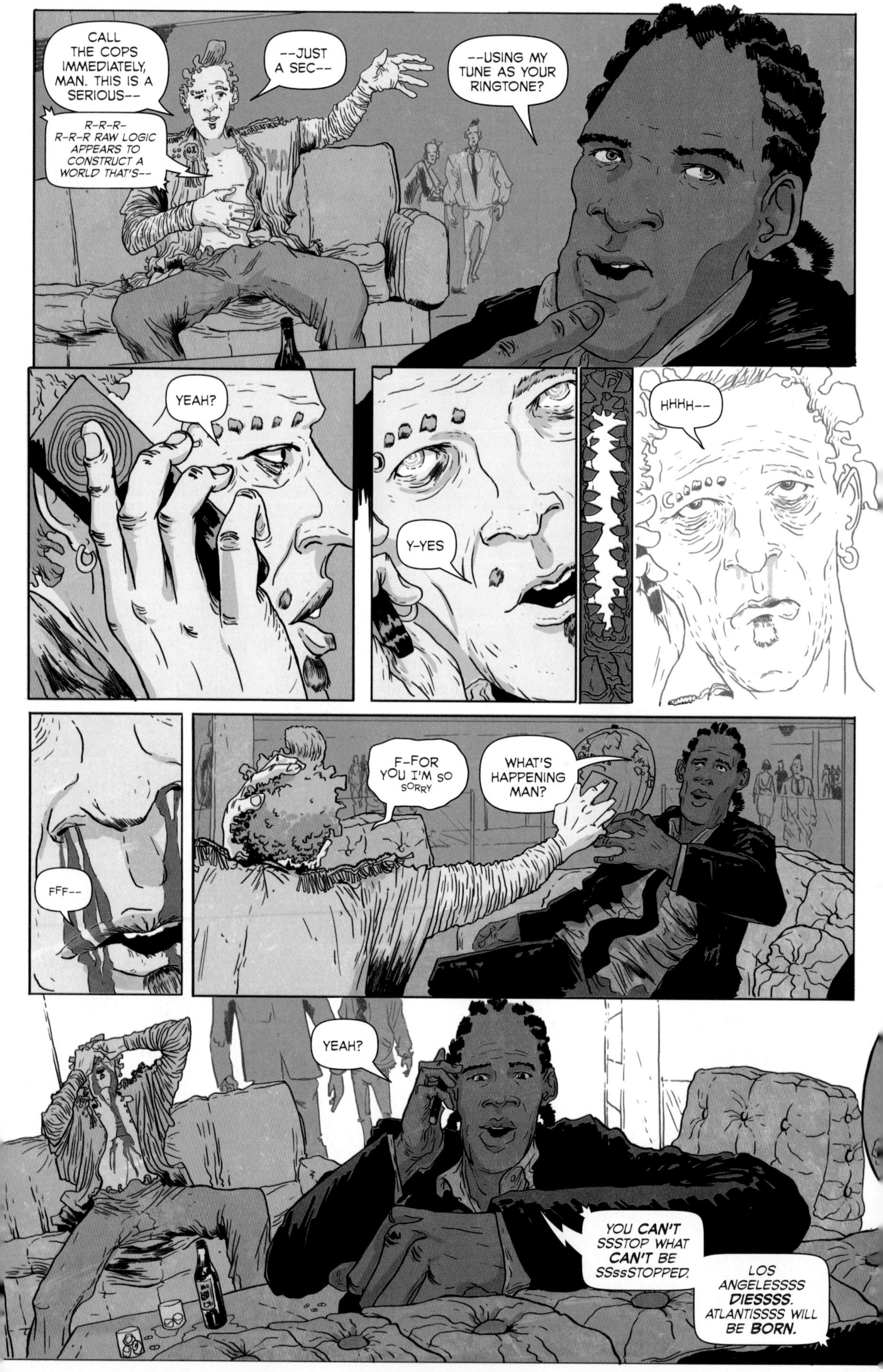
CALL THE COPS IMMEDIATELY, MAN. THIS IS A SERIOUS--
R-R-R-R-R-R RAW LOGIC APPEARS TO CONSTRUCT A WORLD THAT'S--
--JUST A SEC--
--USING MY TUNE AS YOUR RINGTONE?
YEAH?
Y-YES
HHHH--
FFF--
F-FOR YOU I'M SO SORRY
WHAT'S HAPPENING MAN?
YEAH?
YOU CAN'T SSSTOP WHAT CAN'T BE SSssSTOPPED.
LOS ANGELESSSS DIESSSS. ATLANTISSSS WILL BE BORN.

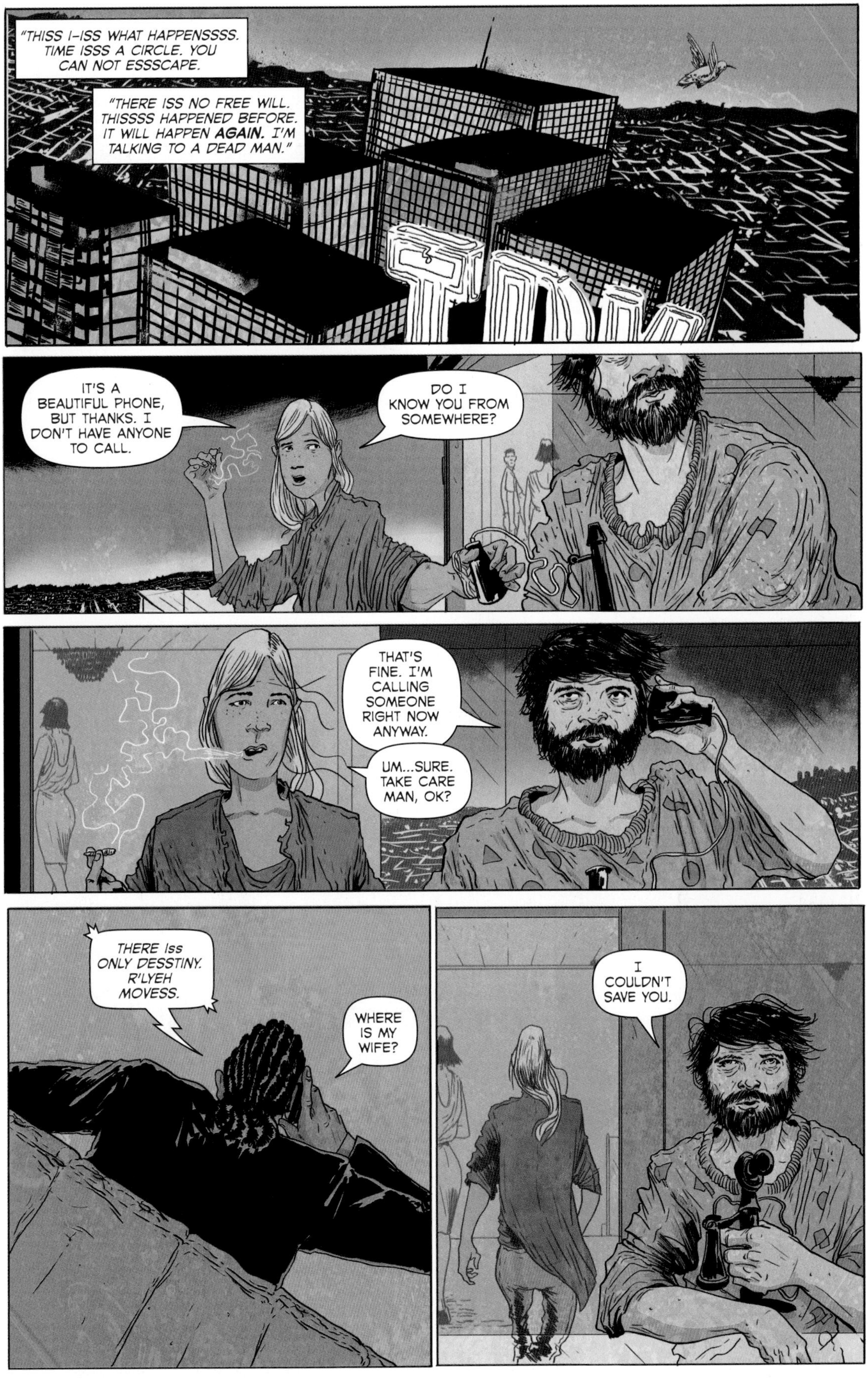
"THISS I-ISS WHAT HAPPENSSSS. TIME ISSS A CIRCLE. YOU CAN NOT ESSSCAPE.
"THERE ISS NO FREE WILL. THISSSS HAPPENED BEFORE. IT WILL HAPPEN **AGAIN.** I'M TALKING TO A DEAD MAN."
IT'S A BEAUTIFUL PHONE, BUT THANKS. I DON'T HAVE ANYONE TO CALL.
DO I KNOW YOU FROM SOMEWHERE?
THAT'S FINE. I'M CALLING SOMEONE RIGHT NOW ANYWAY.
UM...SURE. TAKE CARE MAN, OK?
THERE Iss ONLY DESSTINY. R'LYEH MOVESS.
WHERE IS MY WIFE?
I COULDN'T SAVE YOU.

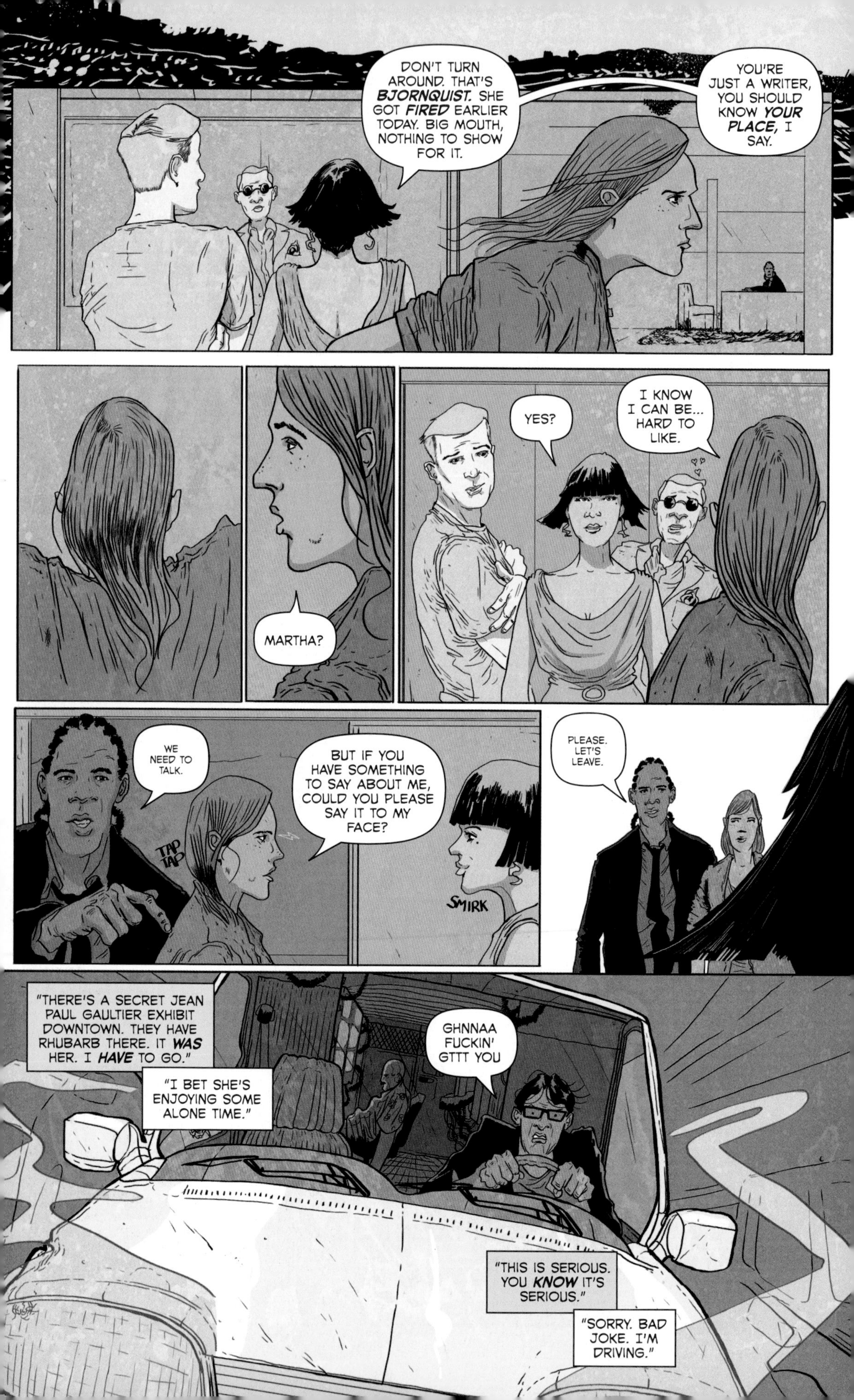

DON'T TURN AROUND. THAT'S BJORNQUIST. SHE GOT FIRED EARLIER TODAY. BIG MOUTH, NOTHING TO SHOW FOR IT.
YOU'RE JUST A WRITER, YOU SHOULD KNOW YOUR PLACE, I SAY.
MARTHA?
YES?
I KNOW I CAN BE... HARD TO LIKE.
WE NEED TO TALK.
TAP TAP
BUT IF YOU HAVE SOMETHING TO SAY ABOUT ME, COULD YOU PLEASE SAY IT TO MY FACE?
SMIRK
PLEASE. LET'S LEAVE.
"THERE'S A SECRET JEAN PAUL GAULTIER EXHIBIT DOWNTOWN. THEY HAVE RHUBARB THERE. IT WAS HER. I HAVE TO GO."
"I BET SHE'S ENJOYING SOME ALONE TIME."
GHNNAA FUCKIN' GTTT YOU
"THIS IS SERIOUS. YOU KNOW IT'S SERIOUS."
"SORRY. BAD JOKE. I'M DRIVING."

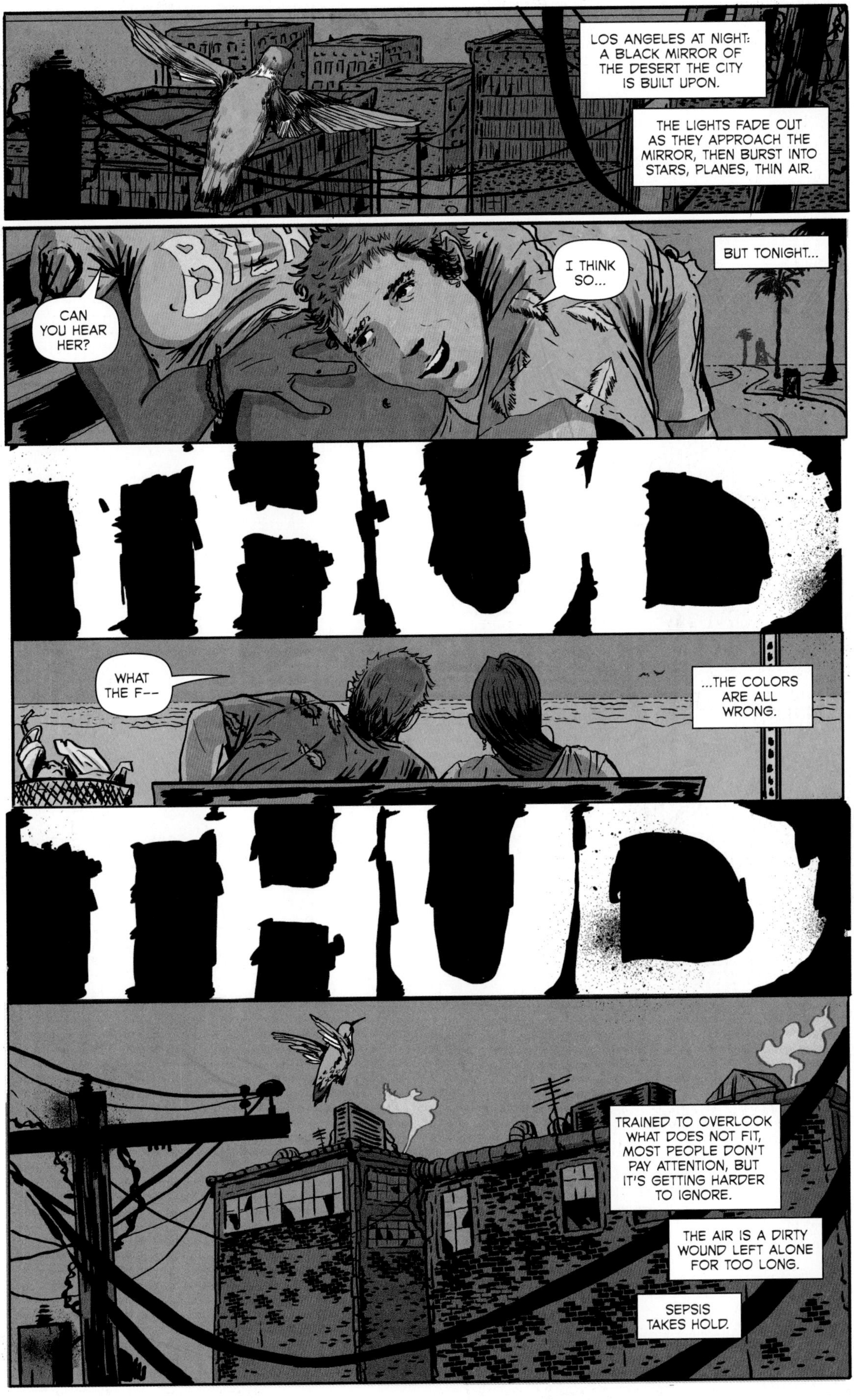
LOS ANGELES AT NIGHT: A BLACK MIRROR OF THE DESERT THE CITY IS BUILT UPON.
THE LIGHTS FADE OUT AS THEY APPROACH THE MIRROR, THEN BURST INTO STARS, PLANES, THIN AIR.
BUT TONIGHT...
CAN YOU HEAR HER?
I THINK SO...
THUD
WHAT THE F--
...THE COLORS ARE ALL WRONG.
THUD
TRAINED TO OVERLOOK WHAT DOES NOT FIT, MOST PEOPLE DON'T PAY ATTENTION, BUT IT'S GETTING HARDER TO IGNORE.
THE AIR IS A DIRTY WOUND LEFT ALONE FOR TOO LONG.
SEPSIS TAKES HOLD.

THE ASTRONAUT IS
CLOSER NOW.

FALLING,
FALLING,
FALLING.

HAVE TO FIND THE BUTTON.
CONNECT THE WIRES
AGAIN. FORGET THAT
THING IN THE OCEAN.

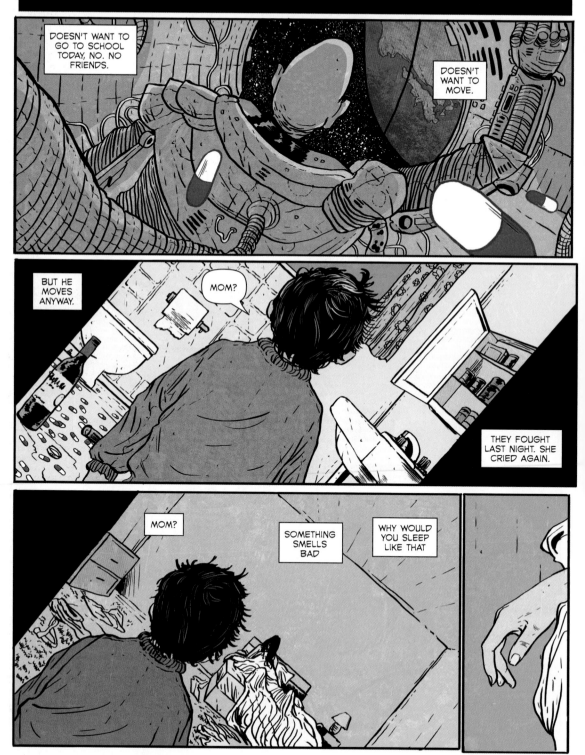

DOESN'T WANT TO
GO TO SCHOOL
TODAY, NO. NO
FRIENDS.

DOESN'T
WANT TO
MOVE.

BUT HE
MOVES
ANYWAY.

MOM?

THEY FOUGHT
LAST NIGHT. SHE
CRIED AGAIN.

MOM?

SOMETHING
SMELLS
BAD

WHY WOULD
YOU SLEEP
LIKE THAT

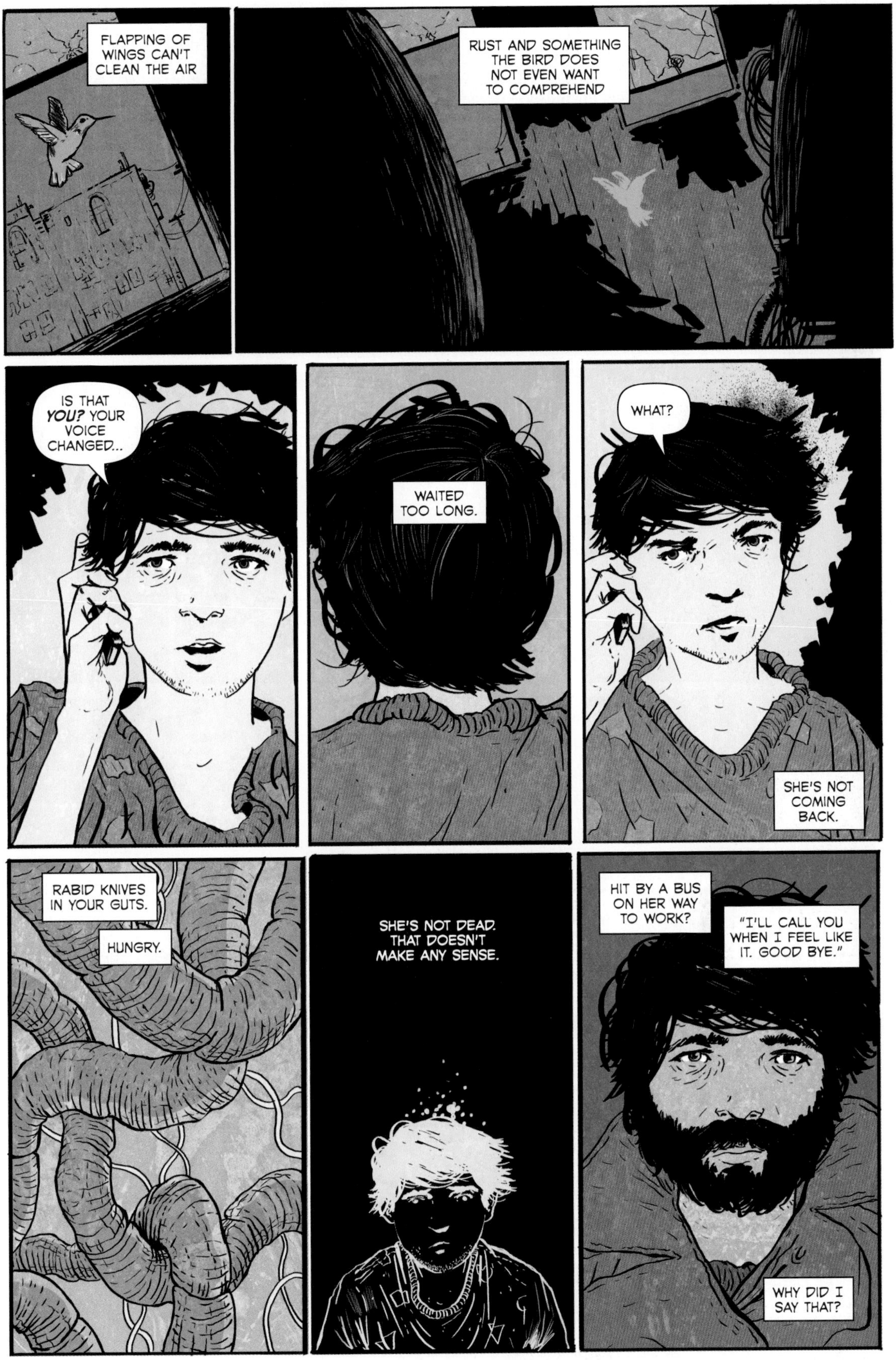
FLAPPING OF WINGS CAN'T CLEAN THE AIR
RUST AND SOMETHING THE BIRD DOES NOT EVEN WANT TO COMPREHEND
IS THAT *YOU?* YOUR VOICE CHANGED...
WAITED TOO LONG.
WHAT?
SHE'S NOT COMING BACK.
RABID KNIVES IN YOUR GUTS.
HUNGRY.
SHE'S NOT DEAD. THAT DOESN'T MAKE ANY SENSE.
HIT BY A BUS ON HER WAY TO WORK?
"I'LL CALL YOU WHEN I FEEL LIKE IT. GOOD BYE."
WHY DID I SAY THAT?

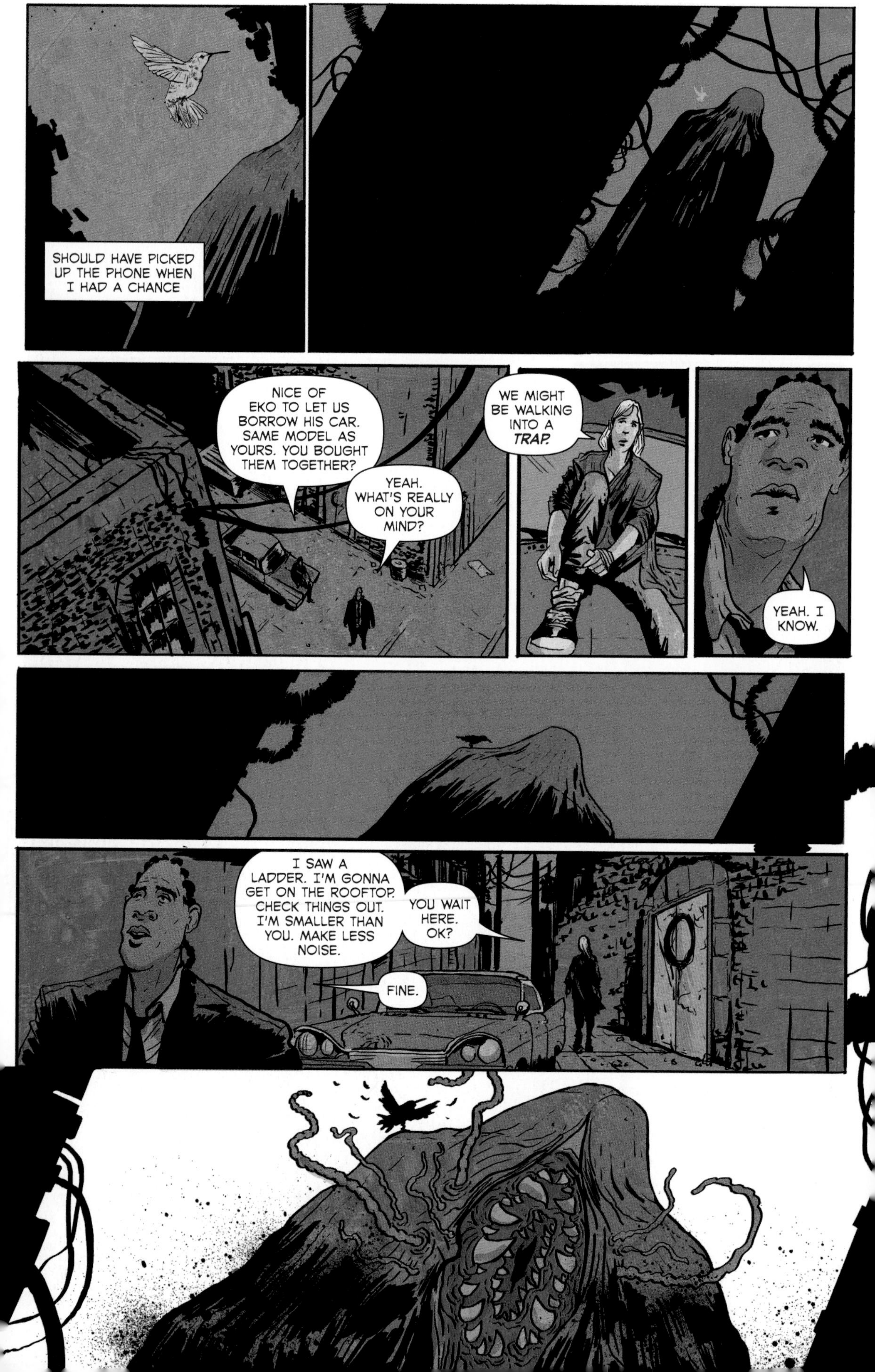

SHOULD HAVE PICKED UP THE PHONE WHEN I HAD A CHANCE
NICE OF EKO TO LET US BORROW HIS CAR. SAME MODEL AS YOURS. YOU BOUGHT THEM TOGETHER?
YEAH. WHAT'S REALLY ON YOUR MIND?
WE MIGHT BE WALKING INTO A *TRAP.*
YEAH. I KNOW.
I SAW A LADDER. I'M GONNA GET ON THE ROOFTOP. CHECK THINGS OUT. I'M SMALLER THAN YOU. MAKE LESS NOISE.
YOU WAIT HERE. OK?
FINE.

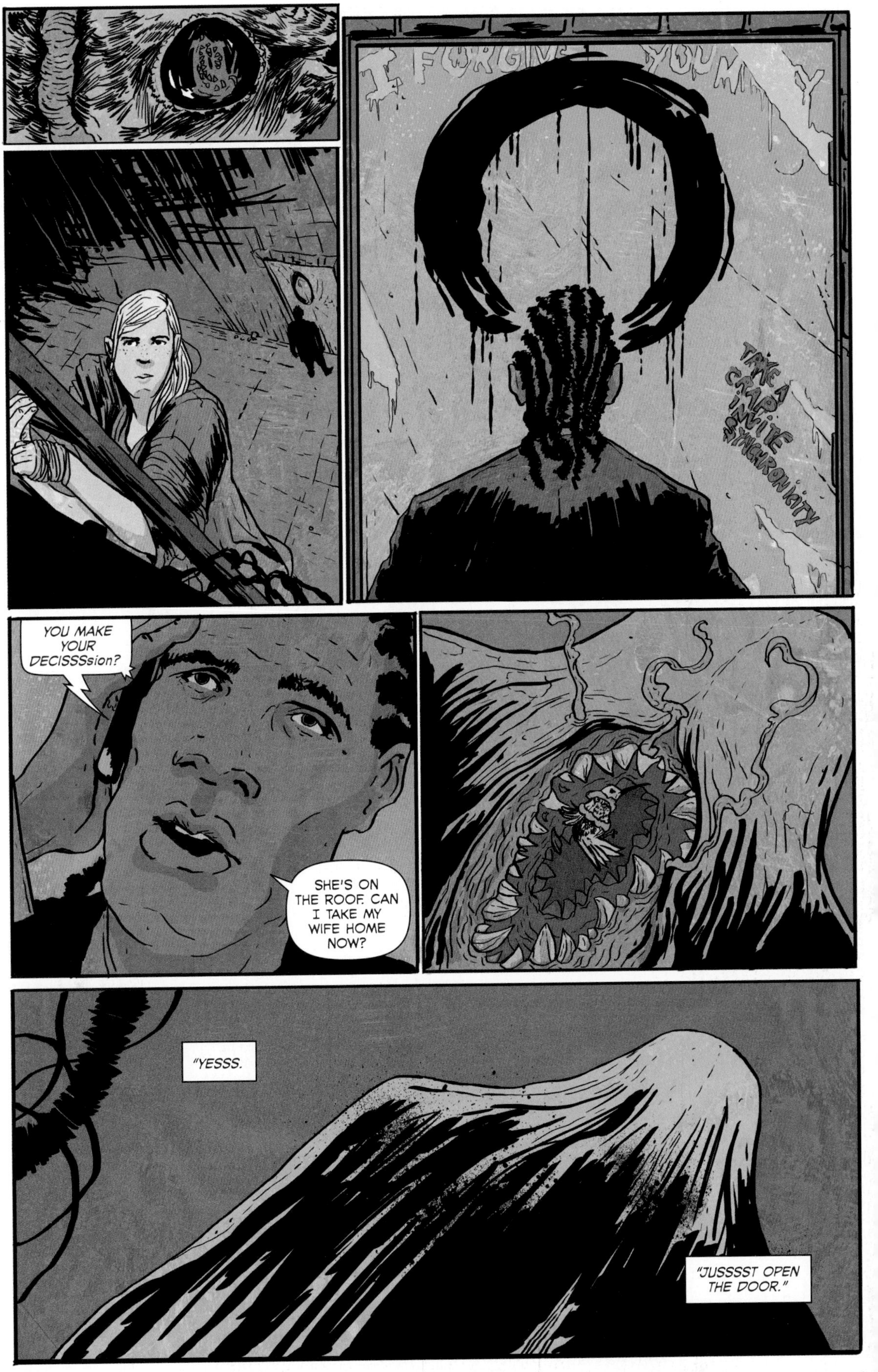
TAKE A CRAP INVITE SYNCHRONICITY
YOU MAKE YOUR DECISSSSsion?
SHE'S ON THE ROOF. CAN I TAKE MY WIFE HOME NOW?
"YESSS.
"JUSSSST OPEN THE DOOR."

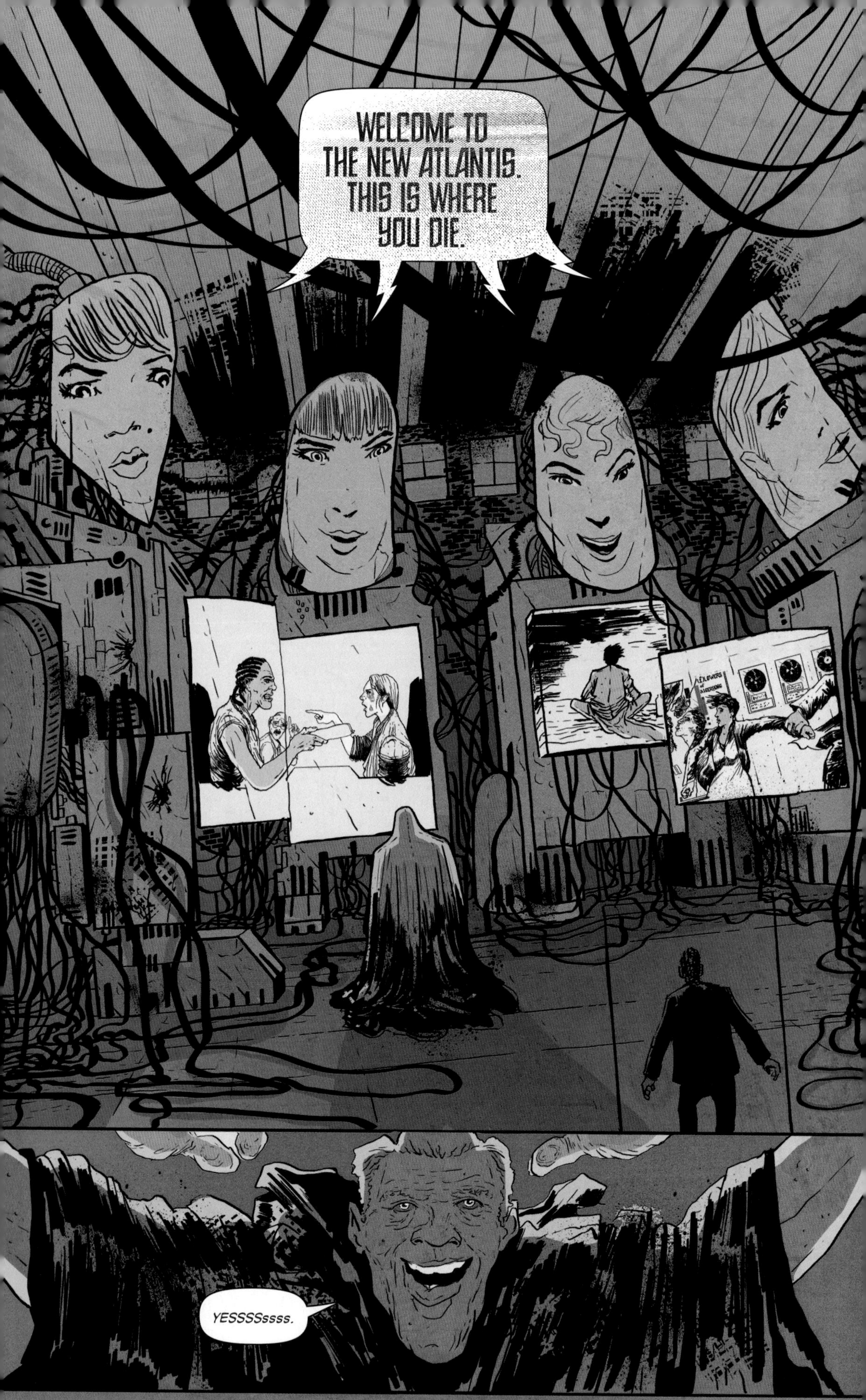
WELCOME TO THE NEW ATLANTIS. THIS IS WHERE YOU DIE.
YESSSSssss.

I leave Sisyphus at the foot of the mountain.
One always finds one's burden again.
But Sisyphus teaches the higher
fidelity that negates the gods and raises
rocks. He too concludes that all is well.
This universe henceforth without a master
seems to him neither sterile nor futile.
Each atom of that stone, each mineral flake of
that night-filled mountain, in itself, forms a world.
The struggle itself toward the heights
is enough to fill a man's heart.
One must imagine Sisyphus happy.

Albert Camus
'The Myth of Sisyphus'

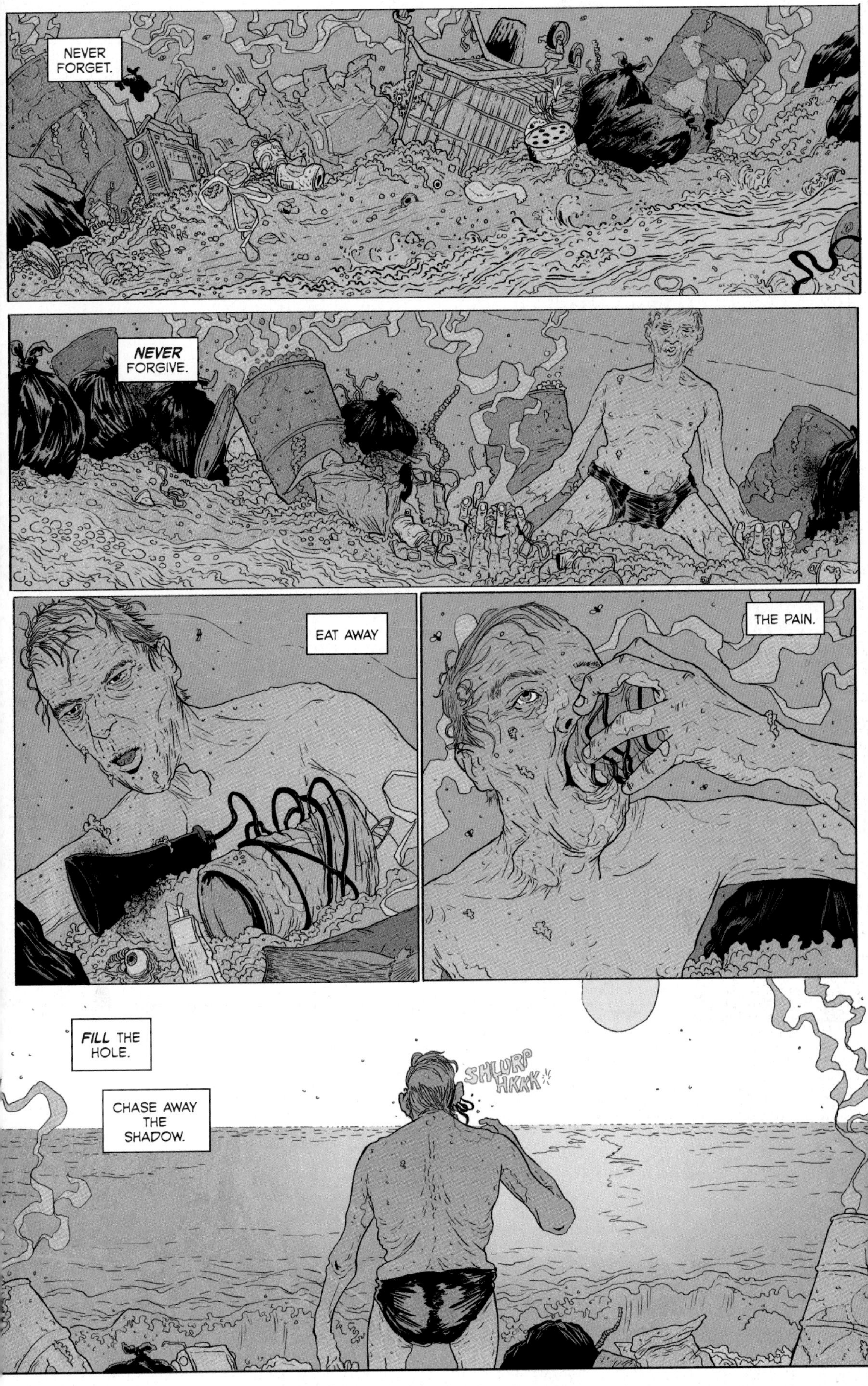
NEVER FORGET.
NEVER FORGIVE.
EAT AWAY
THE PAIN.
FILL THE HOLE.
CHASE AWAY THE SHADOW.
SHLURP
HKKK

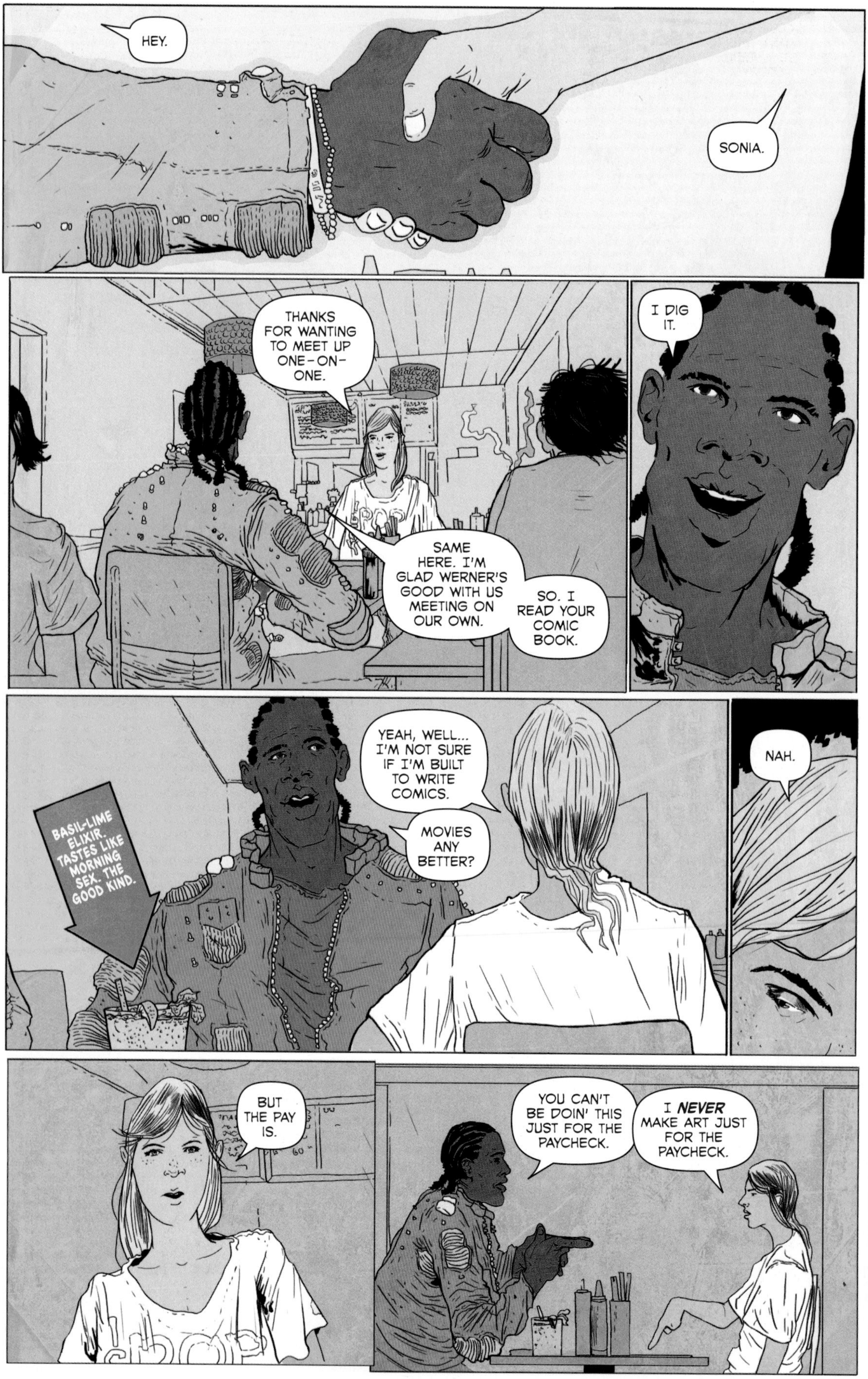
HEY.
SONIA.
THANKS FOR WANTING TO MEET UP ONE-ON-ONE.
SAME HERE. I'M GLAD WERNER'S GOOD WITH US MEETING ON OUR OWN.
SO. I READ YOUR COMIC BOOK.
I DIG IT.
YEAH, WELL... I'M NOT SURE IF I'M BUILT TO WRITE COMICS.
MOVIES ANY BETTER?
BASIL-LIME ELIXIR. TASTES LIKE MORNING SEX. THE GOOD KIND.
NAH.
BUT THE PAY IS.
YOU CAN'T BE DOIN' THIS JUST FOR THE PAYCHECK.
I ***NEVER*** MAKE ART JUST FOR THE PAYCHECK.

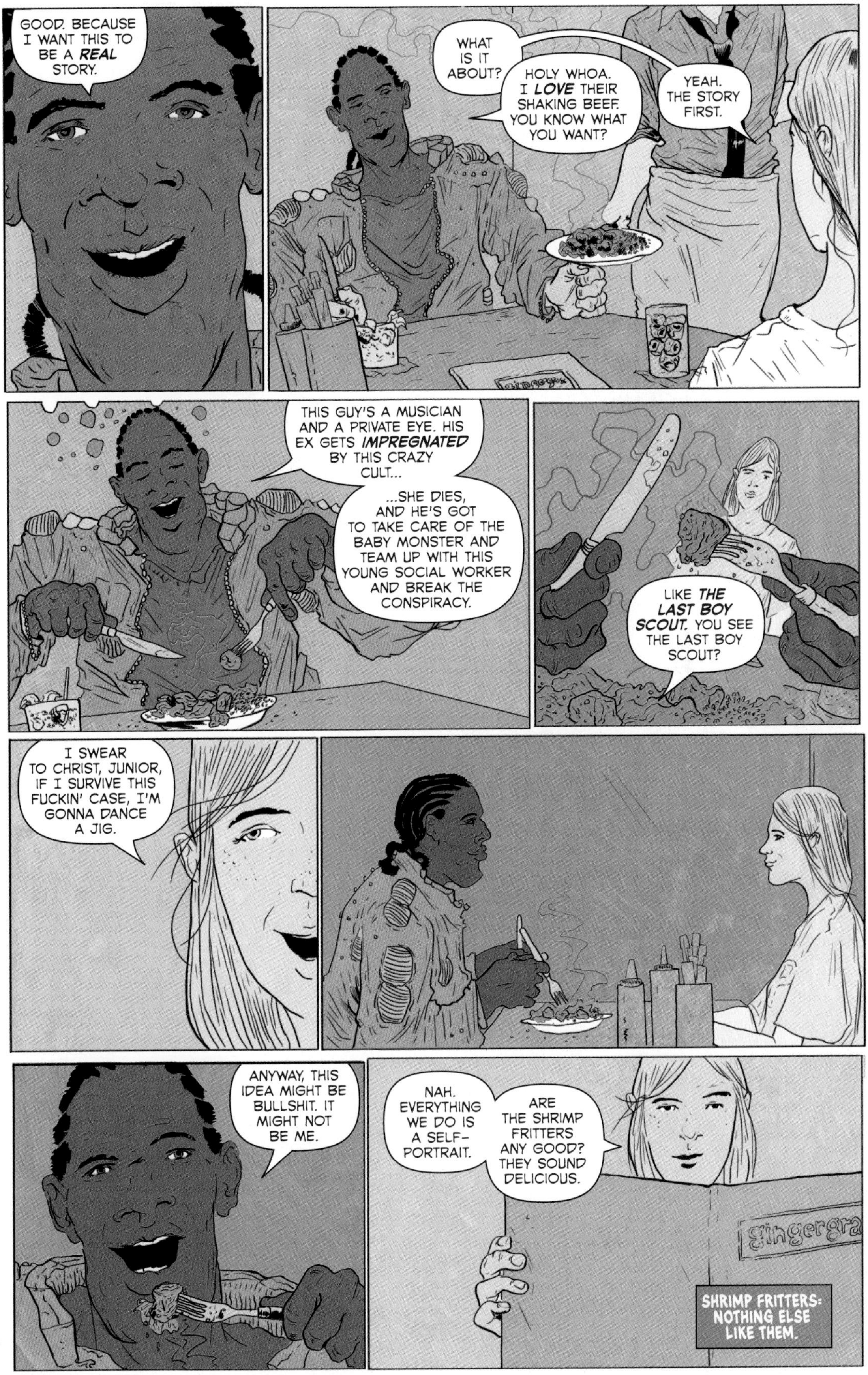
GOOD. BECAUSE I WANT THIS TO BE A *REAL* STORY.
WHAT IS IT ABOUT?
HOLY WHOA. I *LOVE* THEIR SHAKING BEEF. YOU KNOW WHAT YOU WANT?
YEAH. THE STORY FIRST.
THIS GUY'S A MUSICIAN AND A PRIVATE EYE. HIS EX GETS *IMPREGNATED* BY THIS CRAZY CULT...
...SHE DIES, AND HE'S GOT TO TAKE CARE OF THE BABY MONSTER AND TEAM UP WITH THIS YOUNG SOCIAL WORKER AND BREAK THE CONSPIRACY.
LIKE ***THE LAST BOY SCOUT.*** YOU SEE THE LAST BOY SCOUT?
I SWEAR TO CHRIST, JUNIOR, IF I SURVIVE THIS FUCKIN' CASE, I'M GONNA DANCE A JIG.
ANYWAY, THIS IDEA MIGHT BE BULLSHIT. IT MIGHT NOT BE ME.
NAH. EVERYTHING WE DO IS A SELF-PORTRAIT.
ARE THE SHRIMP FRITTERS ANY GOOD? THEY SOUND DELICIOUS.
gingergra
SHRIMP FRITTERS: NOTHING ELSE LIKE THEM.

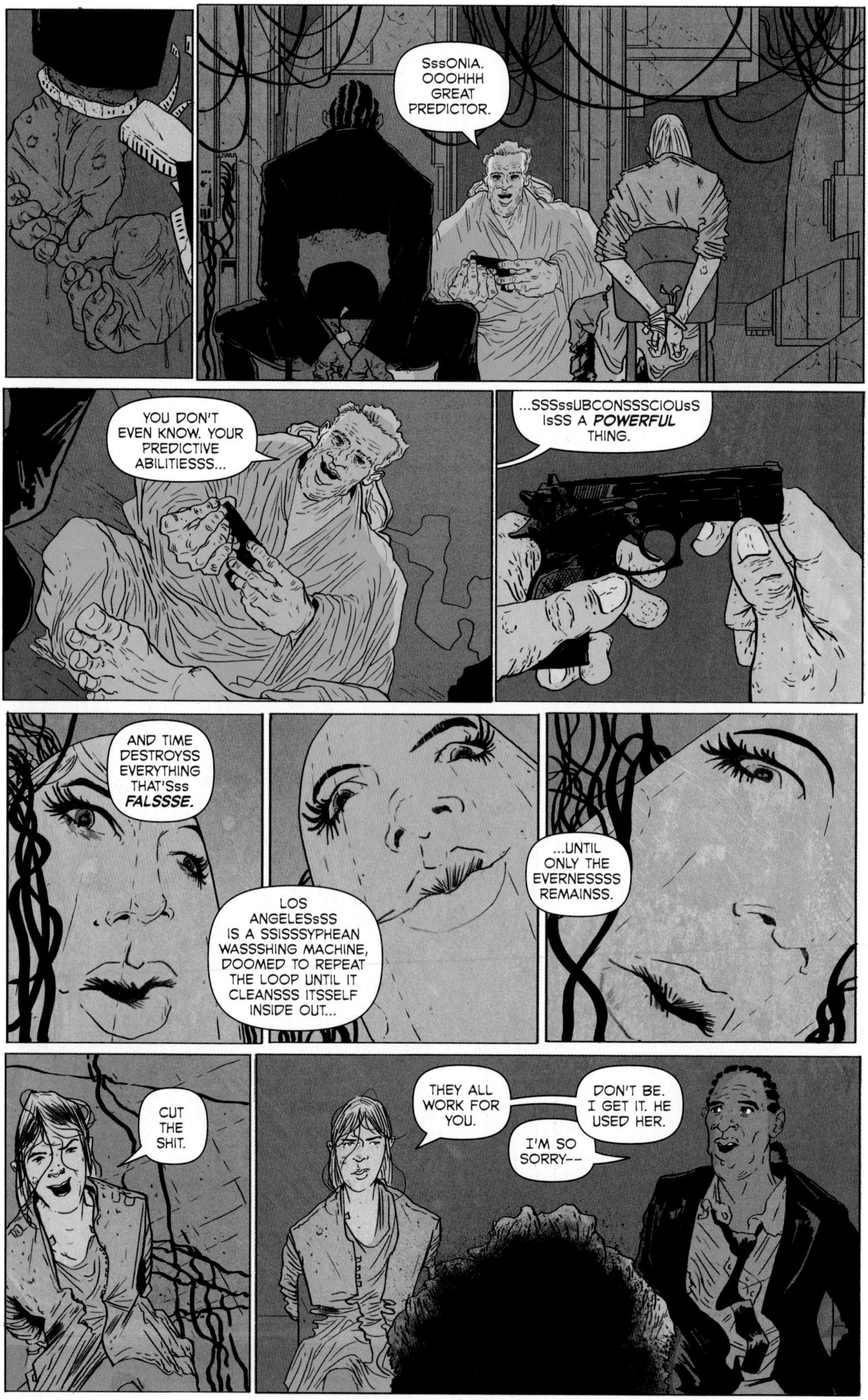
SssONIA. OOOHHH GREAT PREDICTOR.
YOU DON'T EVEN KNOW. YOUR PREDICTIVE ABILITIESSS...
...SSSssUBCONSSSCIOUsS IsSS A **POWERFUL** THING.
AND TIME DESTROYSS EVERYTHING THAT'Sss **FALSSSE.**
LOS ANGELESsSS IS A SSISSSYPHEAN WASSSHING MACHINE, DOOMED TO REPEAT THE LOOP UNTIL IT CLEANSSS ITSSELF INSIDE OUT...
...UNTIL ONLY THE EVERNESSSS REMAINSS.
CUT THE SHIT.
THEY ALL WORK FOR YOU.
I'M SO SORRY--
DON'T BE. I GET IT. HE USED HER.

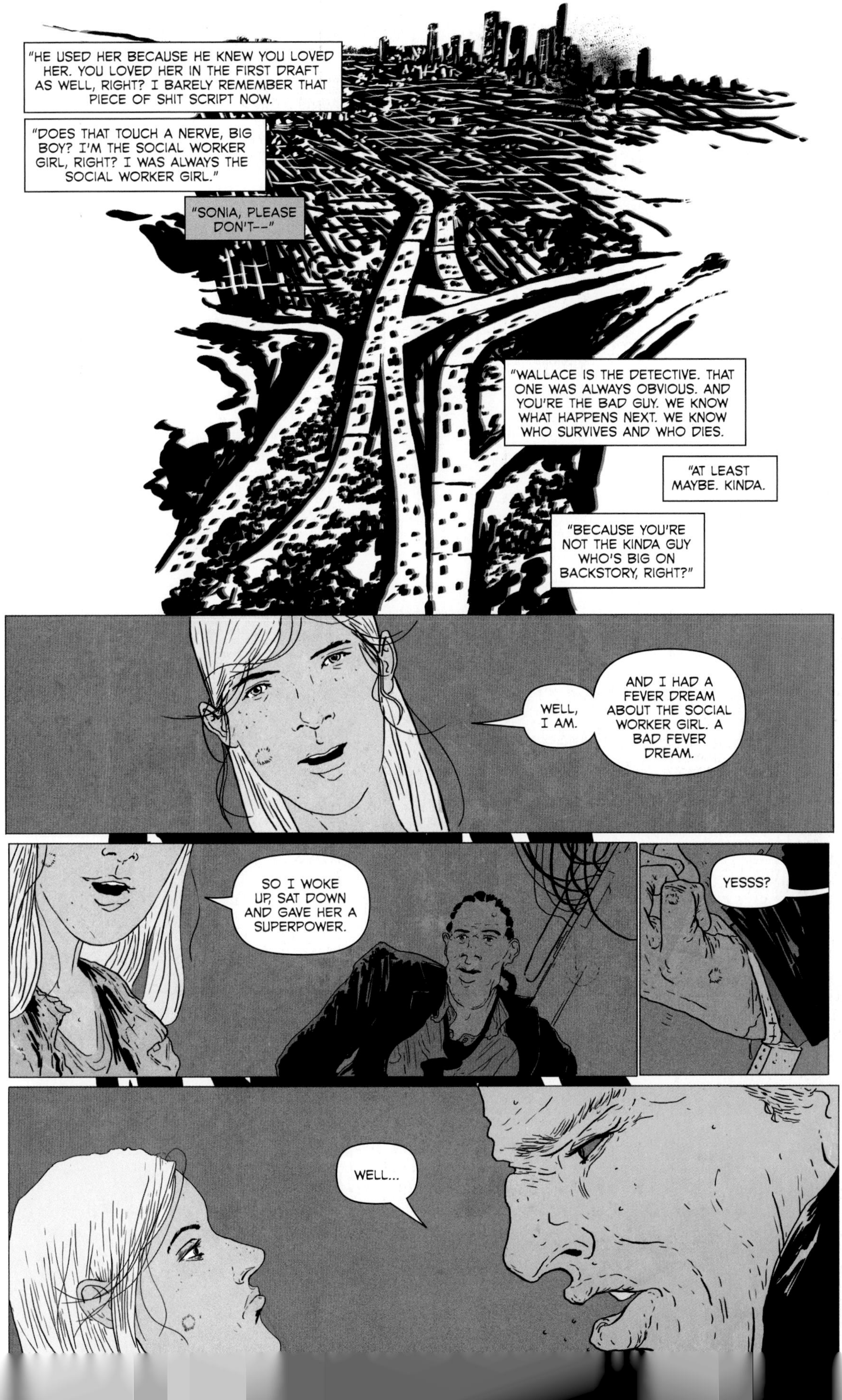
"HE USED HER BECAUSE HE KNEW YOU LOVED HER. YOU LOVED HER IN THE FIRST DRAFT AS WELL, RIGHT? I BARELY REMEMBER THAT PIECE OF SHIT SCRIPT NOW.
"DOES THAT TOUCH A NERVE, BIG BOY? I'M THE SOCIAL WORKER GIRL, RIGHT? I WAS ALWAYS THE SOCIAL WORKER GIRL."
"SONIA, PLEASE DON'T--"
"WALLACE IS THE DETECTIVE. THAT ONE WAS ALWAYS OBVIOUS. AND YOU'RE THE BAD GUY. WE KNOW WHAT HAPPENS NEXT. WE KNOW WHO SURVIVES AND WHO DIES.
"AT LEAST MAYBE. KINDA.
"BECAUSE YOU'RE NOT THE KINDA GUY WHO'S BIG ON BACKSTORY, RIGHT?"
WELL, I AM.
AND I HAD A FEVER DREAM ABOUT THE SOCIAL WORKER GIRL. A BAD FEVER DREAM.
SO I WOKE UP, SAT DOWN AND GAVE HER A SUPERPOWER.
YESSS?
WELL...

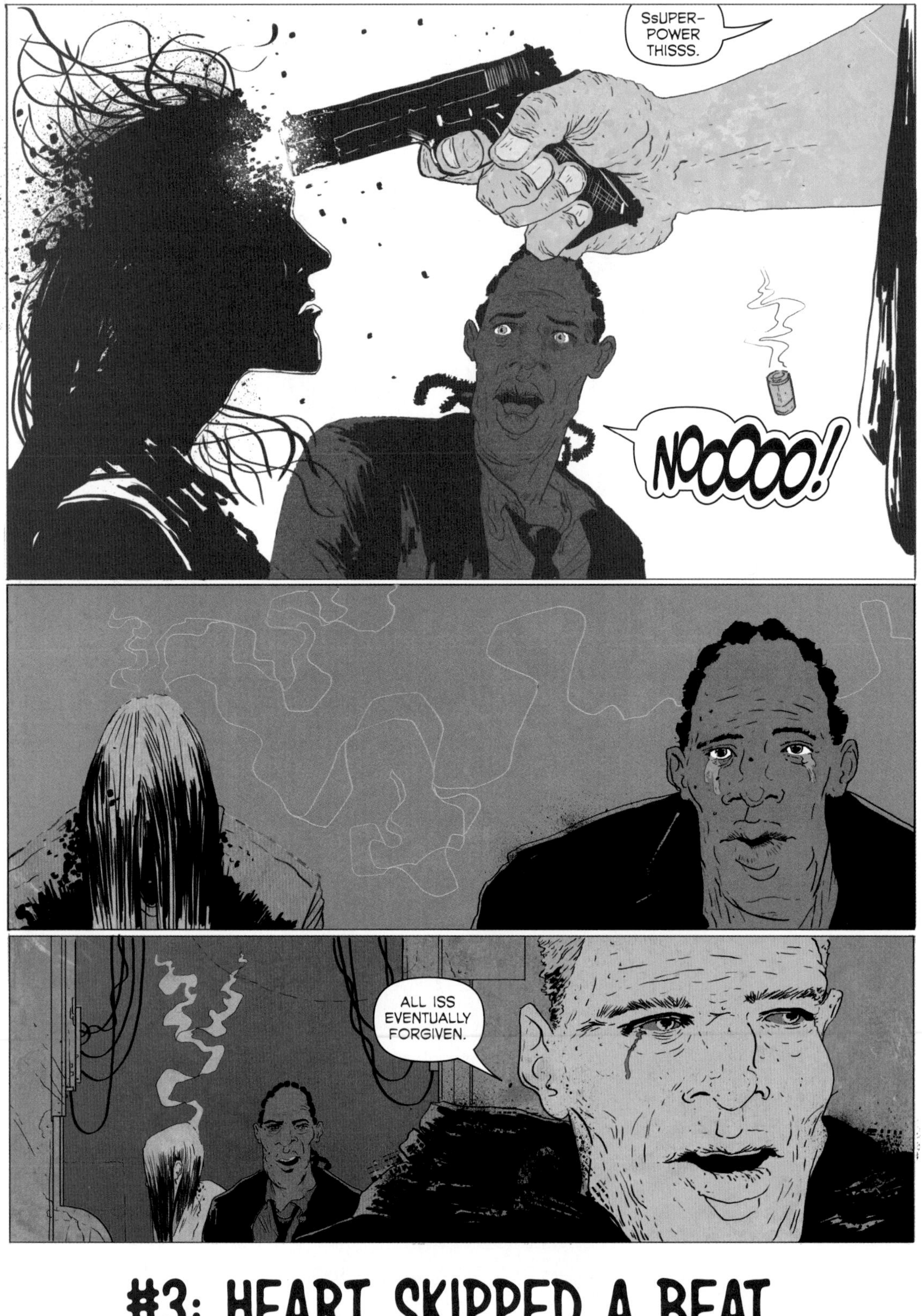
SsUPER-
POWER
THISSS.
NOOOOO!
ALL ISS
EVENTUALLY
FORGIVEN.

#3: HEART SKIPPED A BEAT

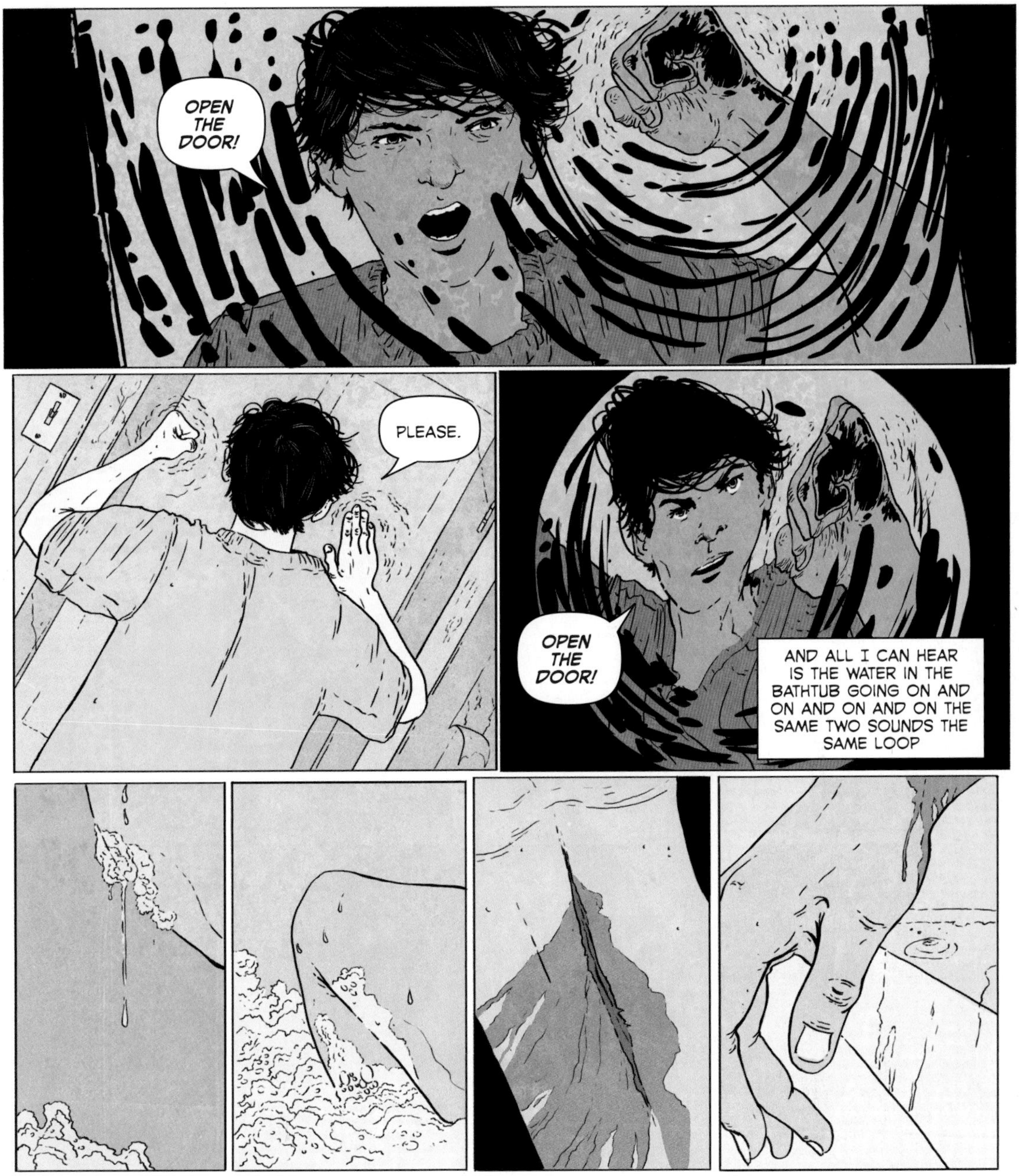
OPEN THE DOOR!
PLEASE.
OPEN THE DOOR!
AND ALL I CAN HEAR IS THE WATER IN THE BATHTUB GOING ON AND ON AND ON AND ON THE SAME TWO SOUNDS THE SAME LOOP

FIVE OR FIFTEEN OR TWENTY MINUTES LATER, I DON'T REALLY KNOW, I SOMEHOW OPEN THE DOOR. I DON'T EVEN REMEMBER WHAT I USED OR HOW IT HAPPENED -- WAS IT THE NEIGHBOR, DID HE HELP ME?

AND I OPEN THE DOOR AND RUN INTO THE BATHROOM TO SEE YOU DEAD BECAUSE THINGS REPEAT THEMSELVES THROUGH TIME IN DIFFERENT VARIATIONS I ***NEVER*** WANT TO GO THROUGH THIS AGAIN WITH ANYONE ELSE

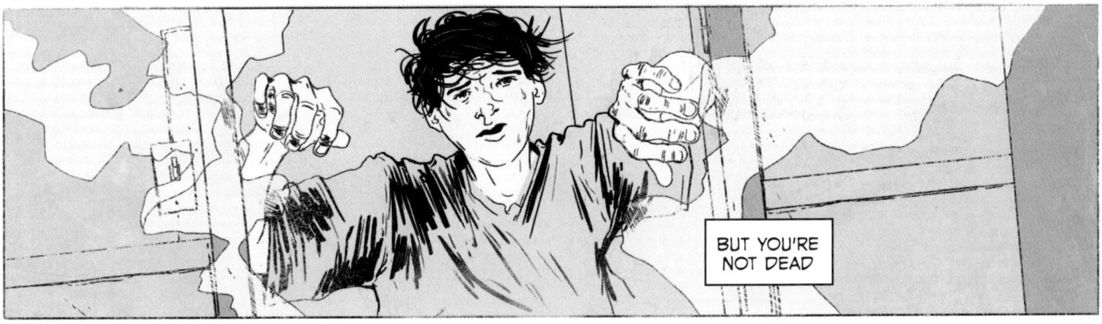
BUT YOU'RE NOT DEAD

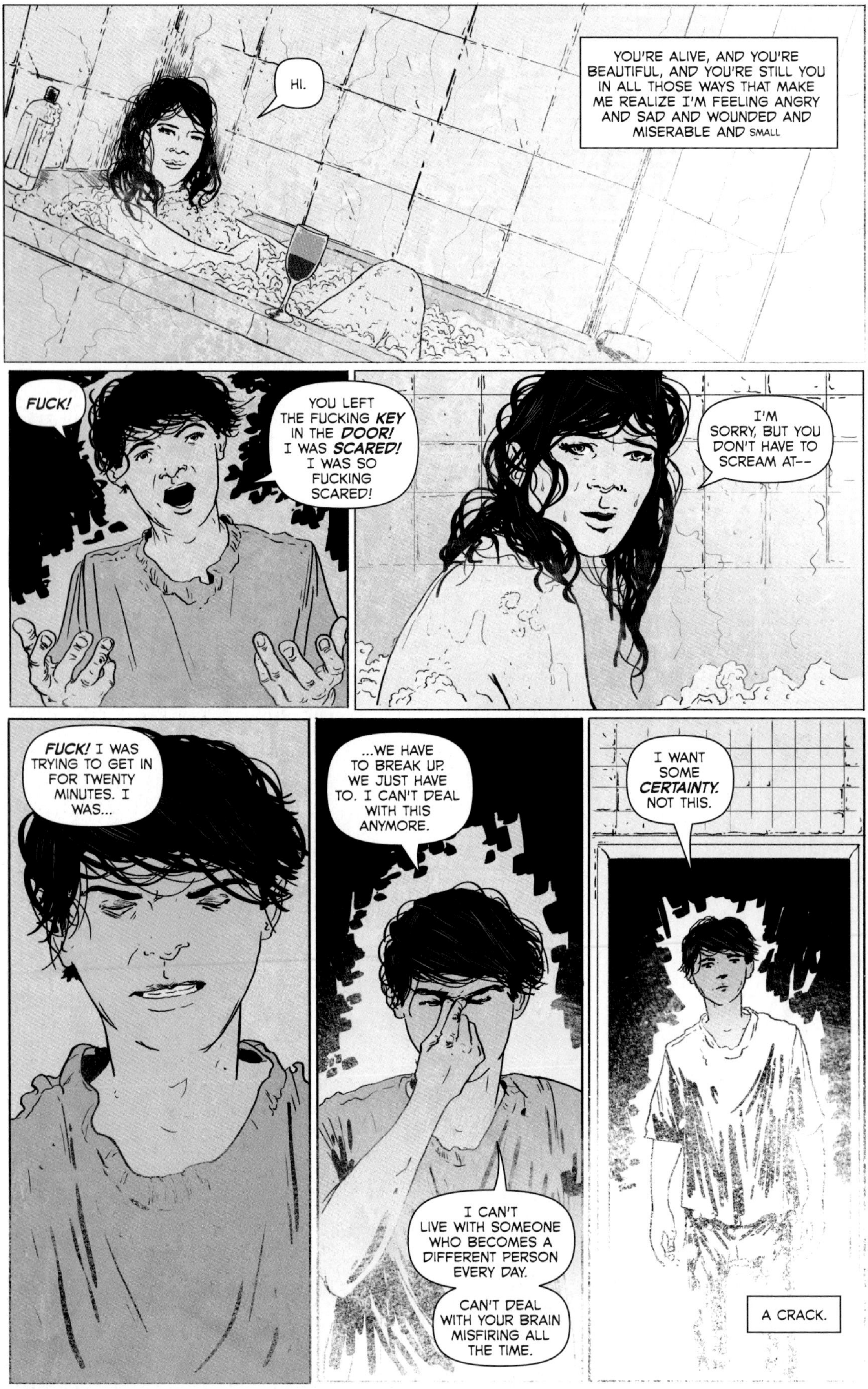

HI.
YOU'RE ALIVE, AND YOU'RE BEAUTIFUL, AND YOU'RE STILL YOU IN ALL THOSE WAYS THAT MAKE ME REALIZE I'M FEELING ANGRY AND SAD AND WOUNDED AND MISERABLE AND SMALL
FUCK!
YOU LEFT THE FUCKING KEY IN THE DOOR! I WAS SCARED! I WAS SO FUCKING SCARED!
I'M SORRY, BUT YOU DON'T HAVE TO SCREAM AT--
FUCK! I WAS TRYING TO GET IN FOR TWENTY MINUTES. I WAS...
...WE HAVE TO BREAK UP. WE JUST HAVE TO. I CAN'T DEAL WITH THIS ANYMORE.
I CAN'T LIVE WITH SOMEONE WHO BECOMES A DIFFERENT PERSON EVERY DAY.
CAN'T DEAL WITH YOUR BRAIN MISFIRING ALL THE TIME.
I WANT SOME CERTAINTY. NOT THIS.
A CRACK.

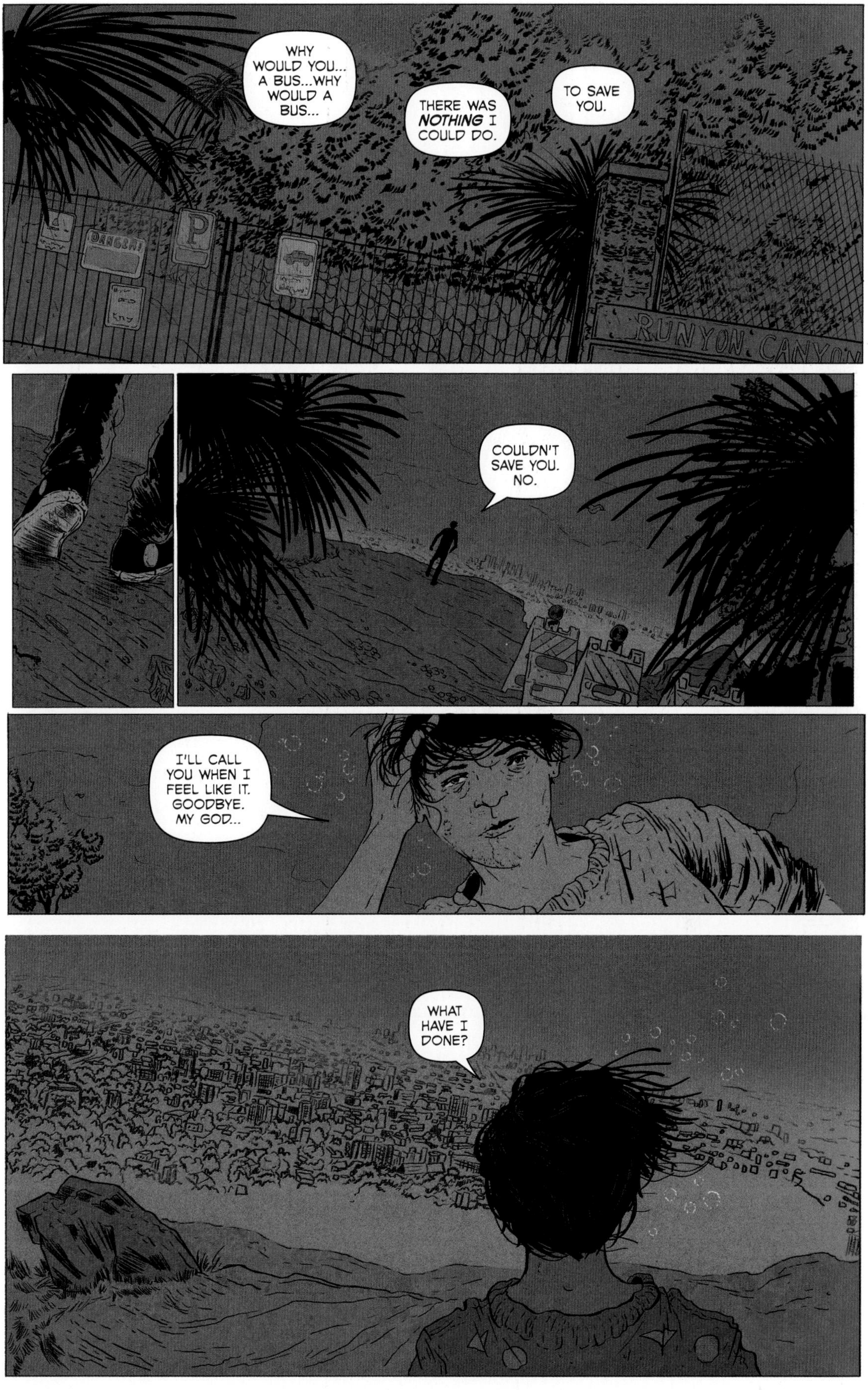
WHY WOULD YOU... A BUS...WHY WOULD A BUS...
THERE WAS *NOTHING* I COULD DO.
TO SAVE YOU.
RUNYON CANYON
COULDN'T SAVE YOU. NO.
I'LL CALL YOU WHEN I FEEL LIKE IT. GOODBYE. MY GOD...
WHAT HAVE I DONE?

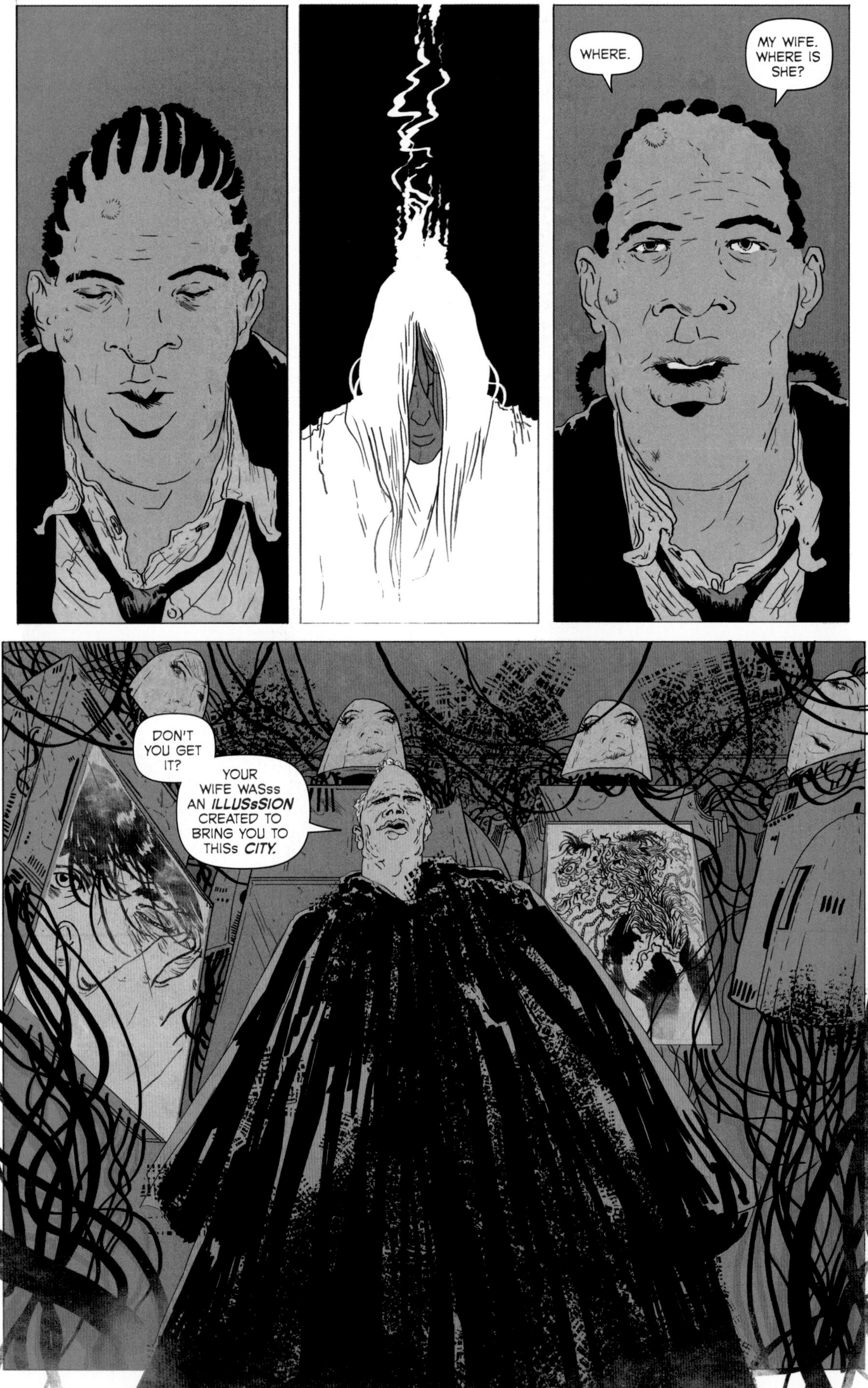
WHERE.
MY WIFE. WHERE IS SHE?
DON'T YOU GET IT?
YOUR WIFE WASss AN *ILLUSsSION* CREATED TO BRING YOU TO THISs *CITY.*

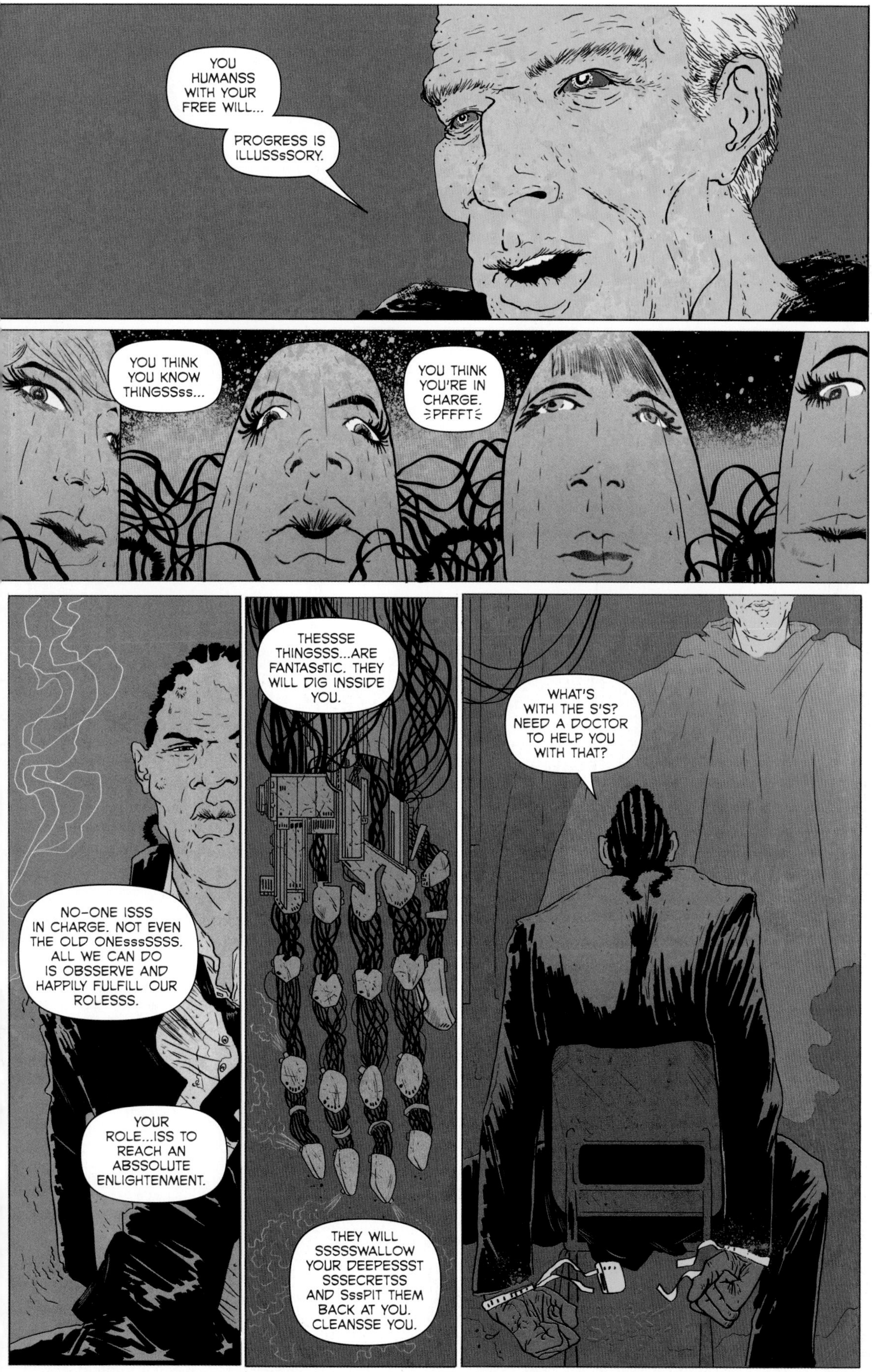
YOU HUMANSS WITH YOUR FREE WILL...
PROGRESS IS ILLUSSsSORY.
YOU THINK YOU KNOW THINGSSss...
YOU THINK YOU'RE IN CHARGE. PFFFT
NO-ONE ISSS IN CHARGE. NOT EVEN THE OLD ONEsssSSSS. ALL WE CAN DO IS OBSSERVE AND HAPPILY FULFILL OUR ROLESSS.
YOUR ROLE...ISS TO REACH AN ABSSOLUTE ENLIGHTENMENT.
THESSSE THINGSSS...ARE FANTASsTIC. THEY WILL DIG INSSIDE YOU.
THEY WILL SSSSSWALLOW YOUR DEEPESSST SSSECRETSS AND SssPIT THEM BACK AT YOU. CLEANSSE YOU.
WHAT'S WITH THE S'S? NEED A DOCTOR TO HELP YOU WITH THAT?

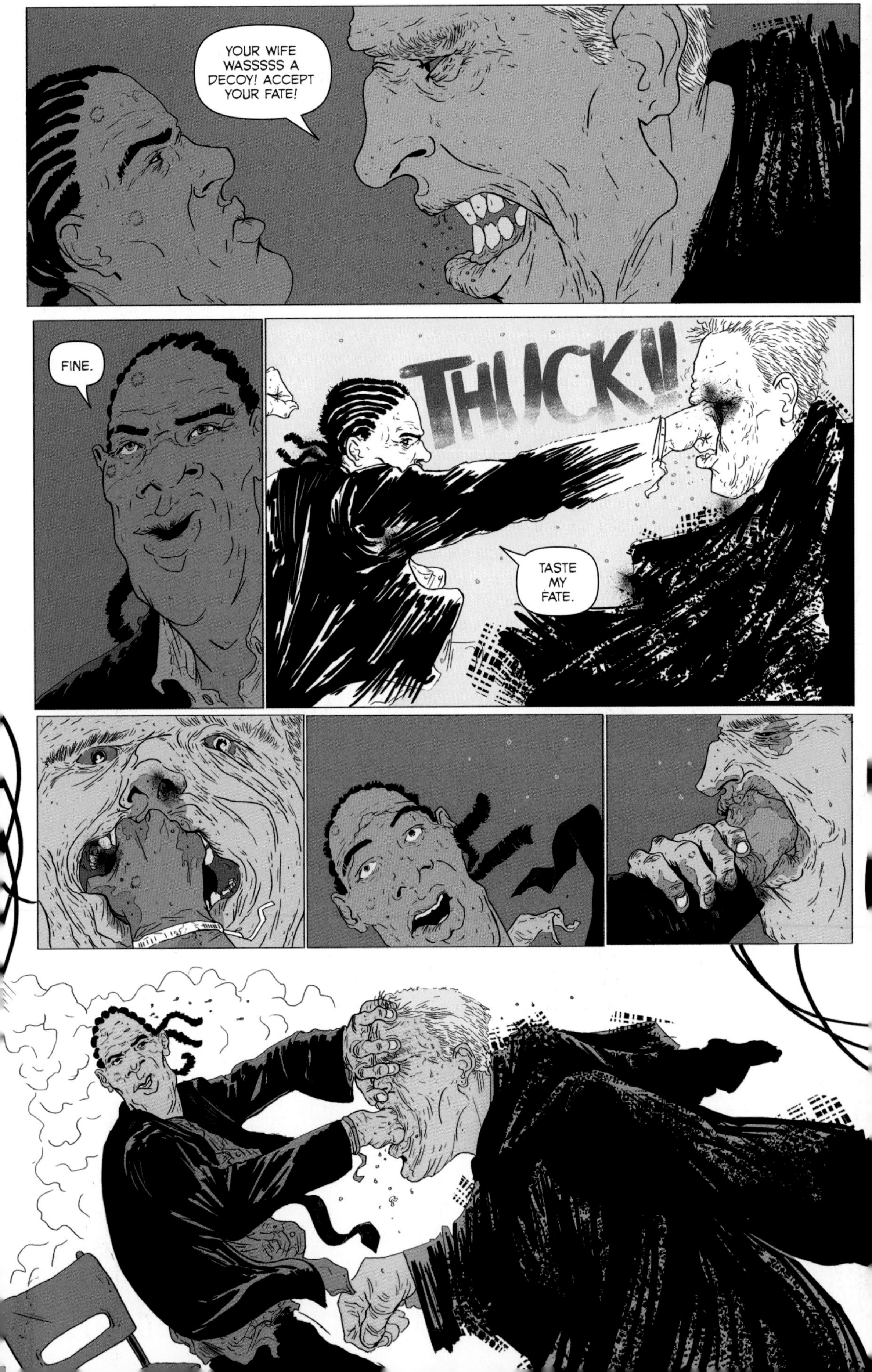
YOUR WIFE WASSSSS A DECOY! ACCEPT YOUR FATE!
FINE.
THUCK!!
TASTE MY FATE.

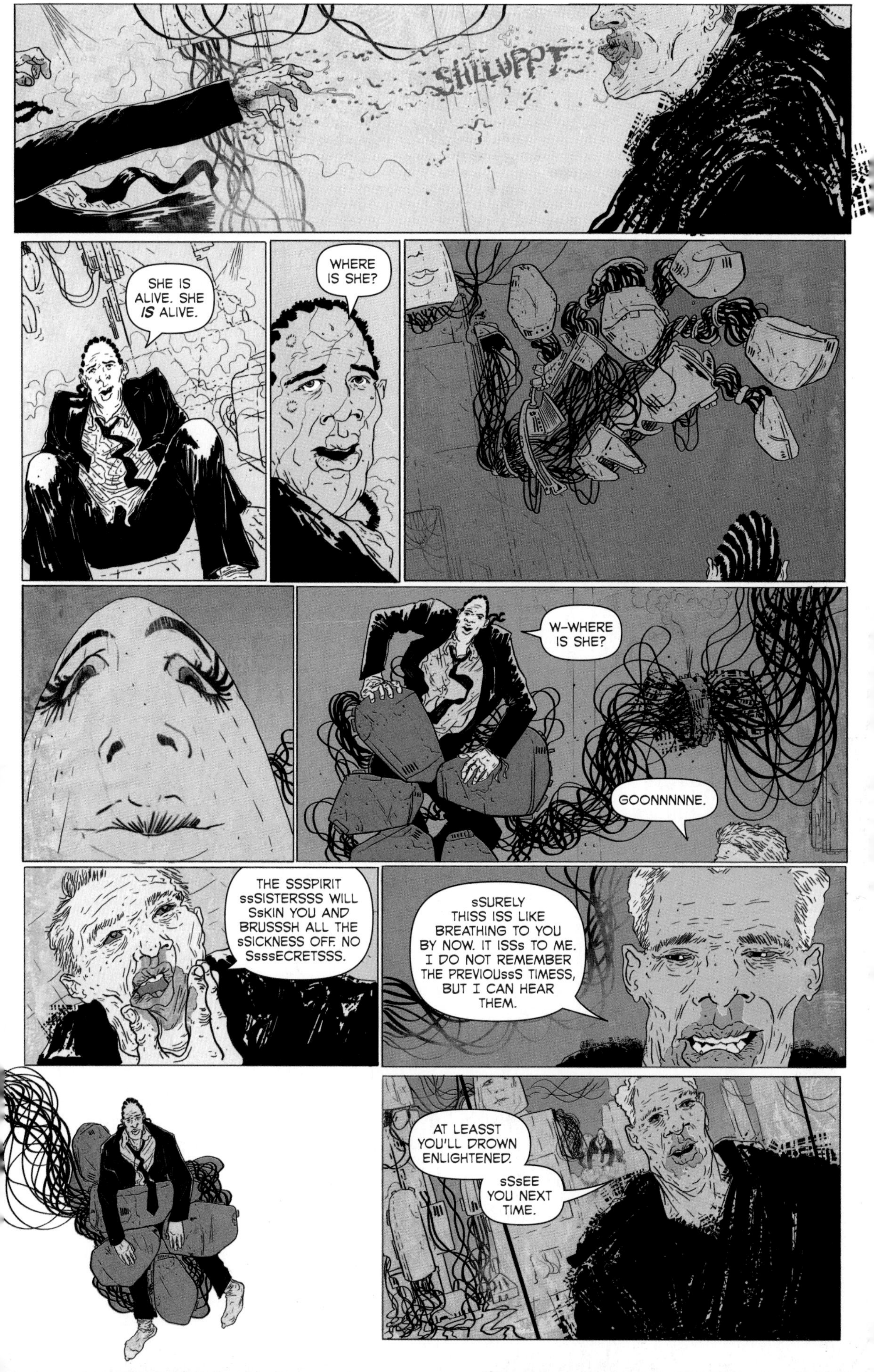
SHLUPPT
SHE IS ALIVE. SHE *IS* ALIVE.
WHERE IS SHE?
W-WHERE IS SHE?
GOONNNNNE.
THE SSSPIRIT ssSISTERSSS WILL SsKIN YOU AND BRUSSSH ALL THE sSICKNESS OFF. NO SsssECRETSSS.
sSURELY THISS ISS LIKE BREATHING TO YOU BY NOW. IT ISSs TO ME. I DO NOT REMEMBER THE PREVIOUssS TIMESS, BUT I CAN HEAR THEM.
AT LEASST YOU'LL DROWN ENLIGHTENED.
sSsEE YOU NEXT TIME.

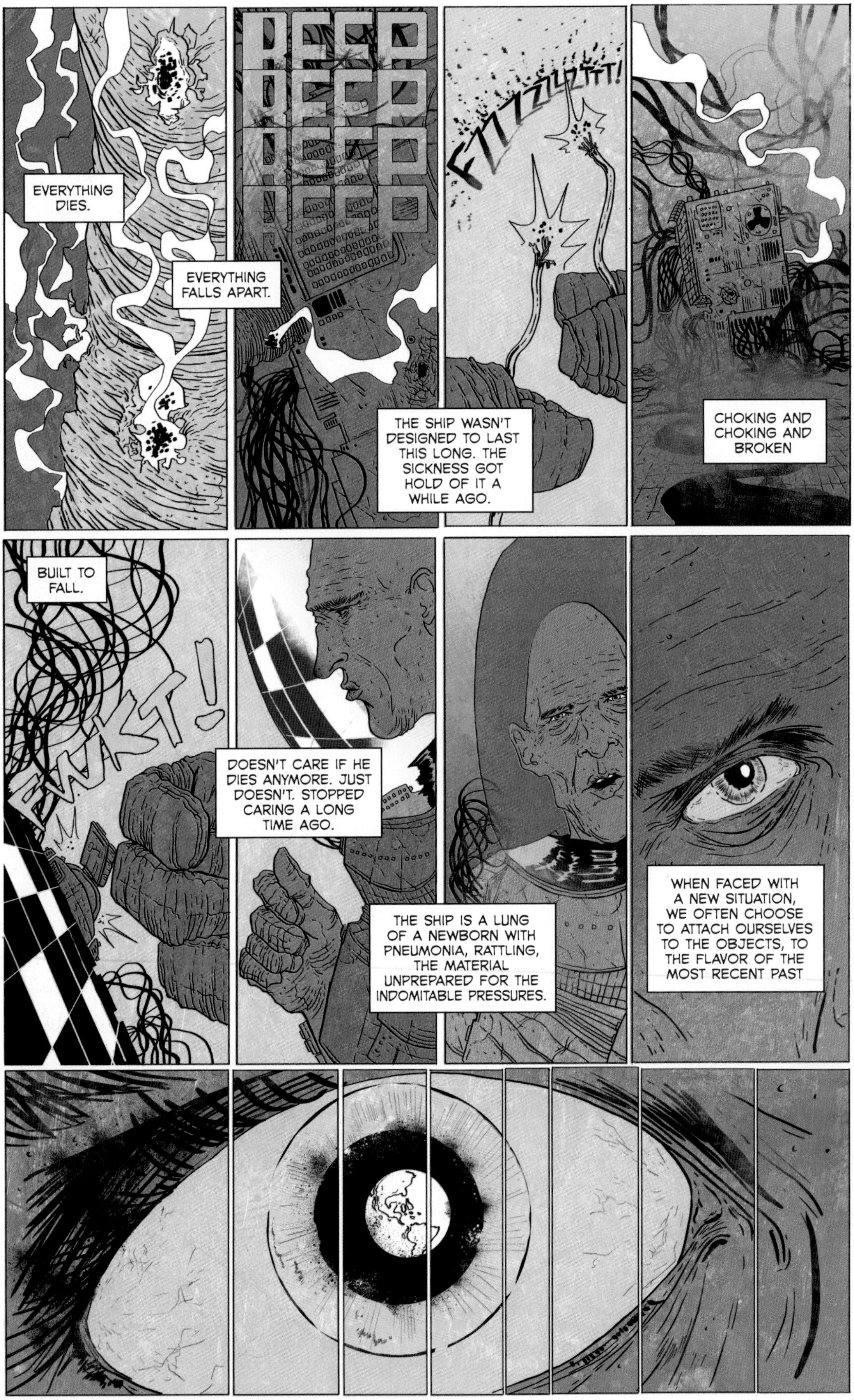
EVERYTHING DIES.
EVERYTHING FALLS APART.
THE SHIP WASN'T DESIGNED TO LAST THIS LONG. THE SICKNESS GOT HOLD OF IT A WHILE AGO.
CHOKING AND CHOKING AND BROKEN
BUILT TO FALL.
DOESN'T CARE IF HE DIES ANYMORE. JUST DOESN'T. STOPPED CARING A LONG TIME AGO.
THE SHIP IS A LUNG OF A NEWBORN WITH PNEUMONIA, RATTLING, THE MATERIAL UNPREPARED FOR THE INDOMITABLE PRESSURES.
WHEN FACED WITH A NEW SITUATION, WE OFTEN CHOOSE TO ATTACH OURSELVES TO THE OBJECTS, TO THE FLAVOR OF THE MOST RECENT PAST

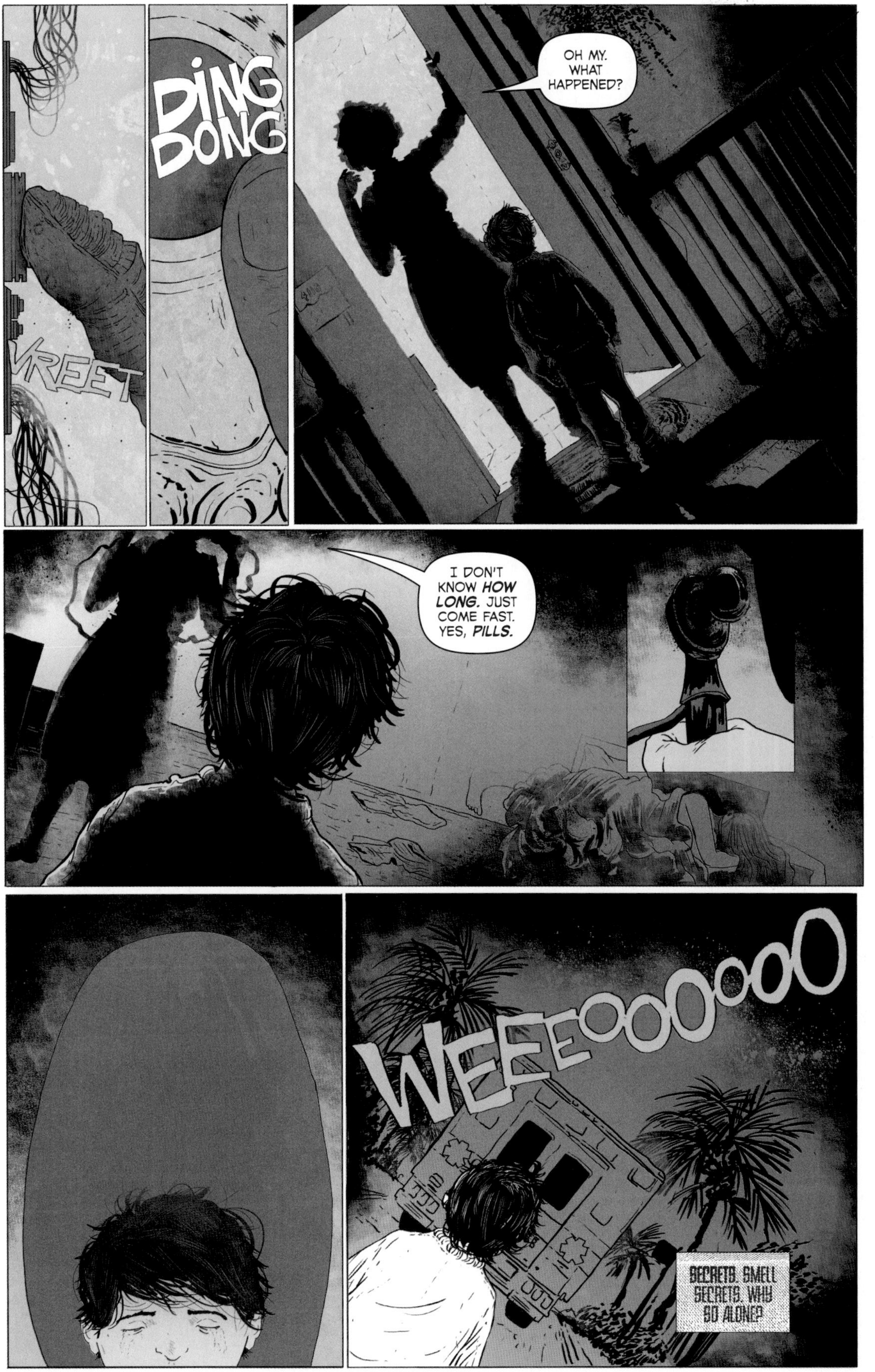
VREEET
DING DONG
OH MY. WHAT HAPPENED?
I DON'T KNOW HOW LONG. JUST COME FAST. YES, PILLS.
WEEEOOOOOO
SECRETS. SMELL SECRETS. WHY SO ALONE?

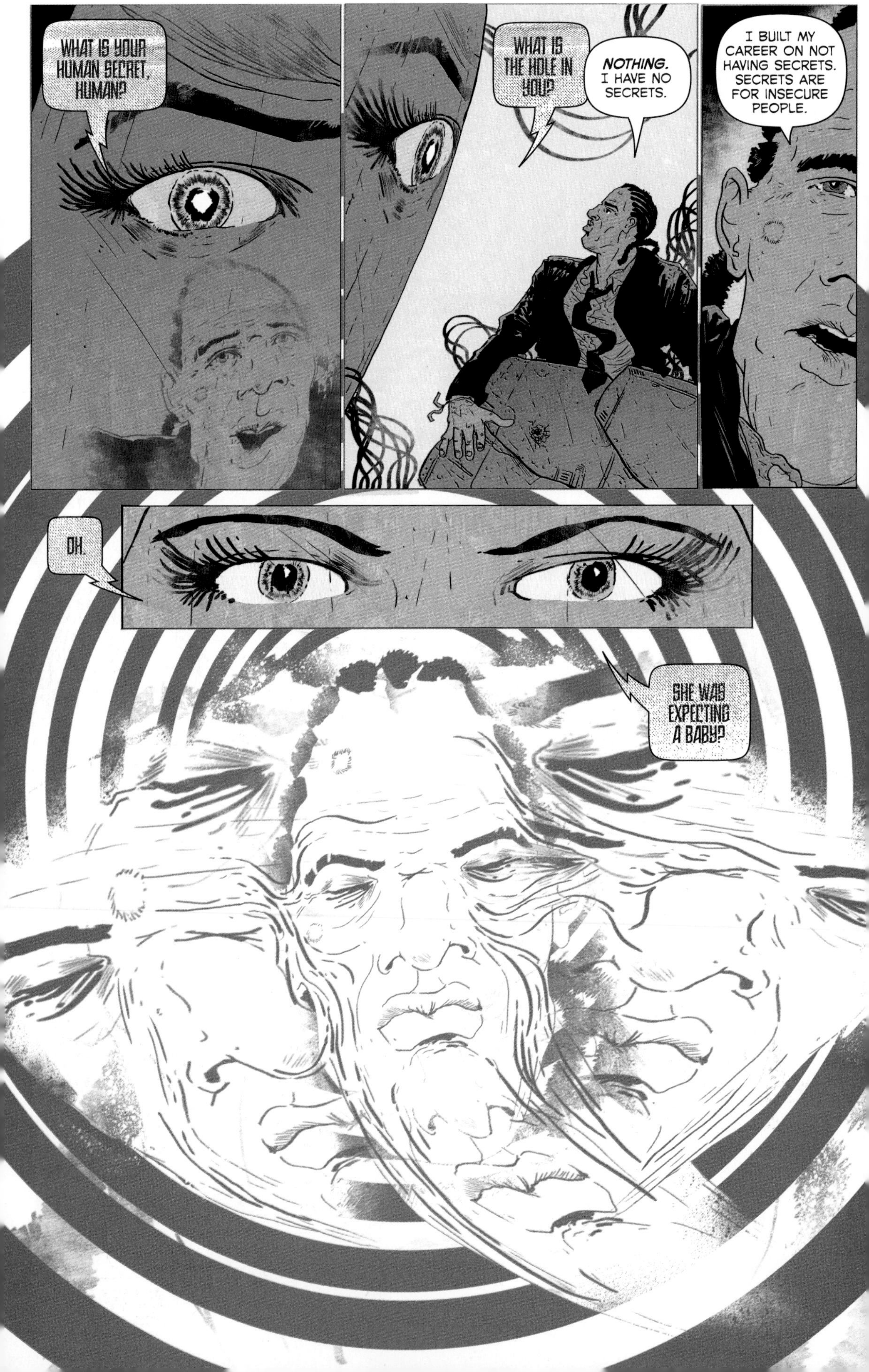
WHAT IS YOUR HUMAN SECRET, HUMAN?
WHAT IS THE HOLE IN YOU?
NOTHING. I HAVE NO SECRETS.
I BUILT MY CAREER ON NOT HAVING SECRETS. SECRETS ARE FOR INSECURE PEOPLE.
OH.
SHE WAS EXPECTING A BABY?

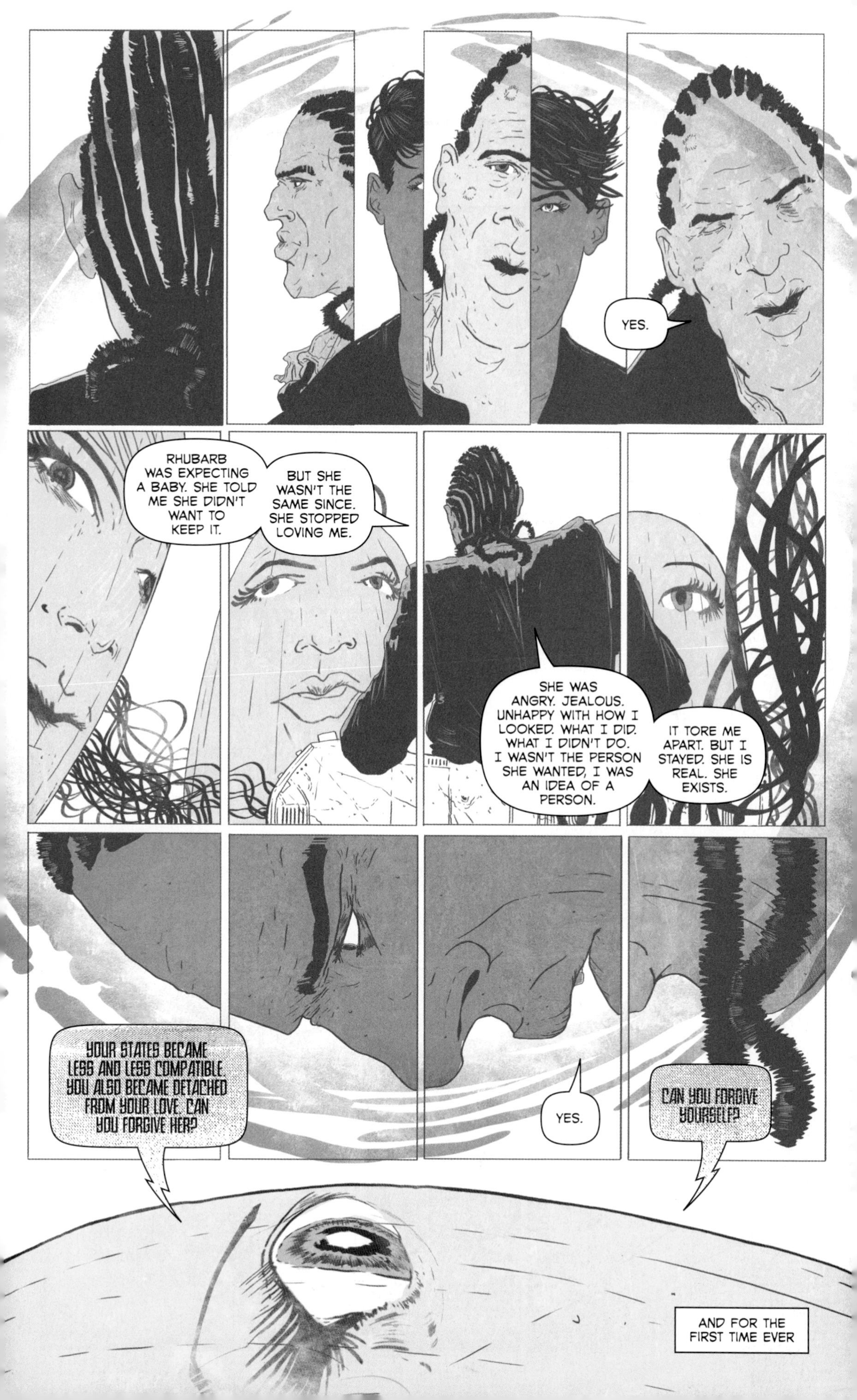
YES.
RHUBARB WAS EXPECTING A BABY. SHE TOLD ME SHE DIDN'T WANT TO KEEP IT.
BUT SHE WASN'T THE SAME SINCE. SHE STOPPED LOVING ME.
SHE WAS ANGRY. JEALOUS. UNHAPPY WITH HOW I LOOKED. WHAT I DID. WHAT I DIDN'T DO. I WASN'T THE PERSON SHE WANTED, I WAS AN IDEA OF A PERSON.
IT TORE ME APART. BUT I STAYED. SHE IS REAL. SHE EXISTS.
YOUR STATES BECAME LESS AND LESS COMPATIBLE. YOU ALSO BECAME DETACHED FROM YOUR LOVE. CAN YOU FORGIVE HER?
YES.
CAN YOU FORGIVE YOURSELF?
AND FOR THE FIRST TIME EVER

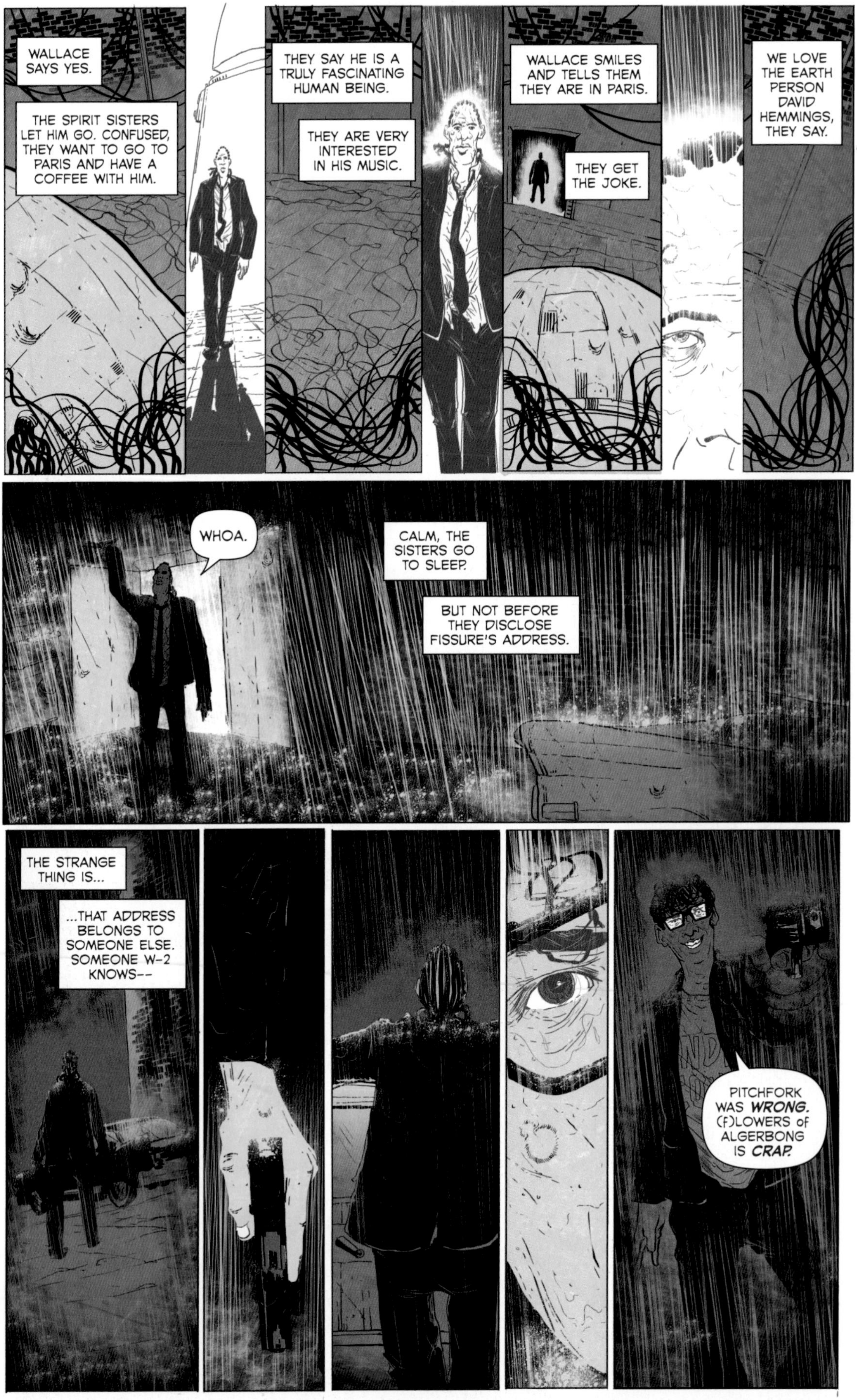
WALLACE SAYS YES.
THE SPIRIT SISTERS LET HIM GO. CONFUSED, THEY WANT TO GO TO PARIS AND HAVE A COFFEE WITH HIM.
THEY SAY HE IS A TRULY FASCINATING HUMAN BEING.
THEY ARE VERY INTERESTED IN HIS MUSIC.
WALLACE SMILES AND TELLS THEM THEY ARE IN PARIS.
THEY GET THE JOKE.
WE LOVE THE EARTH PERSON DAVID HEMMINGS, THEY SAY.
WHOA.
CALM, THE SISTERS GO TO SLEEP.
BUT NOT BEFORE THEY DISCLOSE FISSURE'S ADDRESS.
THE STRANGE THING IS...
...THAT ADDRESS BELONGS TO SOMEONE ELSE. SOMEONE W-2 KNOWS--
PITCHFORK WAS WRONG. (F)LOWERS of ALGERBONG IS CRAP.

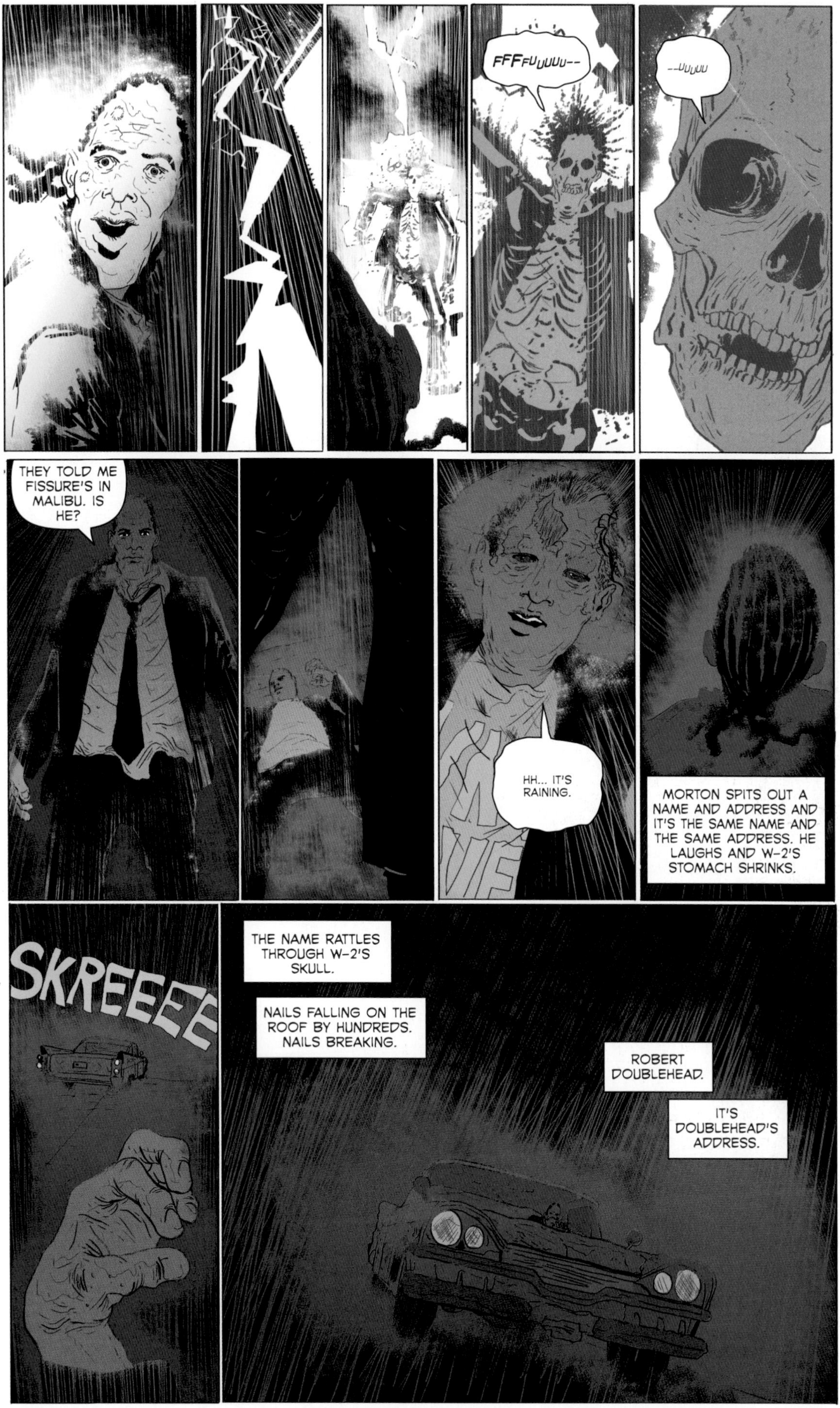
FFFFUUUUU--
--UUUUU
THEY TOLD ME FISSURE'S IN MALIBU. IS HE?
HH... IT'S RAINING.
MORTON SPITS OUT A NAME AND ADDRESS AND IT'S THE SAME NAME AND THE SAME ADDRESS. HE LAUGHS AND W-2'S STOMACH SHRINKS.
SKREEEE
THE NAME RATTLES THROUGH W-2'S SKULL.
NAILS FALLING ON THE ROOF BY HUNDREDS. NAILS BREAKING.
ROBERT DOUBLEHEAD.
IT'S DOUBLEHEAD'S ADDRESS.

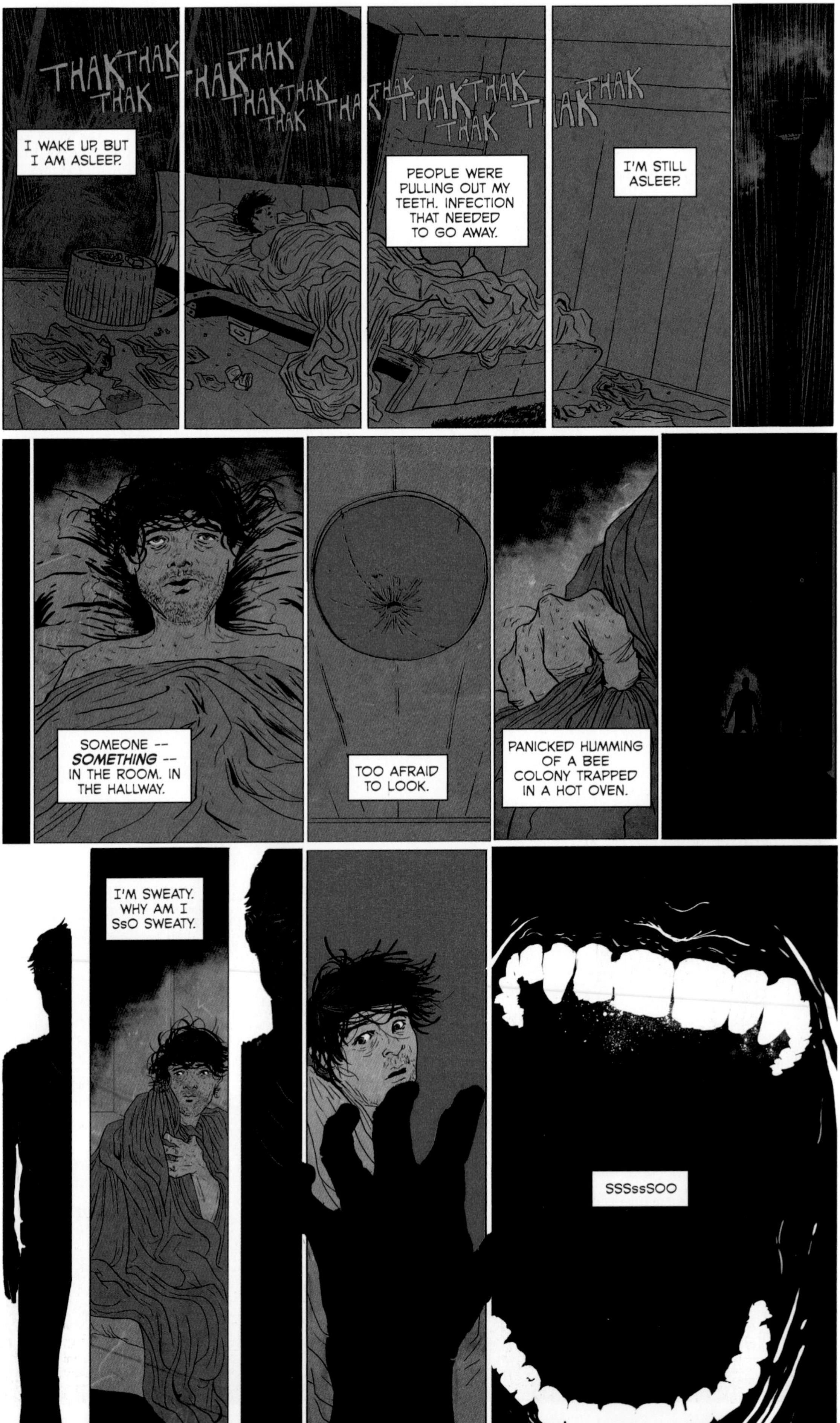
THAKTHAK THAK THAKTHAK THAKTHAK THAK THAKTHAK THAKTHAK THAK THAKTHAK
I WAKE UP, BUT I AM ASLEEP.
PEOPLE WERE PULLING OUT MY TEETH. INFECTION THAT NEEDED TO GO AWAY.
I'M STILL ASLEEP.
SOMEONE -- *SOMETHING* -- IN THE ROOM. IN THE HALLWAY.
TOO AFRAID TO LOOK.
PANICKED HUMMING OF A BEE COLONY TRAPPED IN A HOT OVEN.
I'M SWEATY. WHY AM I SsO SWEATY.
SSSssSOO

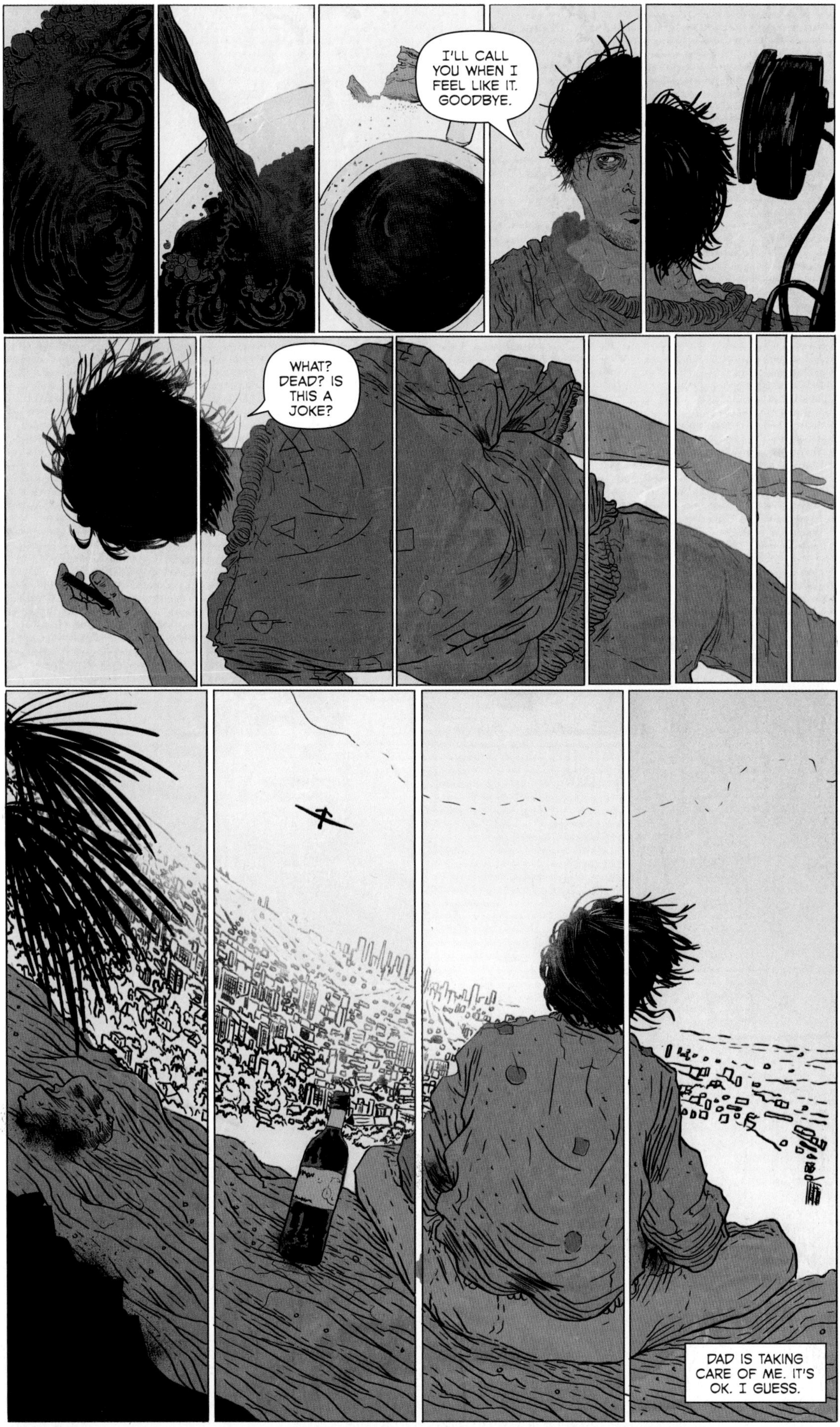

I'LL CALL YOU WHEN I FEEL LIKE IT. GOODBYE.
WHAT? DEAD? IS THIS A JOKE?
DAD IS TAKING CARE OF ME. IT'S OK. I GUESS.

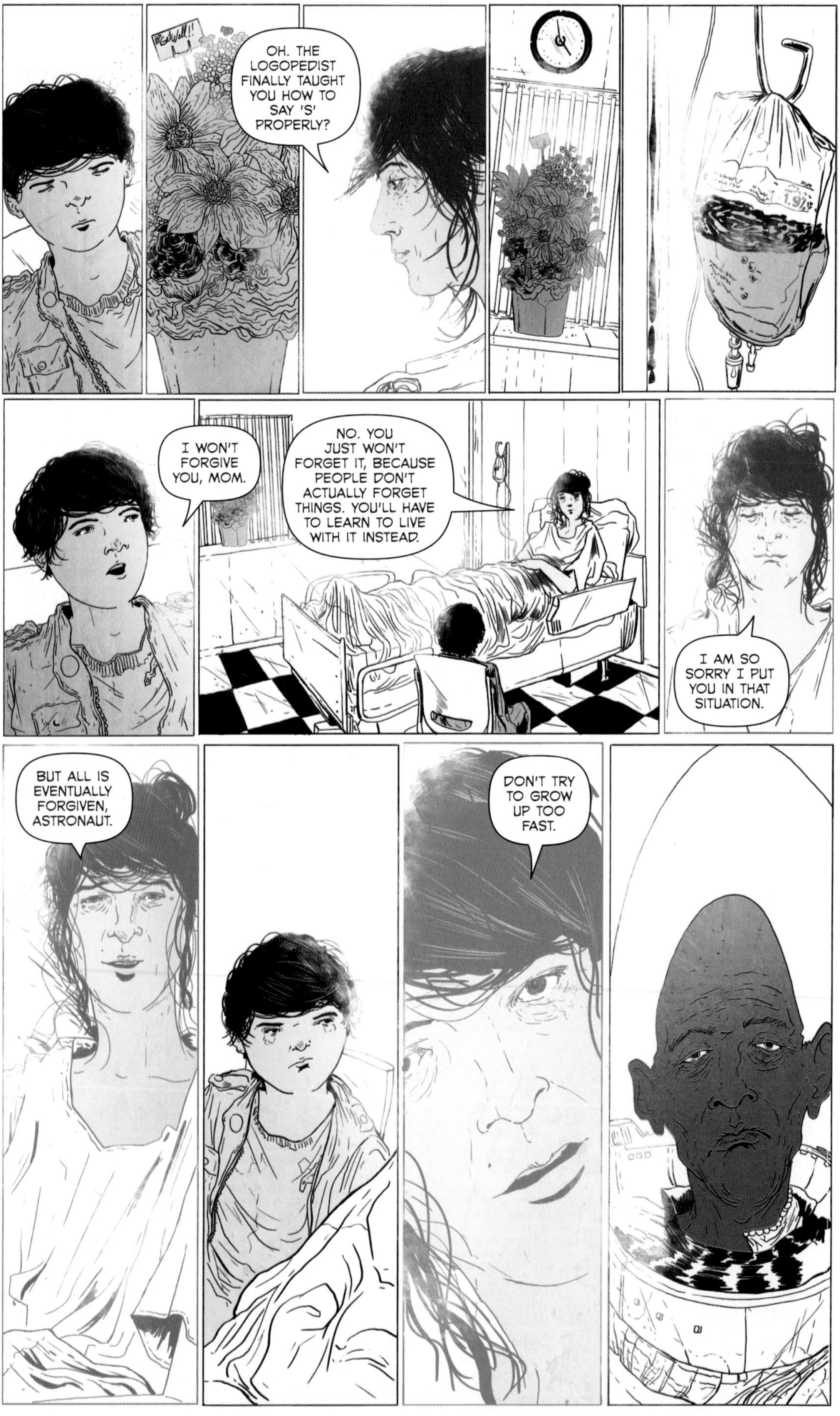
OH. THE LOGOPEDIST FINALLY TAUGHT YOU HOW TO SAY 'S' PROPERLY?
I WON'T FORGIVE YOU, MOM.
NO. YOU JUST WON'T FORGET IT, BECAUSE PEOPLE DON'T ACTUALLY FORGET THINGS. YOU'LL HAVE TO LEARN TO LIVE WITH IT INSTEAD.
I AM SO SORRY I PUT YOU IN THAT SITUATION.
BUT ALL IS EVENTUALLY FORGIVEN, ASTRONAUT.
DON'T TRY TO GROW UP TOO FAST.

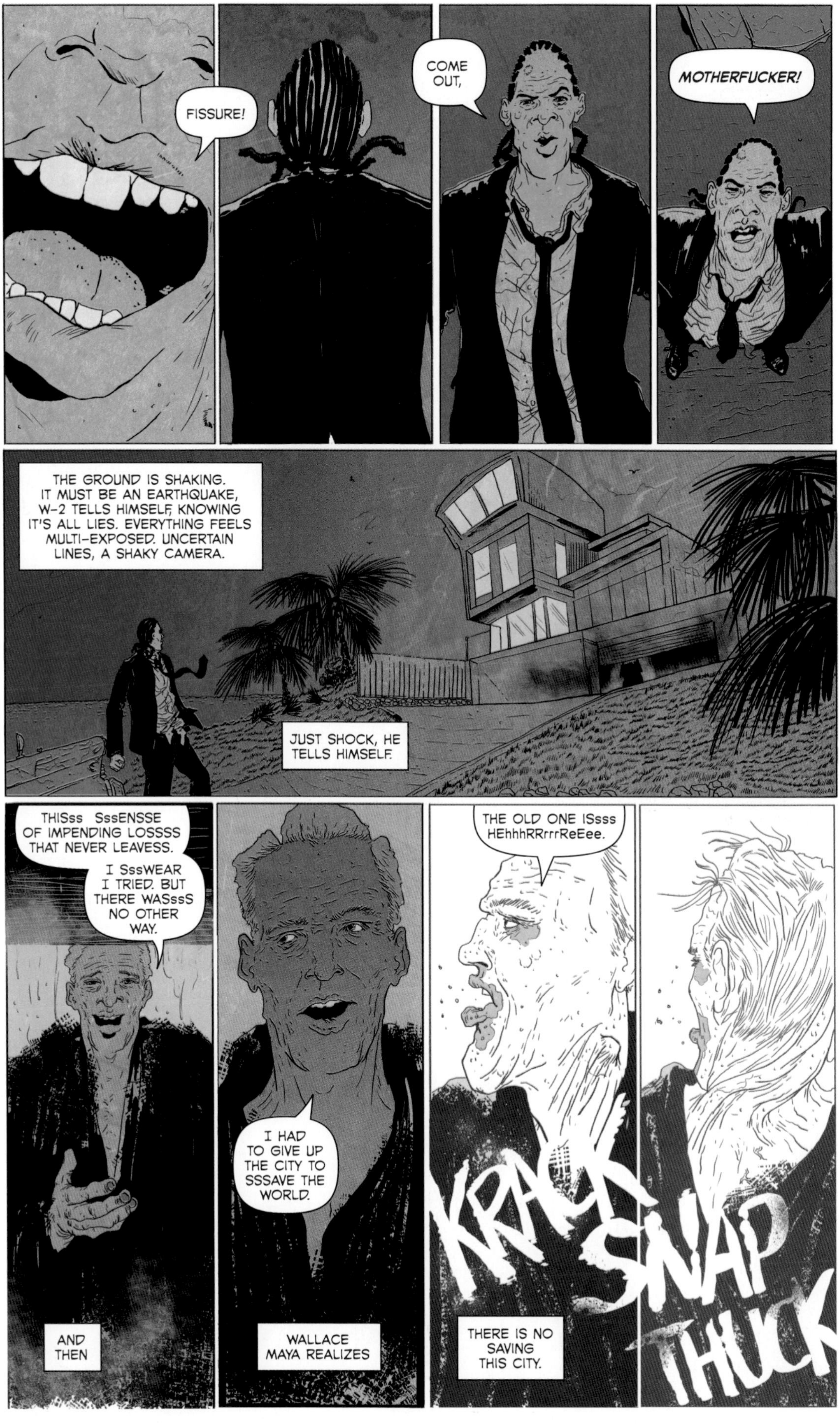
FISSURE!
COME OUT,
MOTHERFUCKER!
THE GROUND IS SHAKING. IT MUST BE AN EARTHQUAKE, W-2 TELLS HIMSELF, KNOWING IT'S ALL LIES. EVERYTHING FEELS MULTI-EXPOSED. UNCERTAIN LINES, A SHAKY CAMERA.
JUST SHOCK, HE TELLS HIMSELF.
THISss SssENSSE OF IMPENDING LOSSSS THAT NEVER LEAVESS.
I SssWEAR I TRIED. BUT THERE WASssS NO OTHER WAY.
AND THEN
I HAD TO GIVE UP THE CITY TO SSSAVE THE WORLD.
WALLACE MAYA REALIZES
THE OLD ONE ISsss HEhhhRRrrrReEee.
KRACK
THERE IS NO SAVING THIS CITY.
SNAP
THUCK

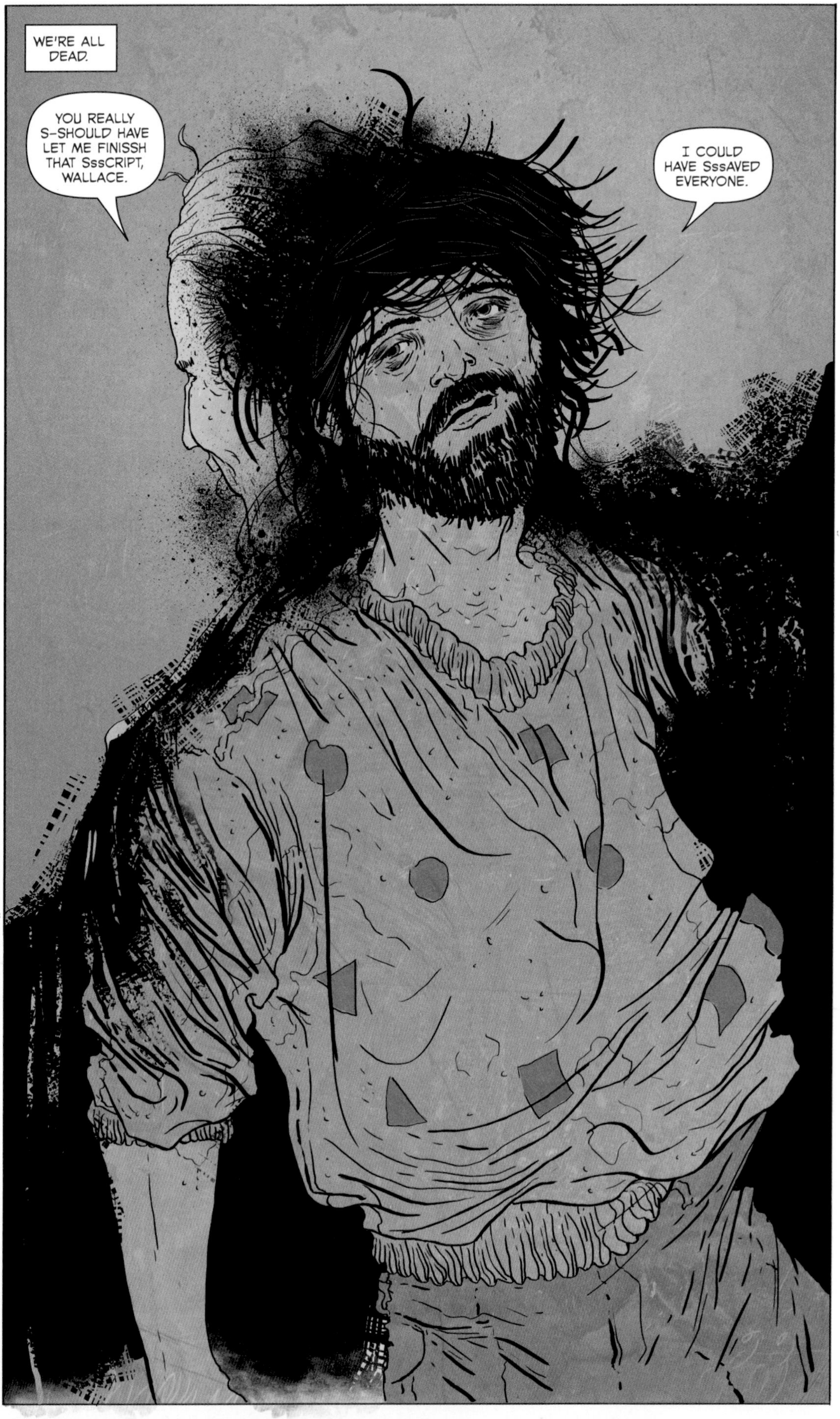
WE'RE ALL DEAD.
YOU REALLY S-SHOULD HAVE LET ME FINISSH THAT SssCRIPT, WALLACE.
I COULD HAVE SssAVED EVERYONE.

SHLURP
HKAK

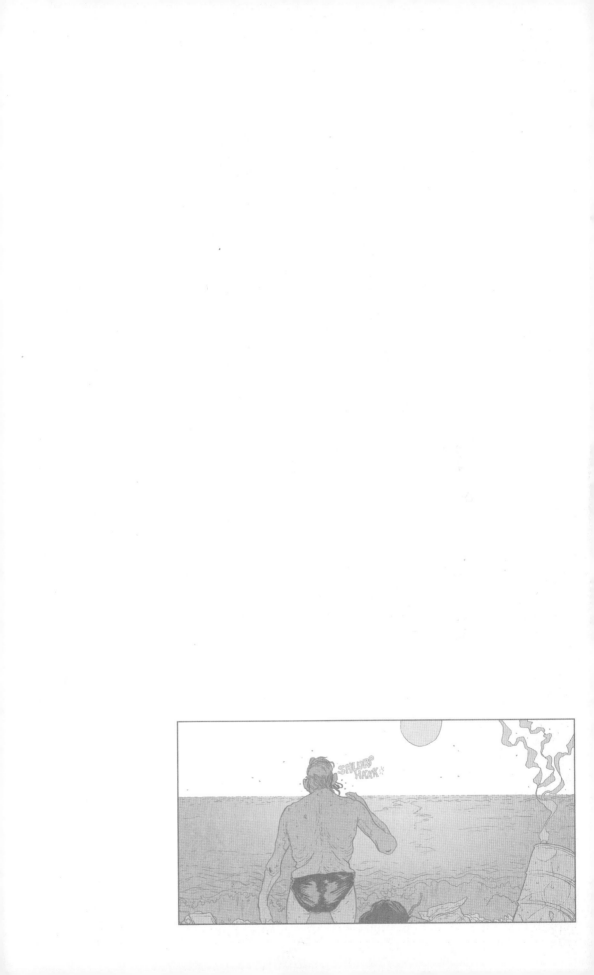

Baby says for all I've forsaken
Make something of all the noise
And the mess you're making
And all the time it's taken

The Kills
'Baby Says'

Only that which
can destroy itself
is truly alive.

Carl Gustav Jung

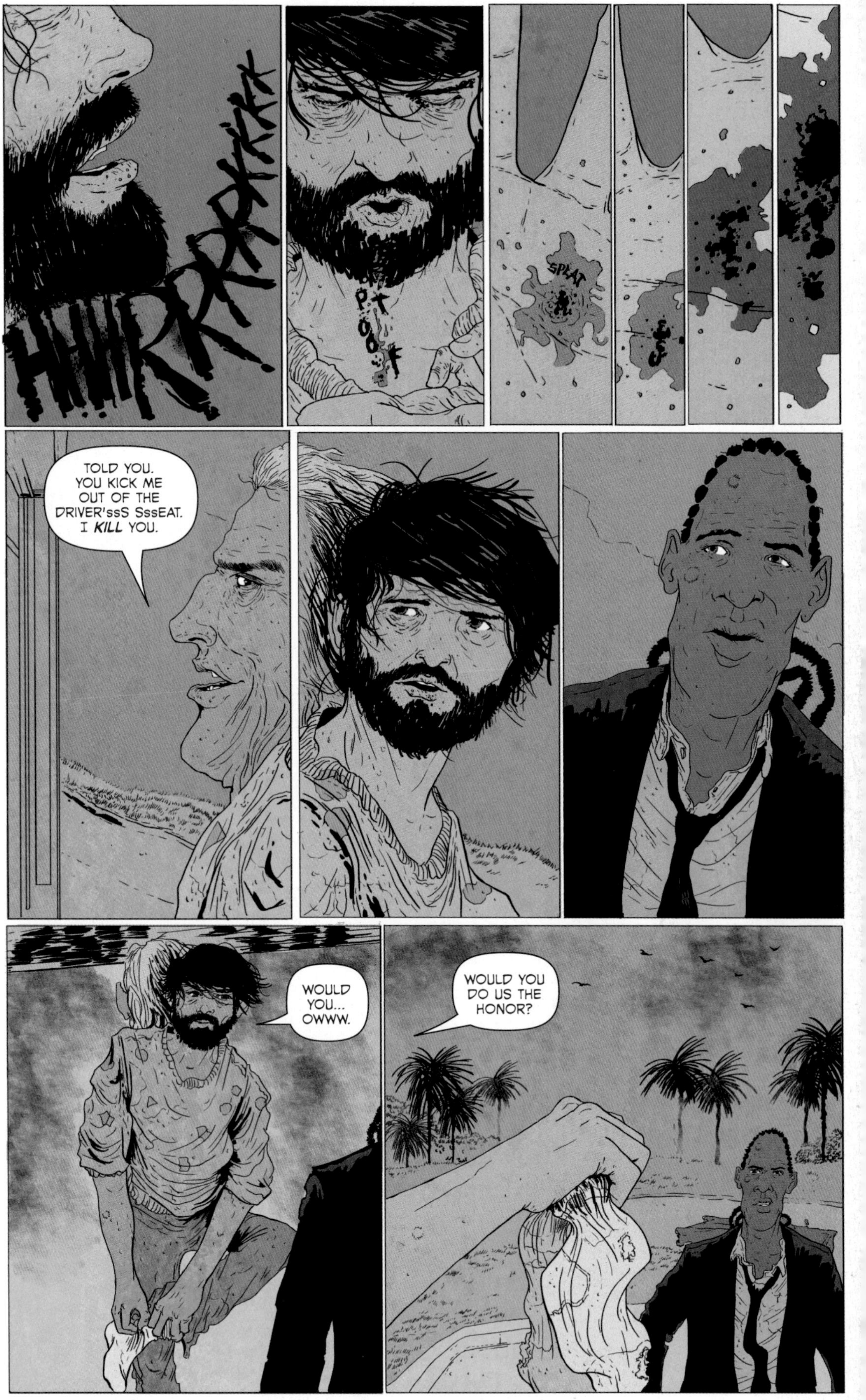
PTOOF
SPLAT
TOLD YOU. YOU KICK ME OUT OF THE DRIVER'ssS SssEAT. I ***KILL*** YOU.
WOULD YOU... OWWW.
WOULD YOU DO US THE HONOR?

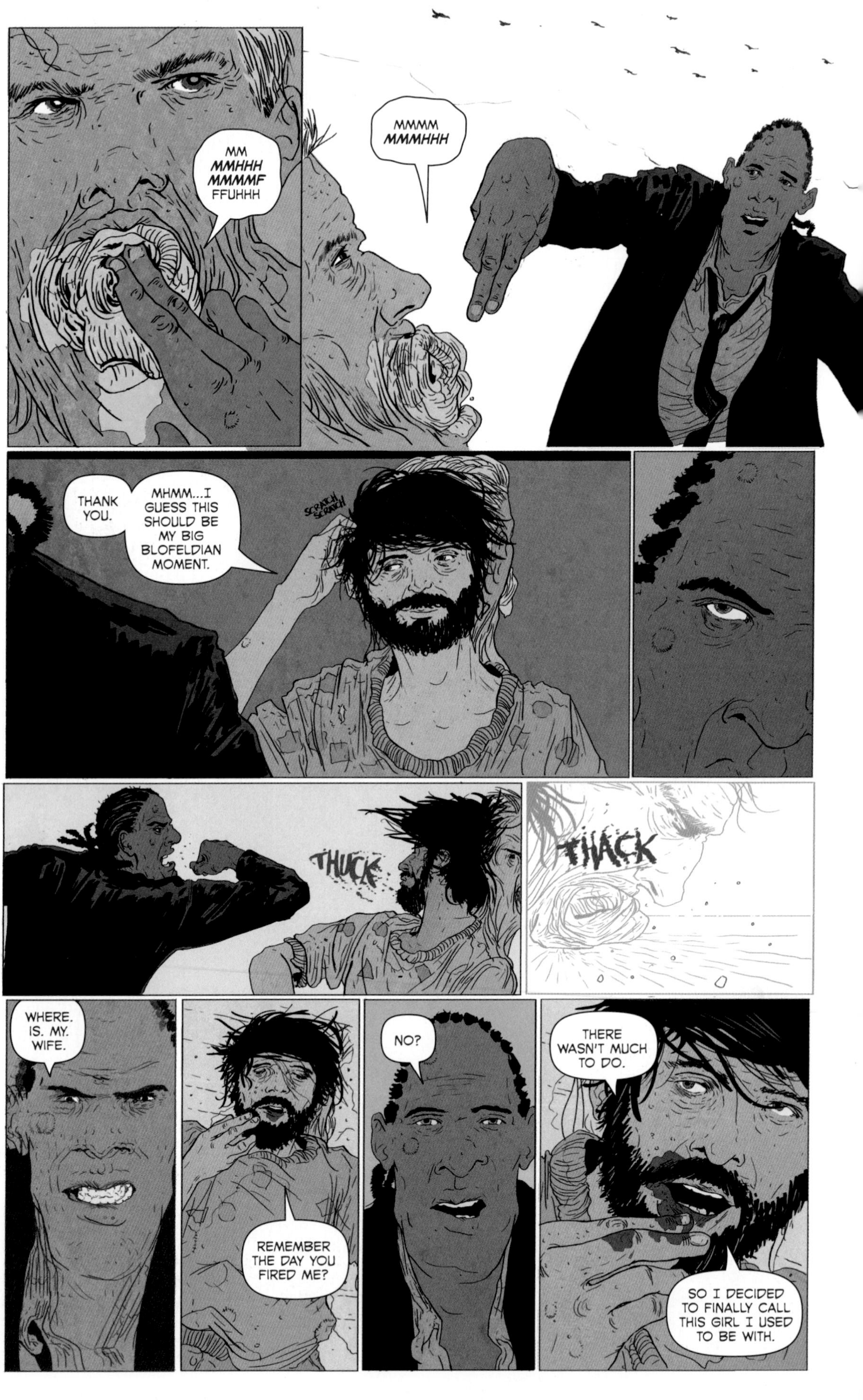
MM
MMHHH
MMMMF
FFUHHH
MMMM
MMMHHH
THANK YOU.
MHMM...I GUESS THIS SHOULD BE MY BIG BLOFELDIAN MOMENT.
SCRATCH SCRATCH
THUCK
THACK
WHERE. IS. MY. WIFE.
REMEMBER THE DAY YOU FIRED ME?
NO?
THERE WASN'T MUCH TO DO.
SO I DECIDED TO FINALLY CALL THIS GIRL I USED TO BE WITH.

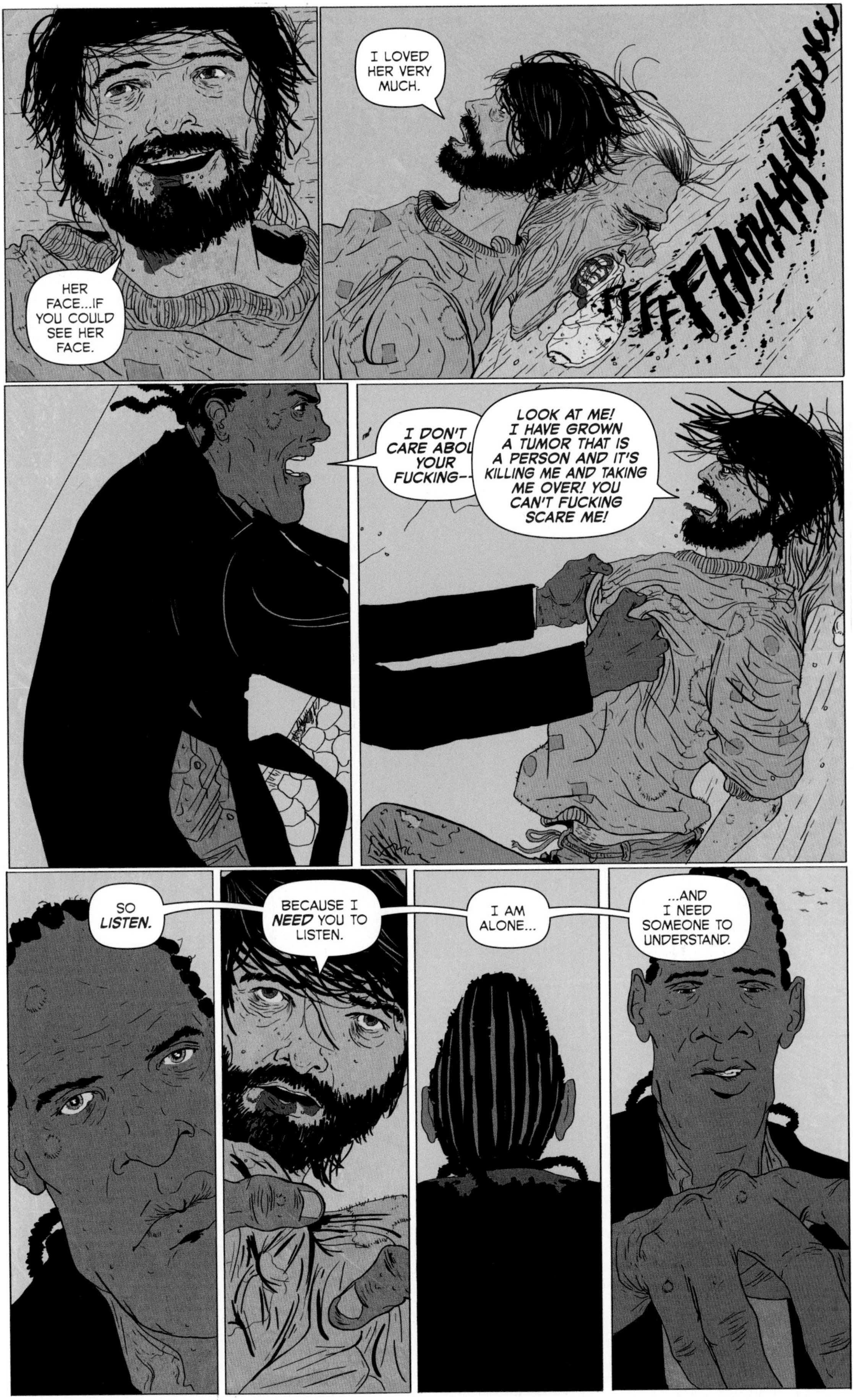
HER FACE...IF YOU COULD SEE HER FACE.
I LOVED HER VERY MUCH.
I DON'T CARE ABOU YOUR FUCKING--
LOOK AT ME! I HAVE GROWN A TUMOR THAT IS A PERSON AND IT'S KILLING ME AND TAKING ME OVER! YOU CAN'T FUCKING SCARE ME!
SO *LISTEN.*
BECAUSE I *NEED* YOU TO LISTEN.
I AM ALONE...
...AND I NEED SOMEONE TO UNDERSTAND.

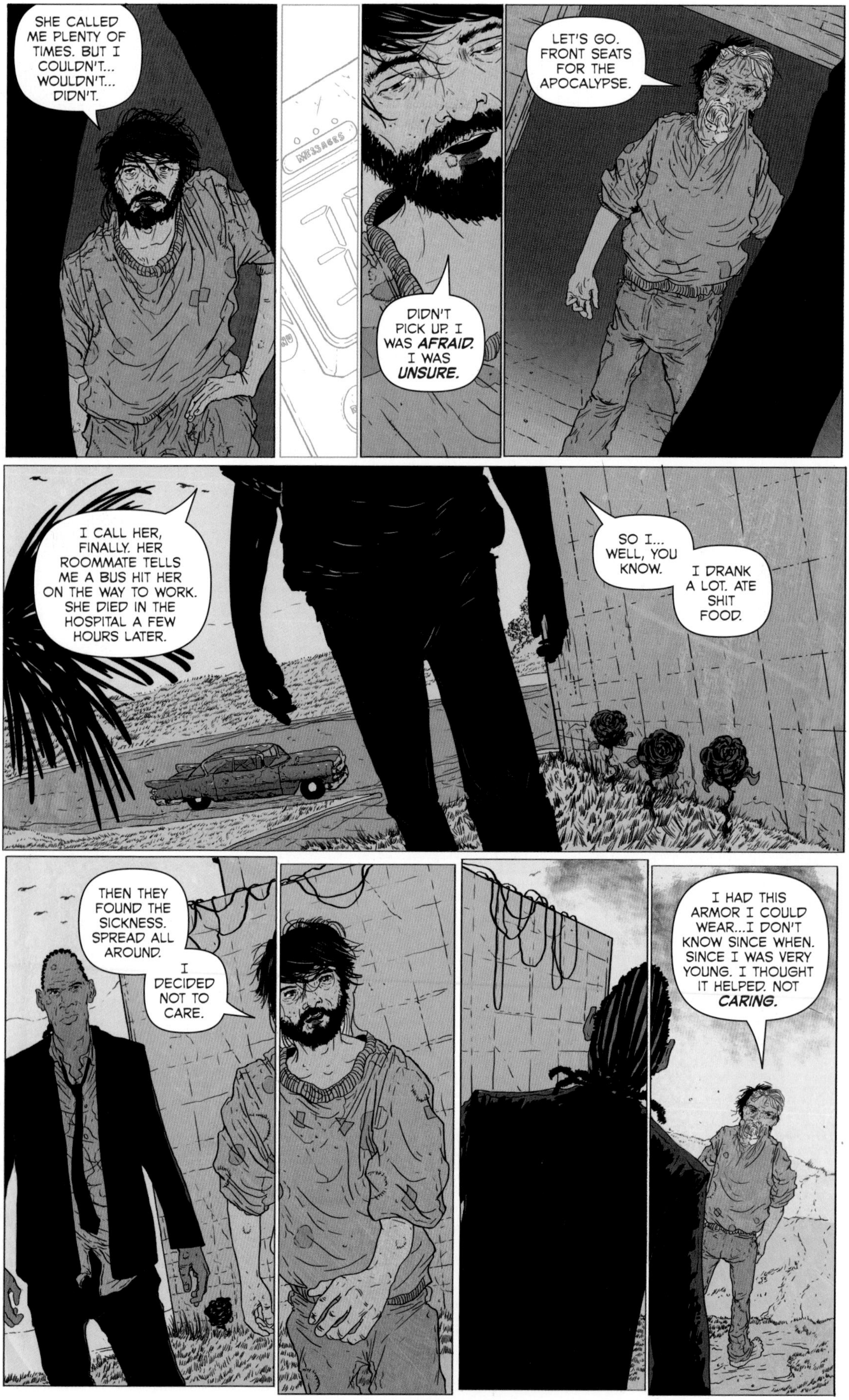
SHE CALLED ME PLENTY OF TIMES. BUT I COULDN'T... WOULDN'T... DIDN'T.
DIDN'T PICK UP. I WAS *AFRAID.* I WAS ***UNSURE.***
LET'S GO. FRONT SEATS FOR THE APOCALYPSE.
I CALL HER, FINALLY. HER ROOMMATE TELLS ME A BUS HIT HER ON THE WAY TO WORK. SHE DIED IN THE HOSPITAL A FEW HOURS LATER.
SO I... WELL, YOU KNOW.
I DRANK A LOT. ATE SHIT FOOD.
THEN THEY FOUND THE SICKNESS. SPREAD ALL AROUND.
I DECIDED NOT TO CARE.
I HAD THIS ARMOR I COULD WEAR...I DON'T KNOW SINCE WHEN. SINCE I WAS VERY YOUNG. I THOUGHT IT HELPED. NOT ***CARING.***

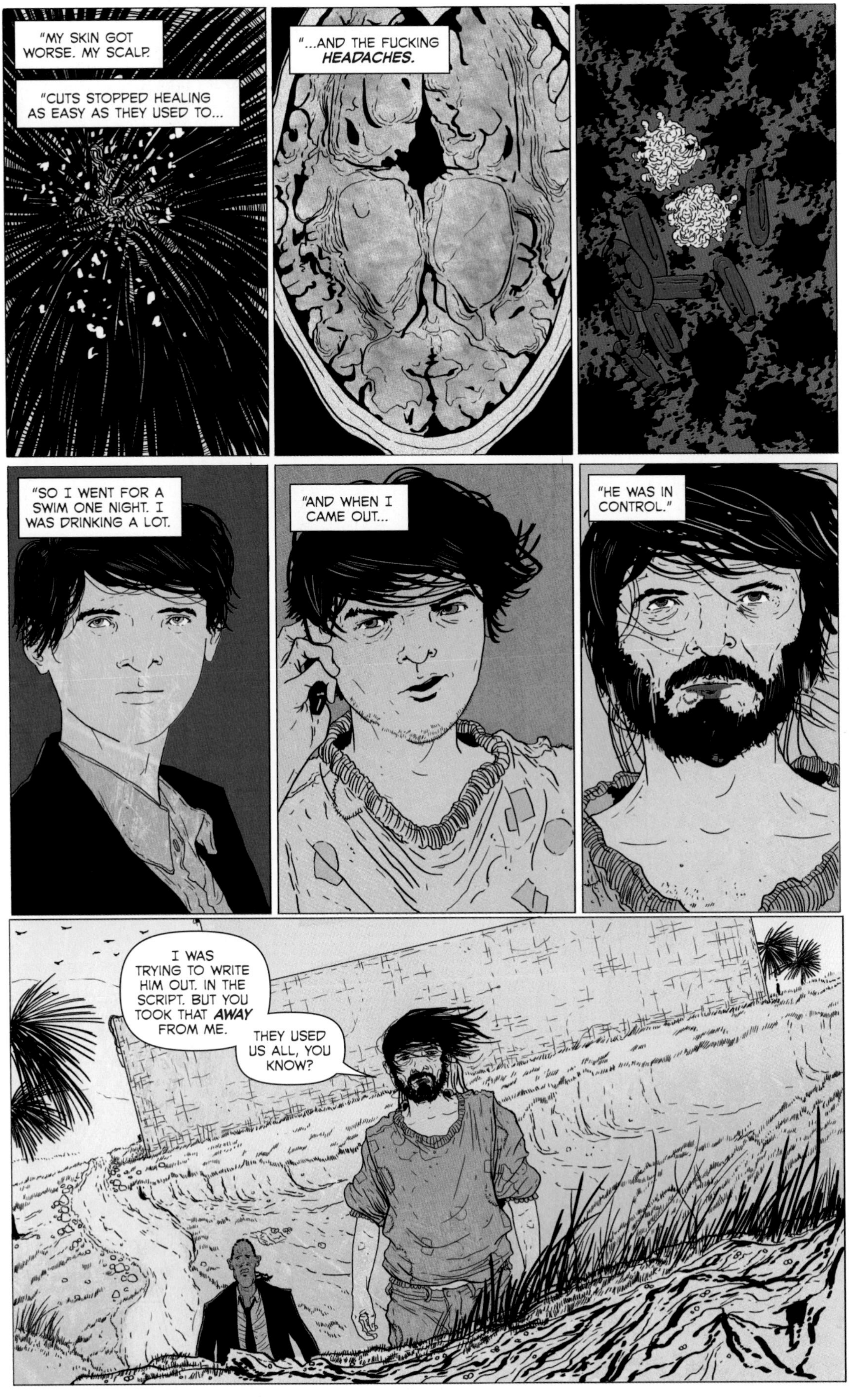
"MY SKIN GOT WORSE. MY SCALP.
"CUTS STOPPED HEALING AS EASY AS THEY USED TO...
"...AND THE FUCKING *HEADACHES.*
"SO I WENT FOR A SWIM ONE NIGHT. I WAS DRINKING A LOT.
"AND WHEN I CAME OUT...
"HE WAS IN CONTROL."
I WAS TRYING TO WRITE HIM OUT. IN THE SCRIPT. BUT YOU TOOK THAT *AWAY* FROM ME.
THEY USED US ALL, YOU KNOW?

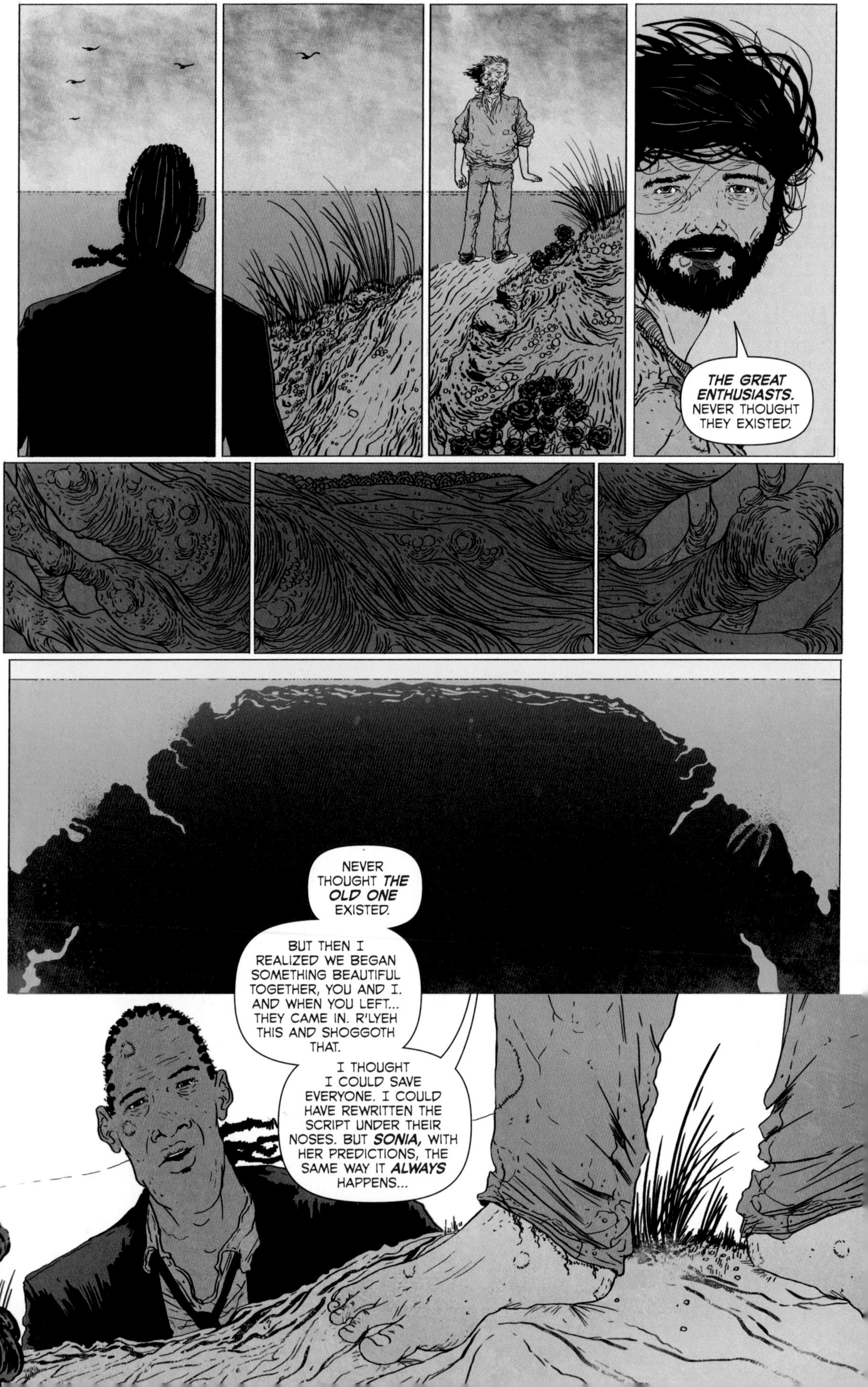
THE GREAT ENTHUSIASTS. NEVER THOUGHT THEY EXISTED.
NEVER THOUGHT THE OLD ONE EXISTED.
BUT THEN I REALIZED WE BEGAN SOMETHING BEAUTIFUL TOGETHER, YOU AND I. AND WHEN YOU LEFT... THEY CAME IN. R'LYEH THIS AND SHOGGOTH THAT.
I THOUGHT I COULD SAVE EVERYONE. I COULD HAVE REWRITTEN THE SCRIPT UNDER THEIR NOSES. BUT SONIA, WITH HER PREDICTIONS, THE SAME WAY IT ALWAYS HAPPENS...

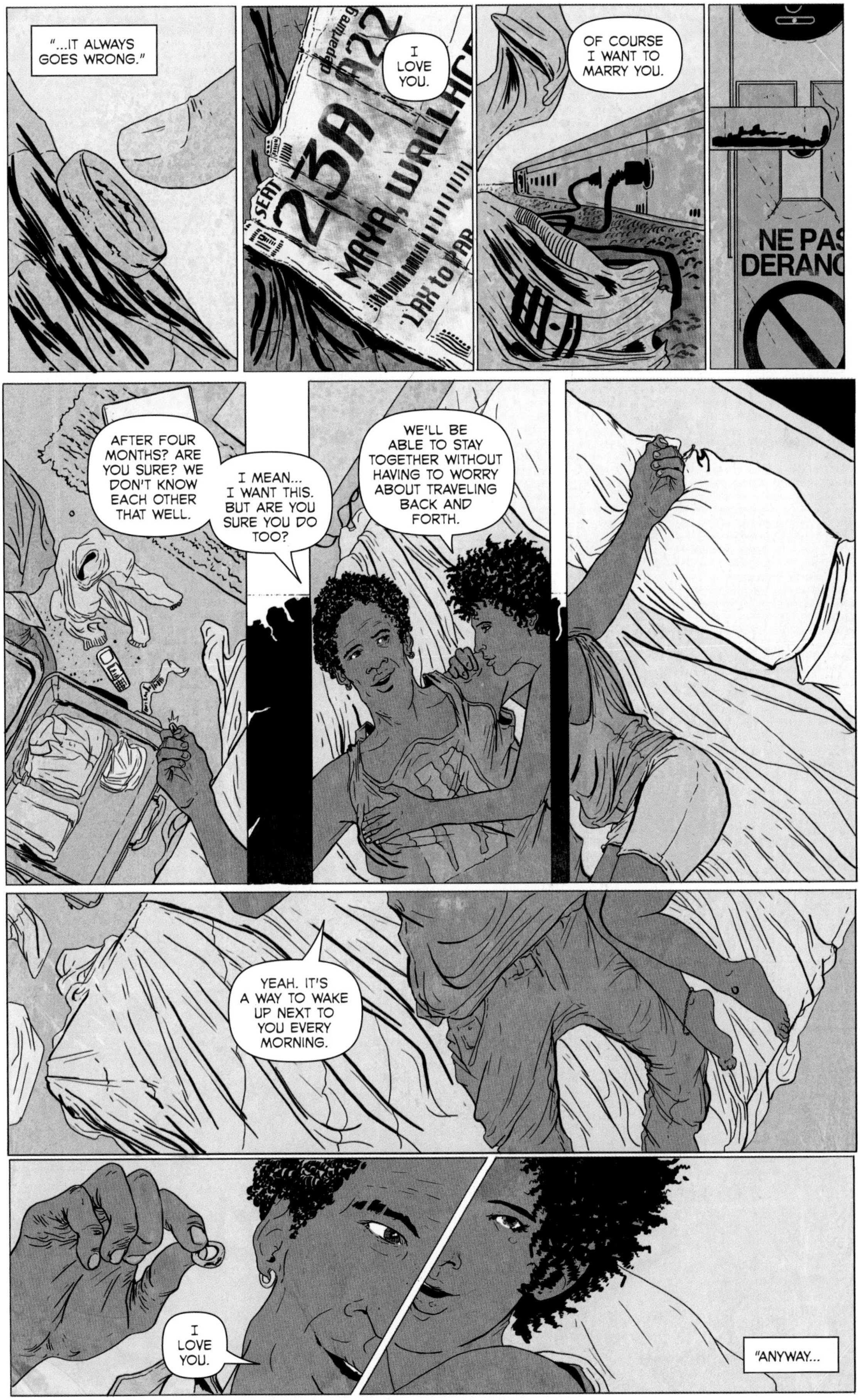
"...IT ALWAYS GOES WRONG."
I LOVE YOU.
OF COURSE I WANT TO MARRY YOU.
NE PAS DERANG
AFTER FOUR MONTHS? ARE YOU SURE? WE DON'T KNOW EACH OTHER THAT WELL.
I MEAN... I WANT THIS. BUT ARE YOU SURE YOU DO TOO?
WE'LL BE ABLE TO STAY TOGETHER WITHOUT HAVING TO WORRY ABOUT TRAVELING BACK AND FORTH.
YEAH. IT'S A WAY TO WAKE UP NEXT TO YOU EVERY MORNING.
I LOVE YOU.
"ANYWAY...

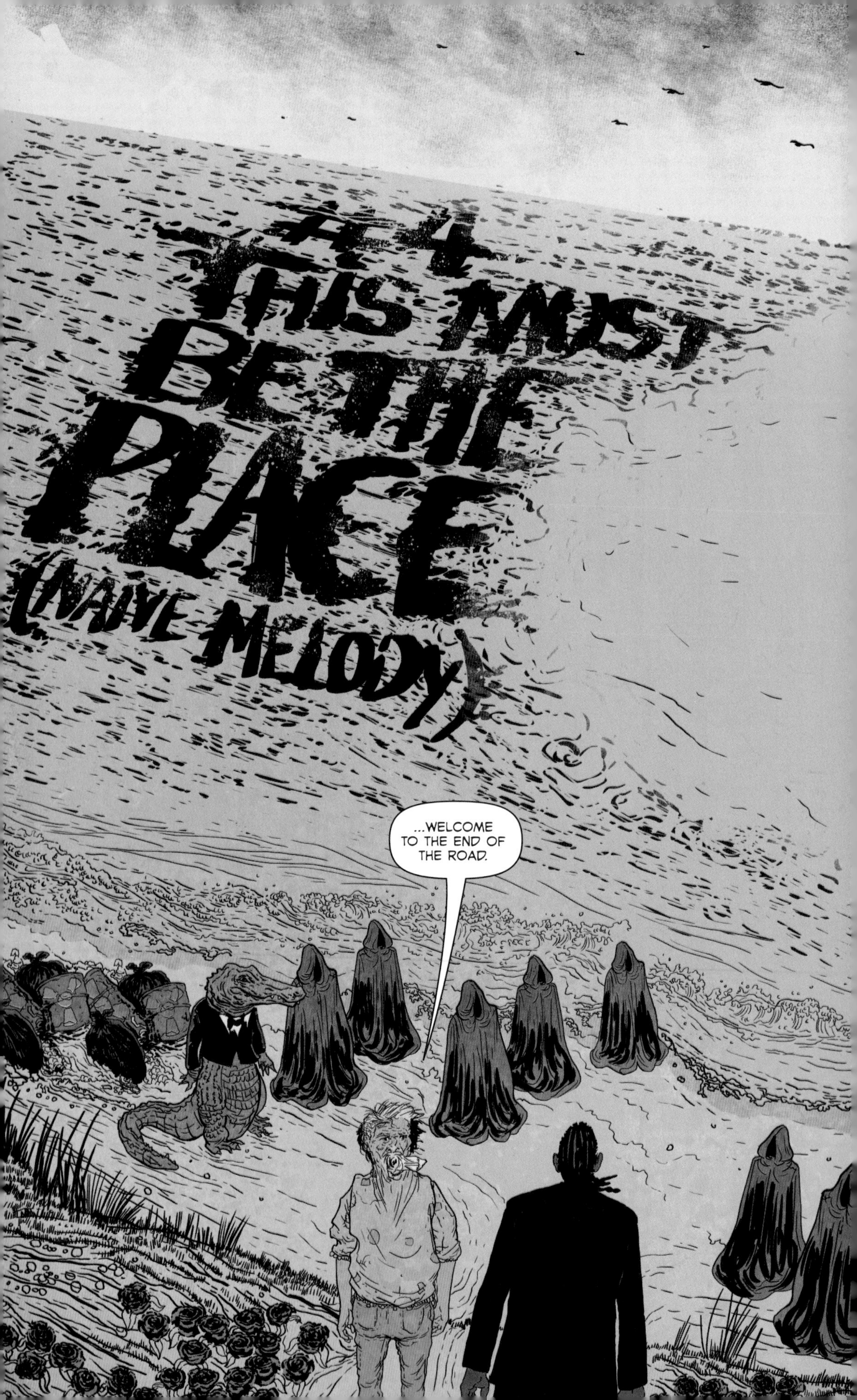
#4
THIS MUST BE THE PLACE
(NAIVE MELODY)
...WELCOME TO THE END OF THE ROAD.

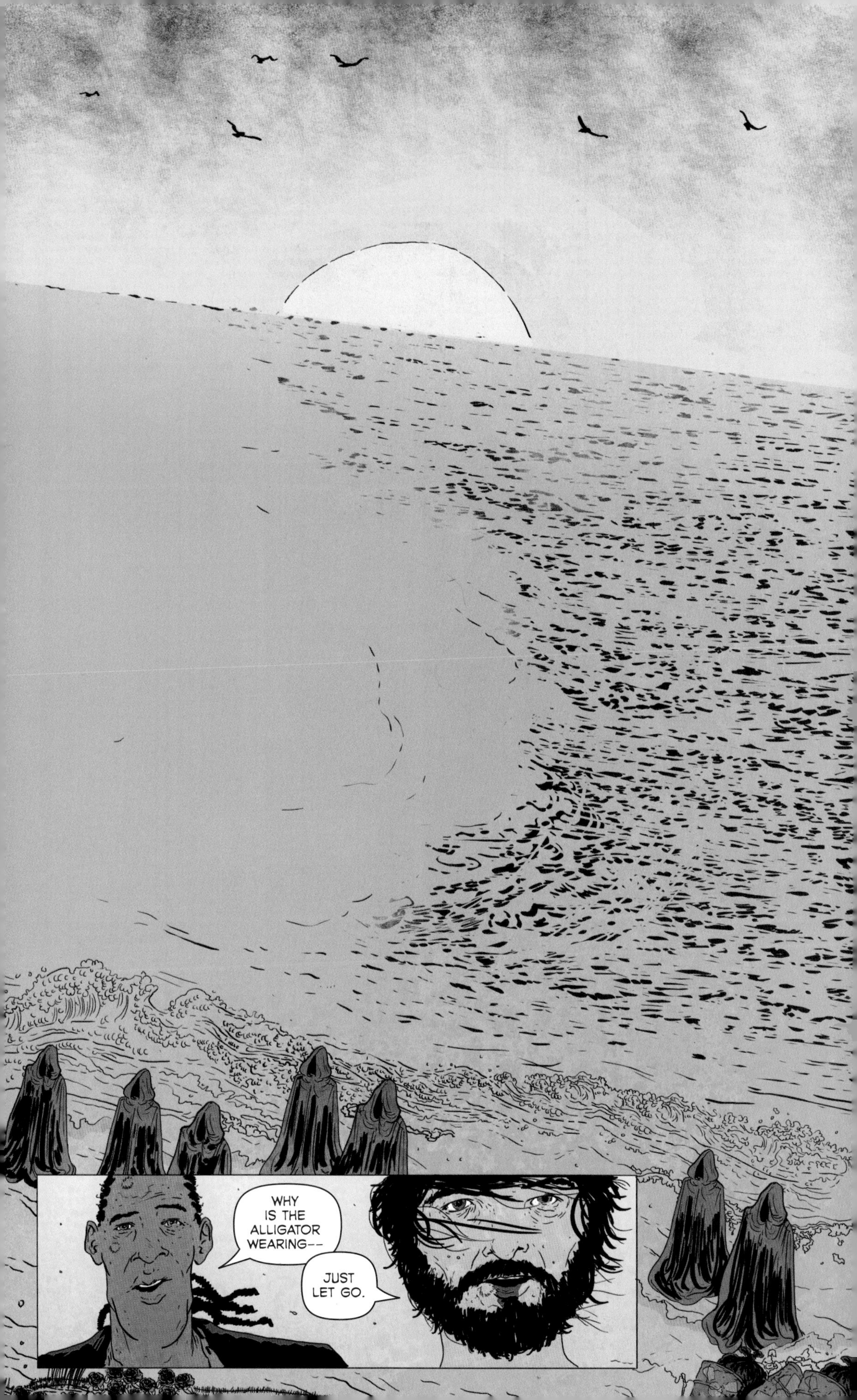
WHY IS THE ALLIGATOR WEARING--
JUST LET GO.

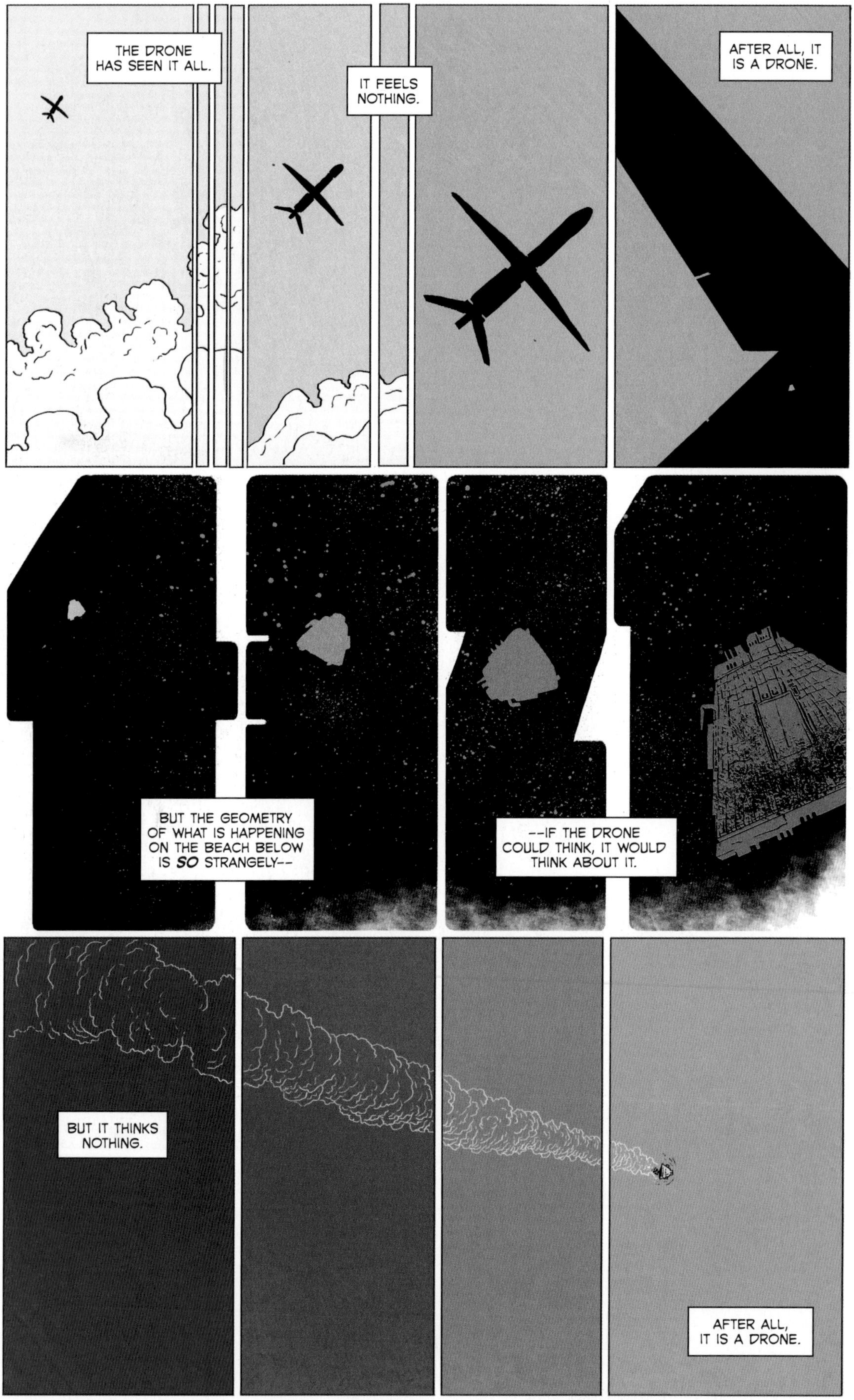
THE DRONE HAS SEEN IT ALL.
IT FEELS NOTHING.
AFTER ALL, IT IS A DRONE.
BUT THE GEOMETRY OF WHAT IS HAPPENING ON THE BEACH BELOW IS *SO* STRANGELY--
--IF THE DRONE COULD THINK, IT WOULD THINK ABOUT IT.
BUT IT THINKS NOTHING.
AFTER ALL, IT IS A DRONE.

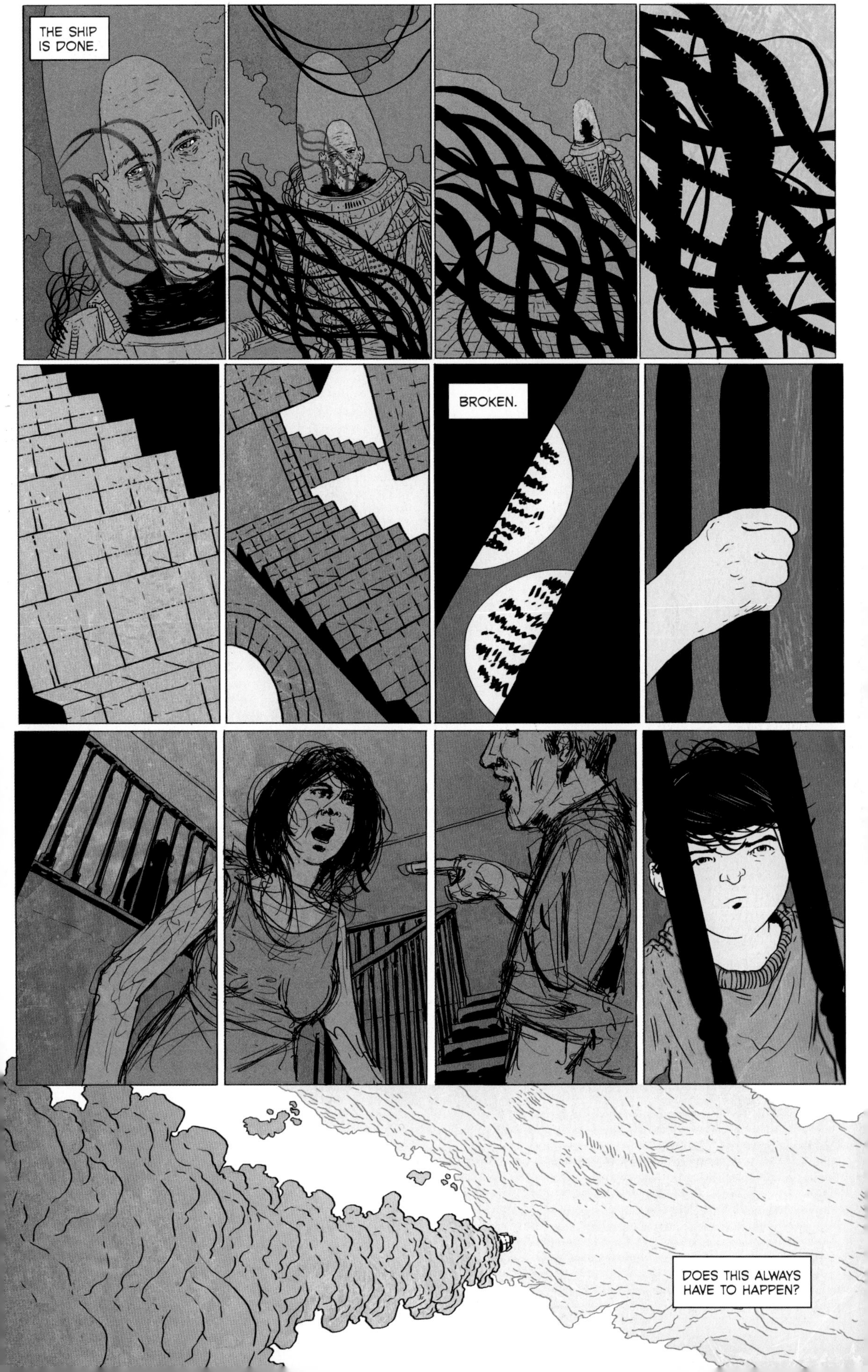
THE SHIP IS DONE.
BROKEN.
DOES THIS ALWAYS HAVE TO HAPPEN?

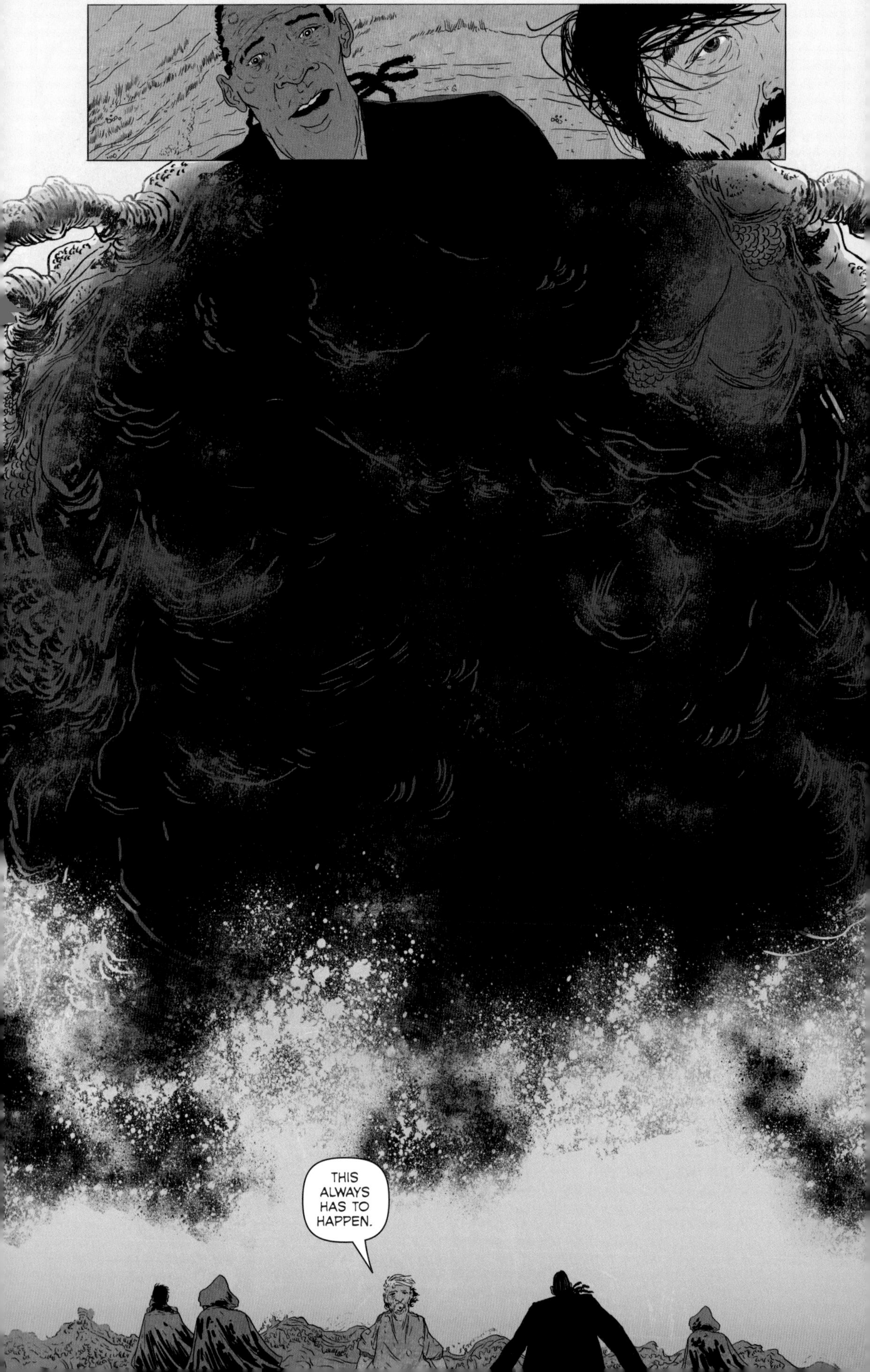
THIS ALWAYS HAS TO HAPPEN.

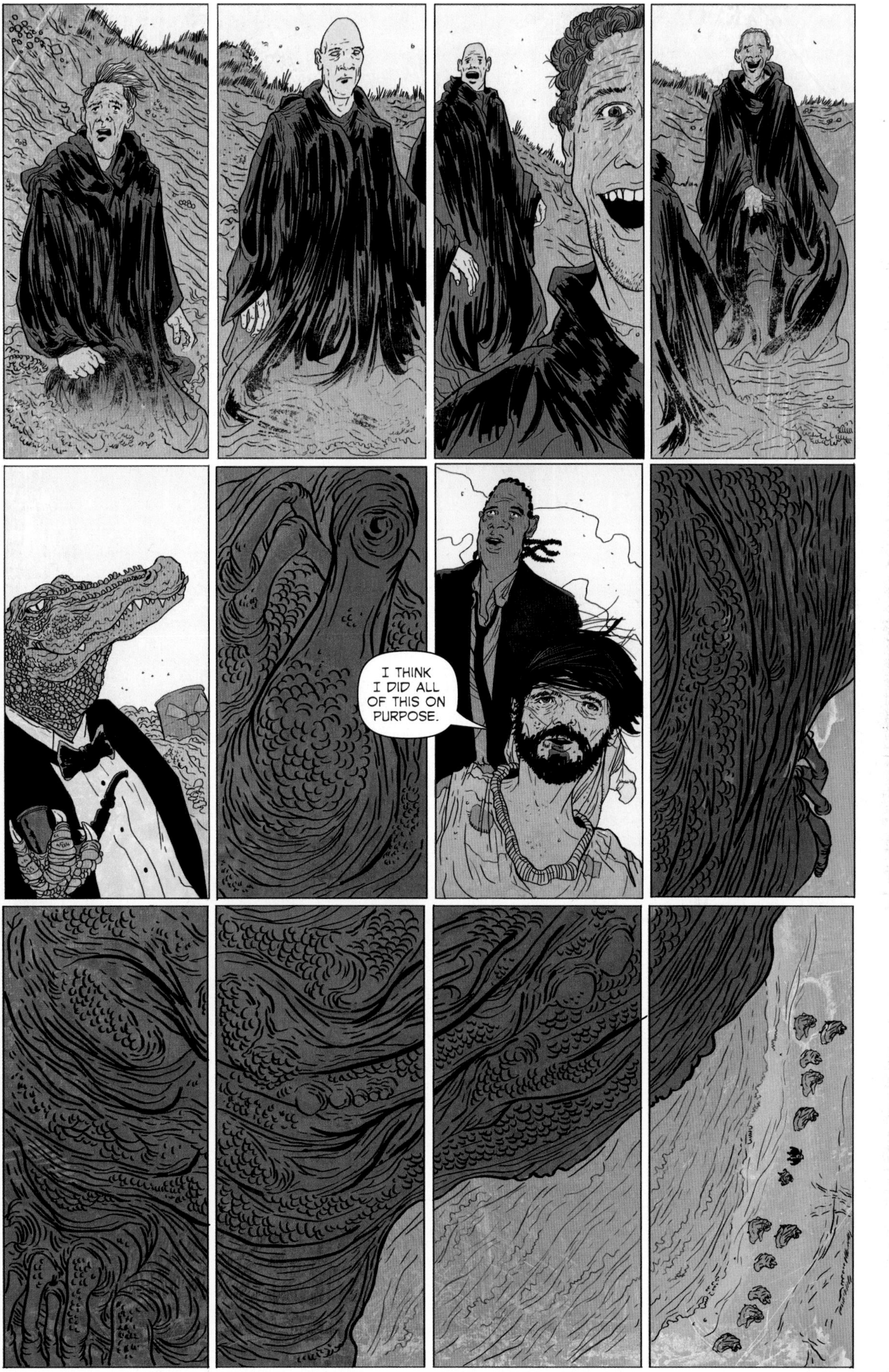
I THINK I DID ALL OF THIS ON PURPOSE.

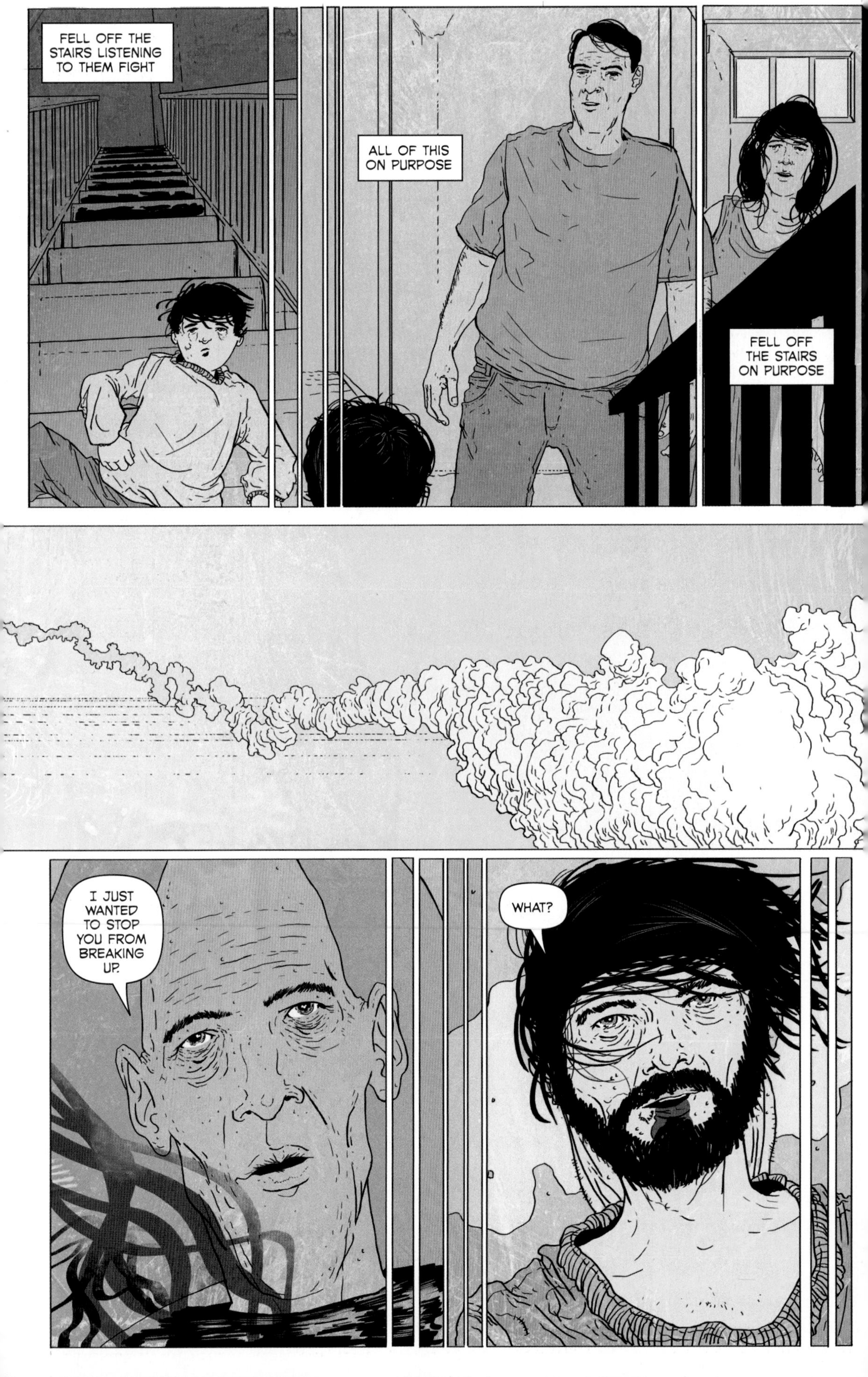
FELL OFF THE STAIRS LISTENING TO THEM FIGHT
ALL OF THIS ON PURPOSE
FELL OFF THE STAIRS ON PURPOSE
I JUST WANTED TO STOP YOU FROM BREAKING UP.
WHAT?

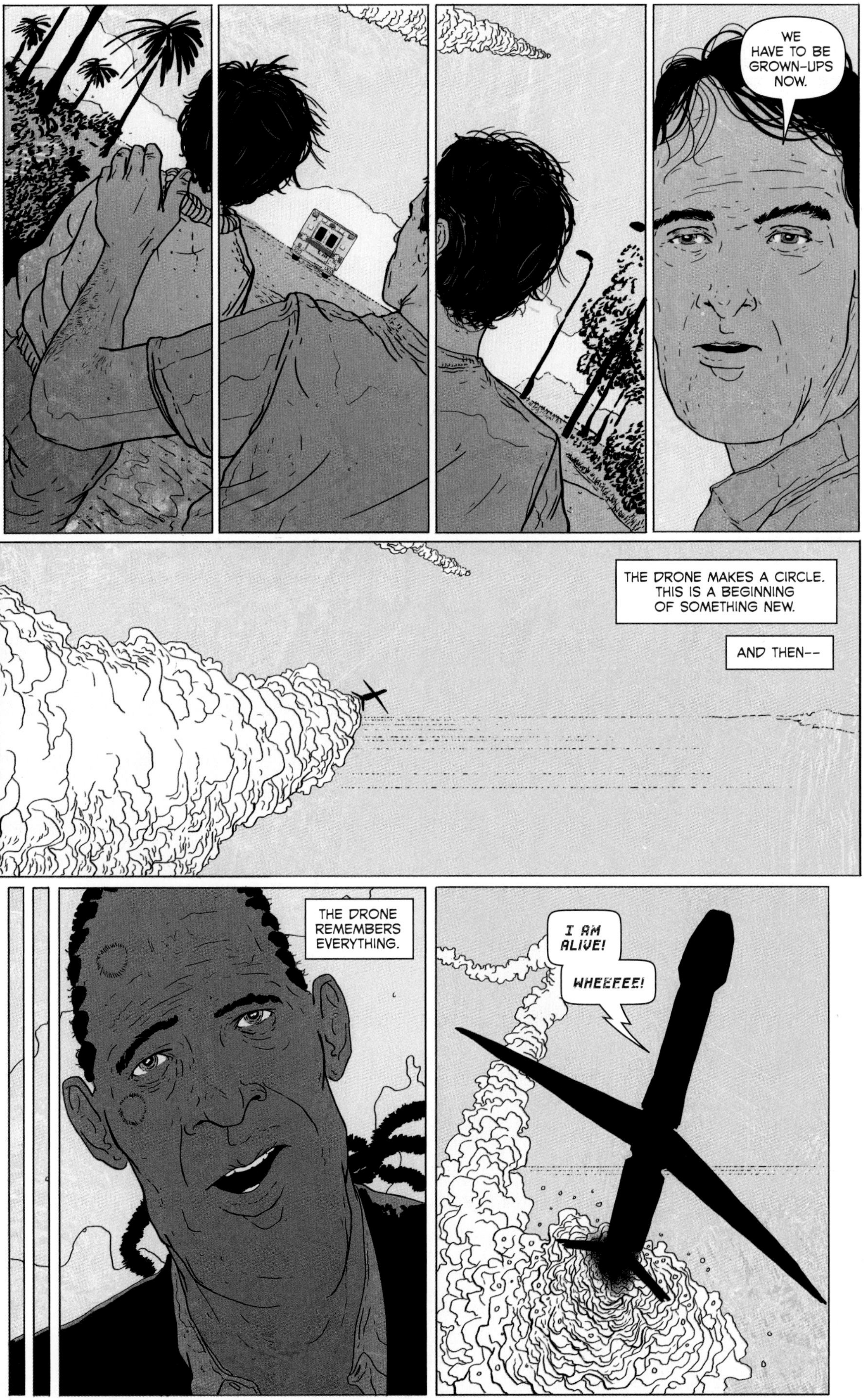
WE HAVE TO BE GROWN-UPS NOW.
THE DRONE MAKES A CIRCLE. THIS IS A BEGINNING OF SOMETHING NEW.
AND THEN--
THE DRONE REMEMBERS EVERYTHING.
I AM ALIVE!
WHEEEEE!

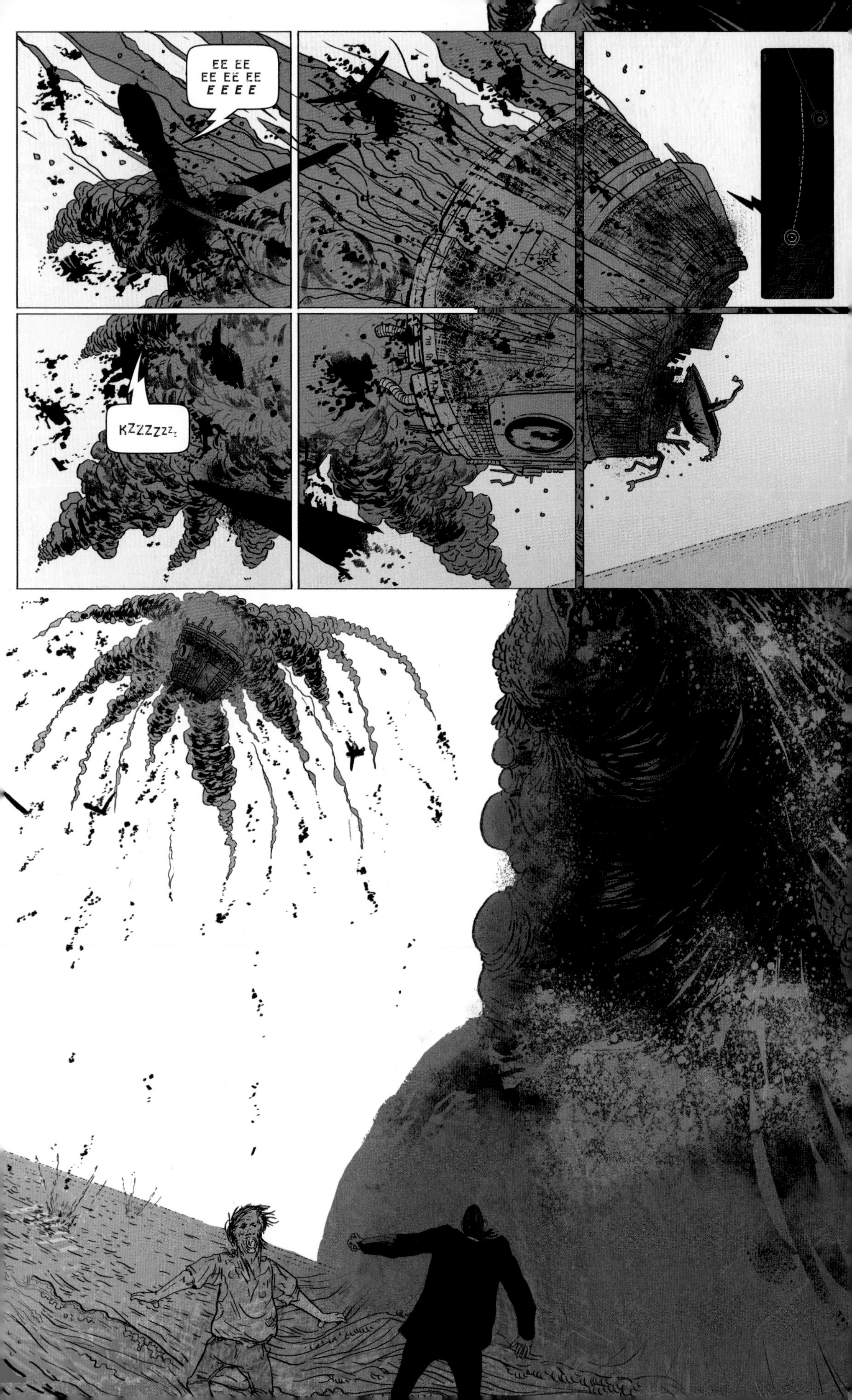
EE EE
EE EE EE
EEEE
KZZZZzz

I NEVER WANTED TO
GROW UP SO FAST

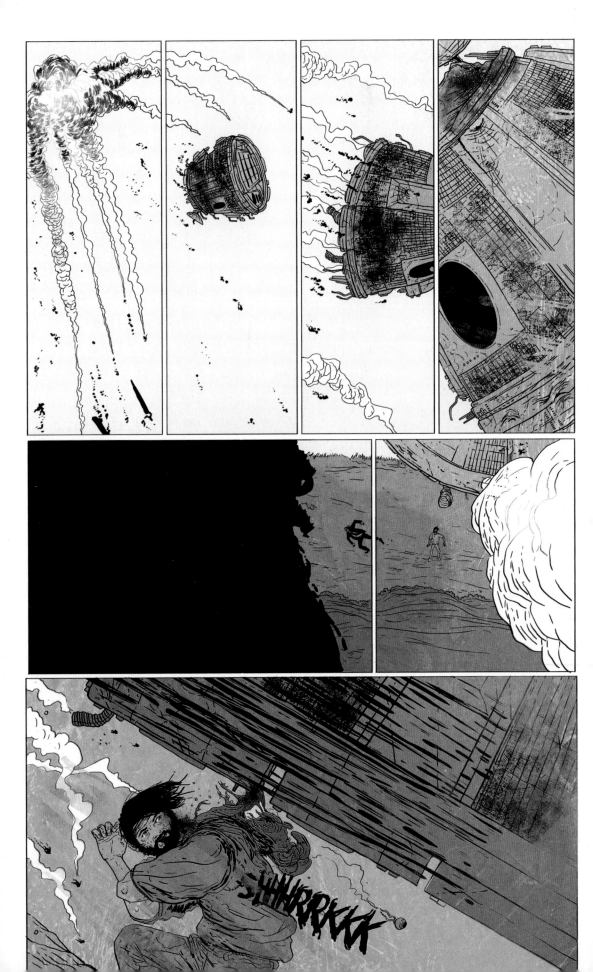

SHHRRKKK

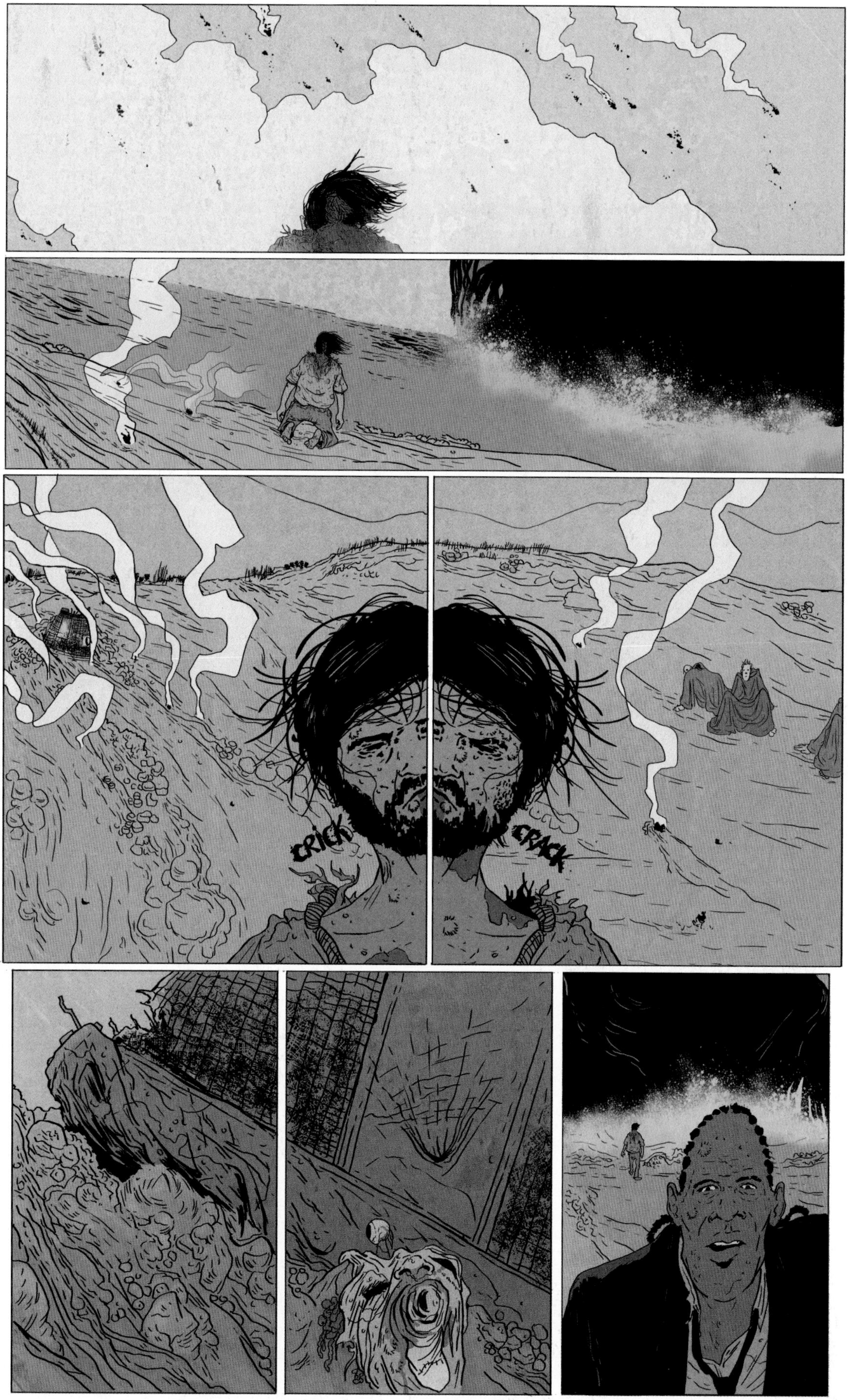
CRICK
CRACK

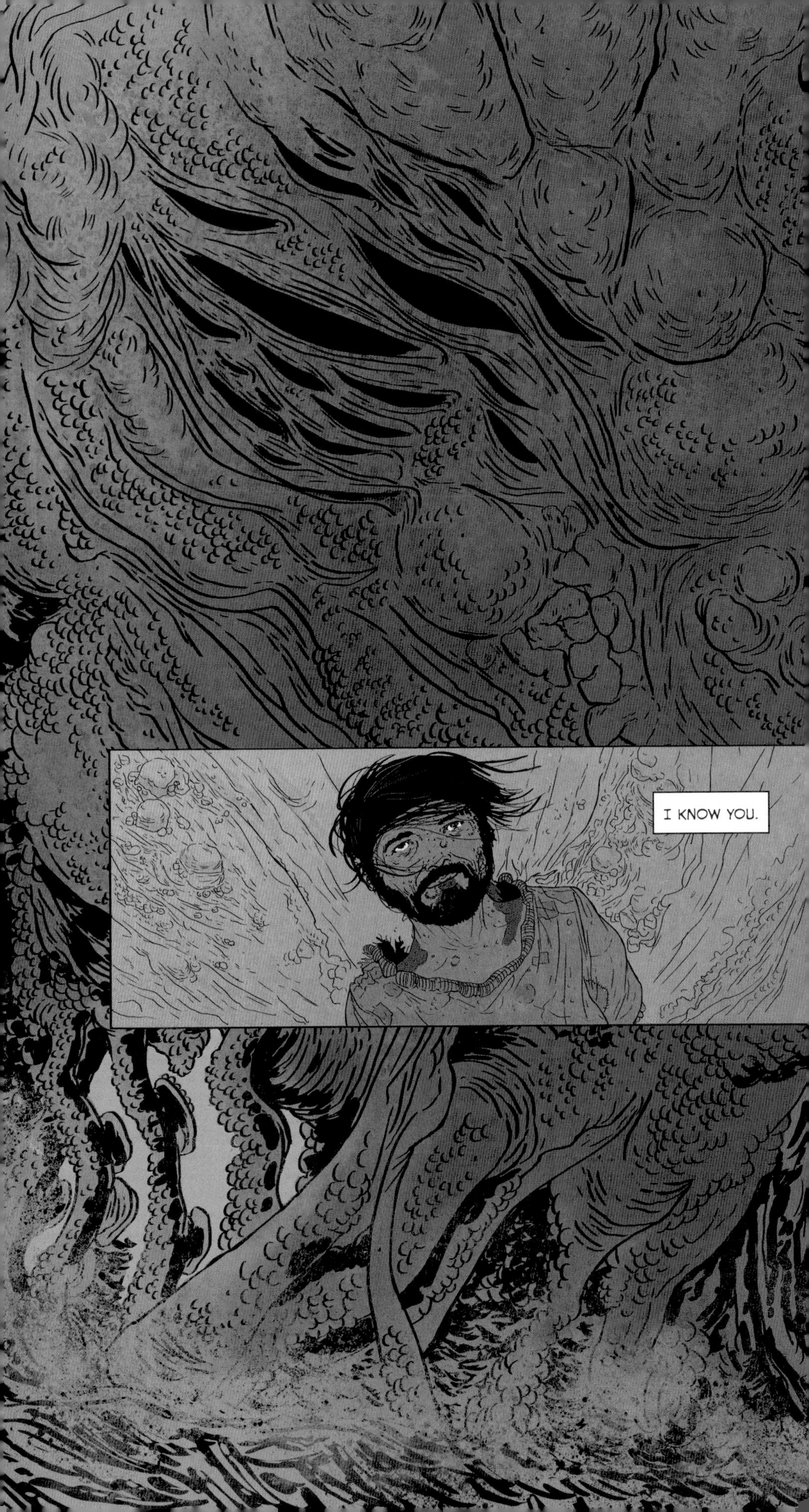
I KNOW YOU.

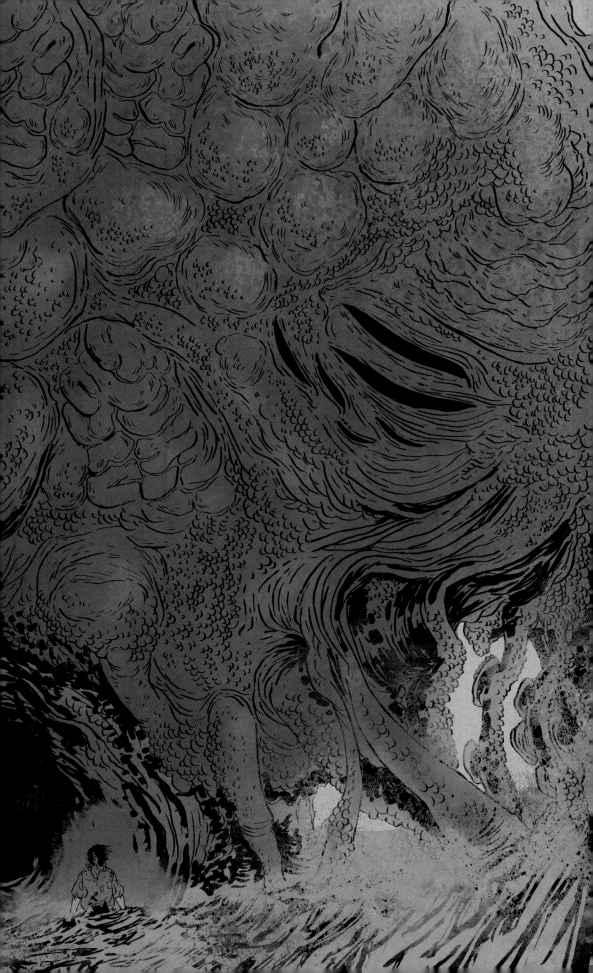

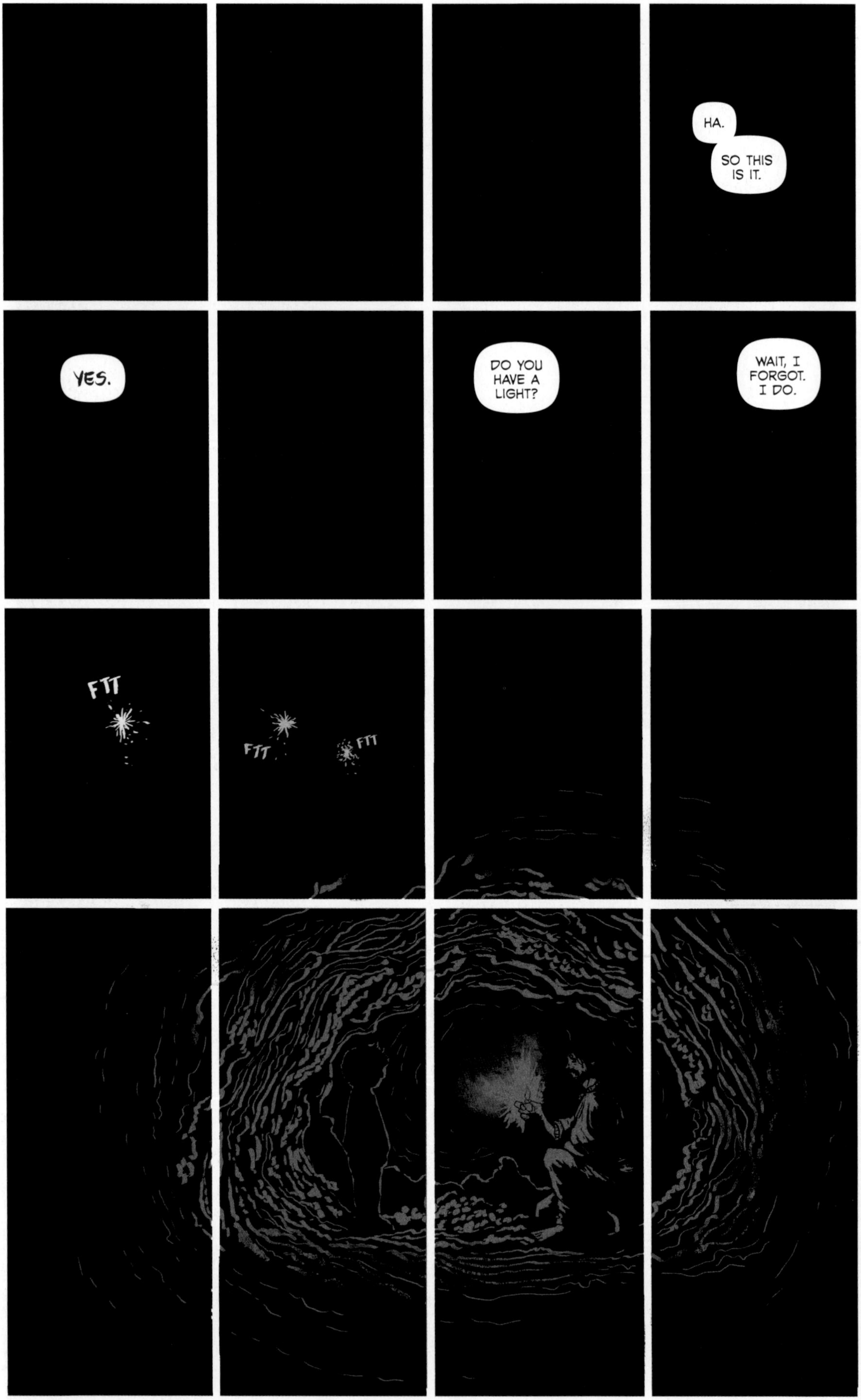
HA.
SO THIS IS IT.
YES.
DO YOU HAVE A LIGHT?
WAIT, I FORGOT. I DO.
FTT
FTT
FTT

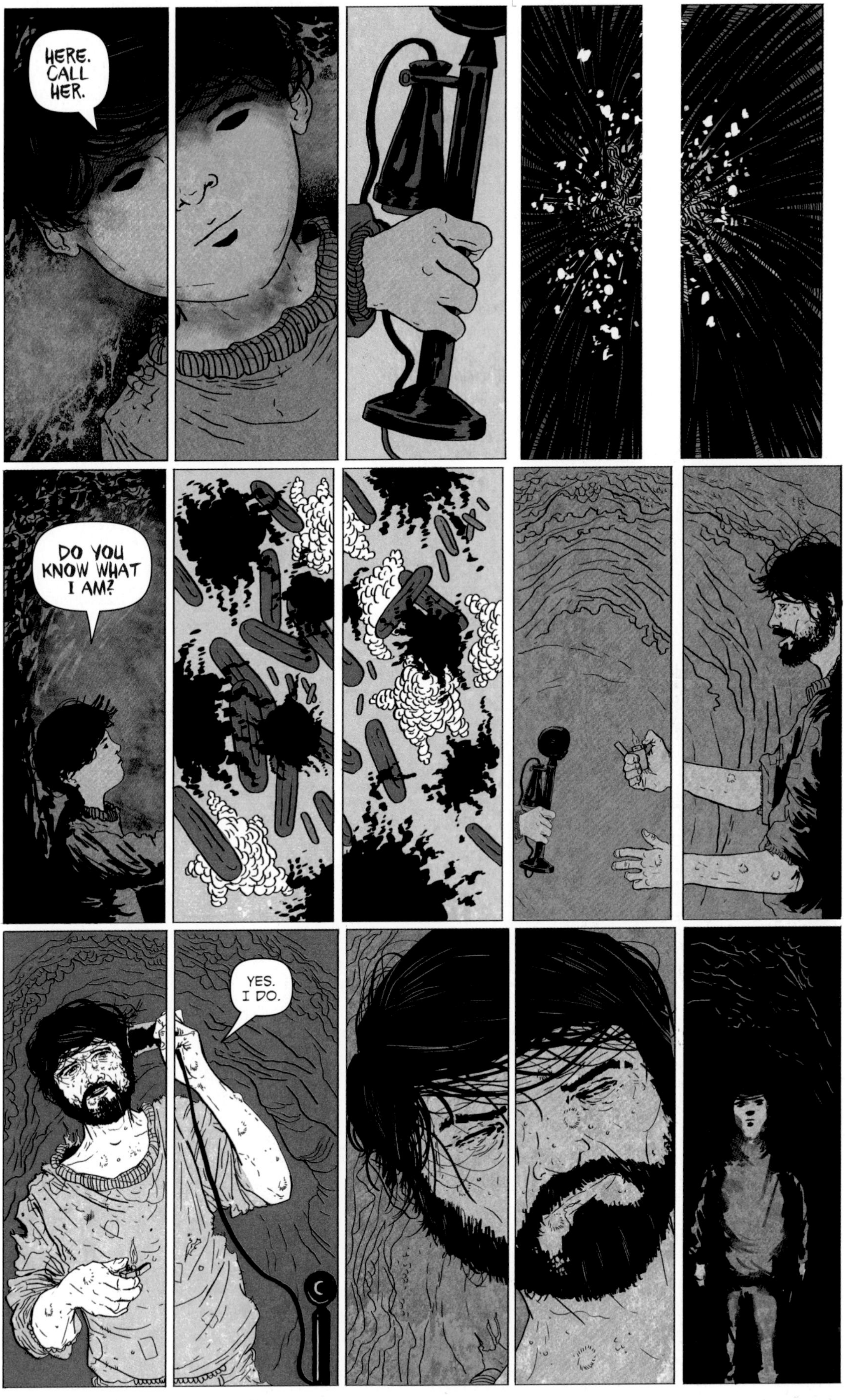
HERE. CALL HER.
DO YOU KNOW WHAT I AM?
YES. I DO.

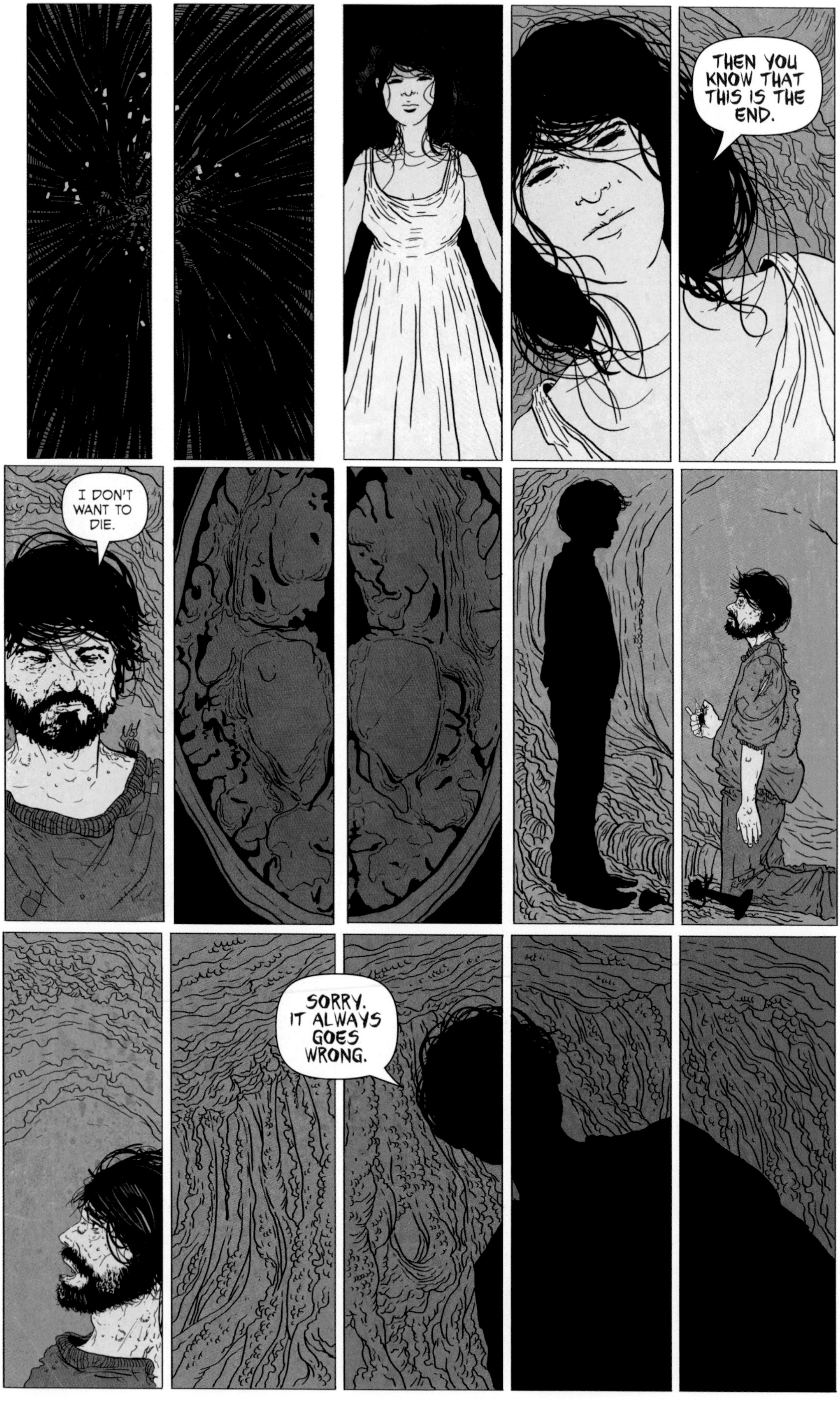
THEN YOU KNOW THAT THIS IS THE END.
I DON'T WANT TO DIE.
SORRY. IT ALWAYS GOES WRONG.

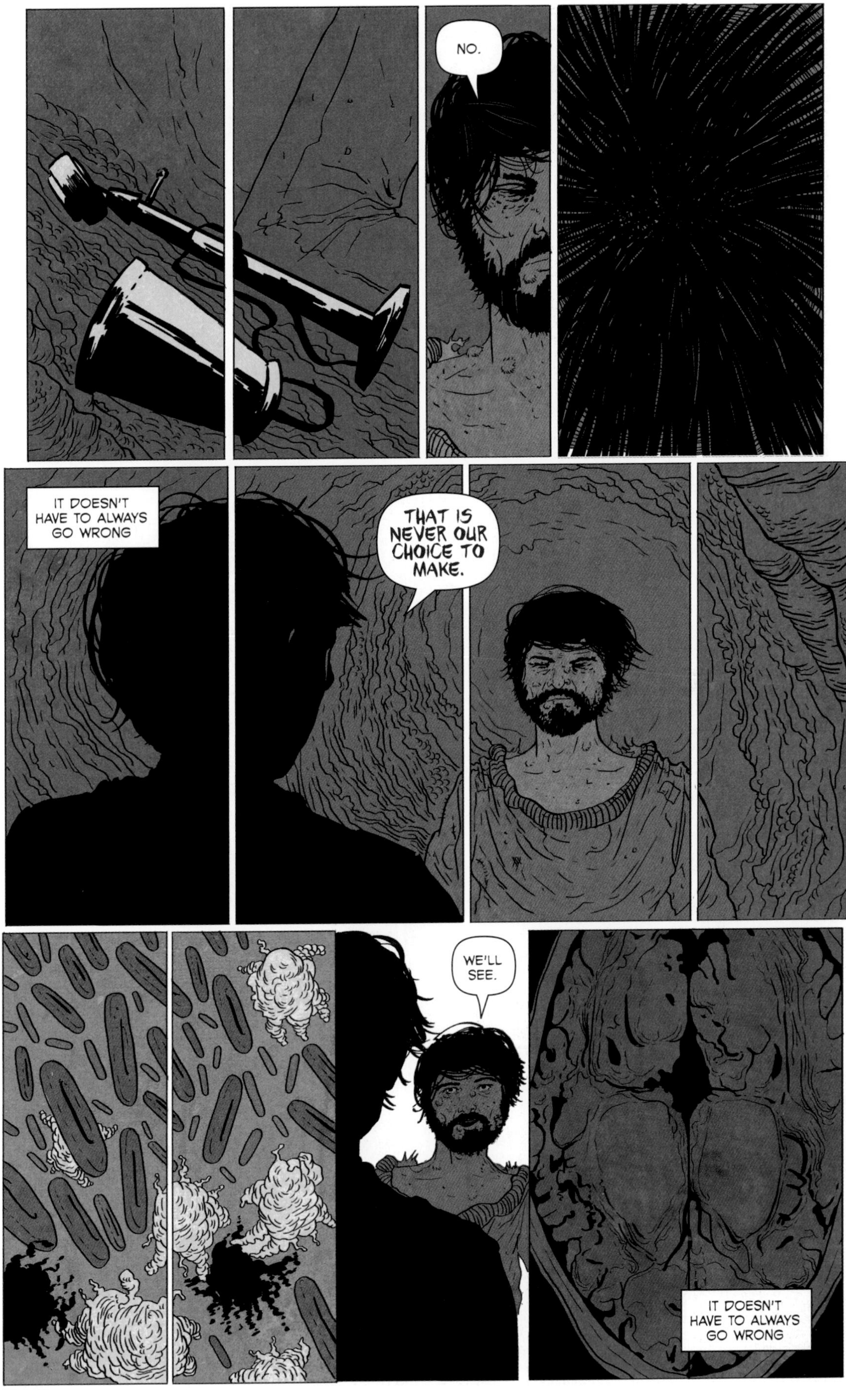
NO.
IT DOESN'T HAVE TO ALWAYS GO WRONG
THAT IS NEVER OUR CHOICE TO MAKE.
WE'LL SEE.
IT DOESN'T HAVE TO ALWAYS GO WRONG

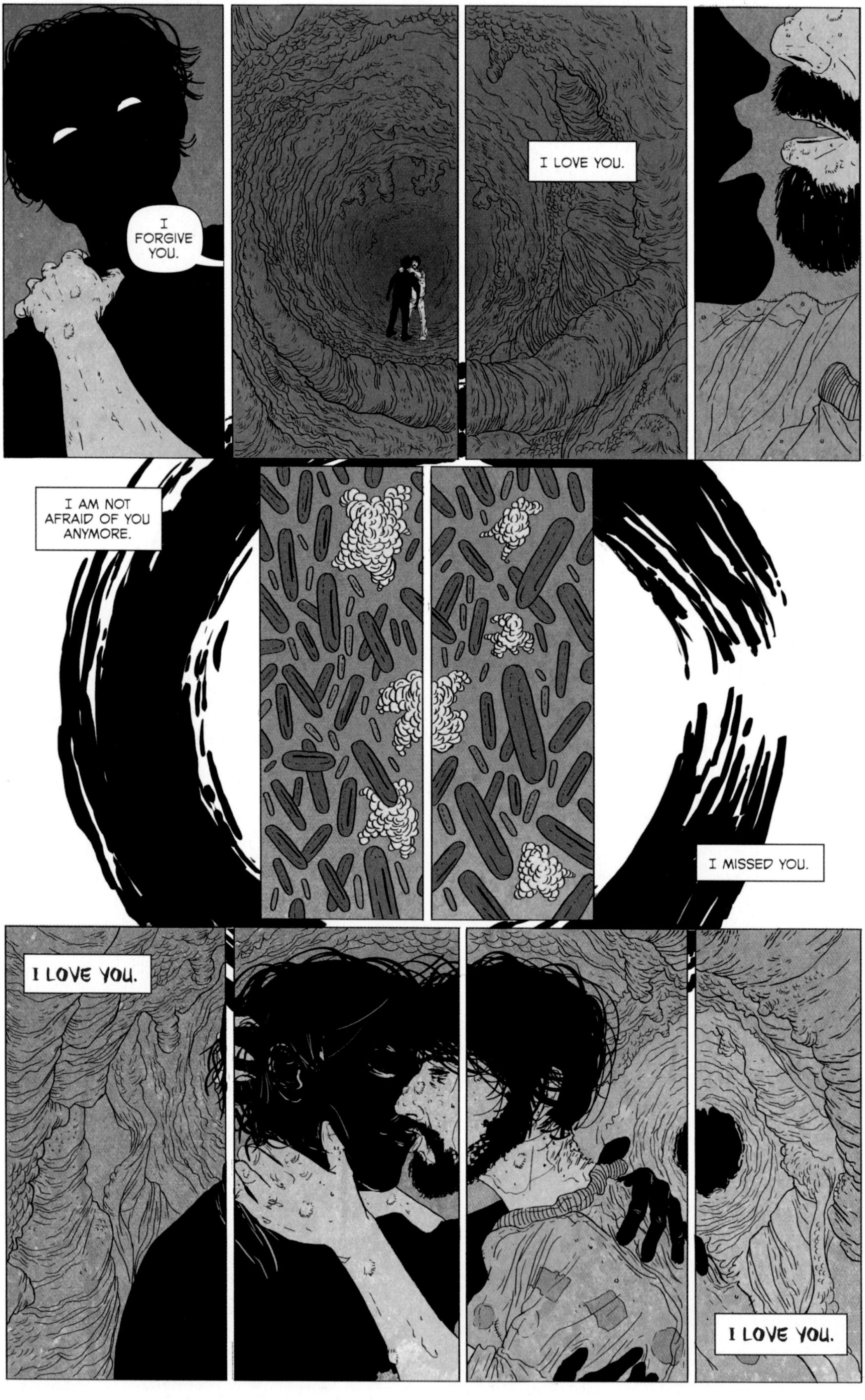
I FORGIVE YOU.
I LOVE YOU.
I AM NOT AFRAID OF YOU ANYMORE.
I MISSED YOU.
I LOVE YOU.
I LOVE YOU.

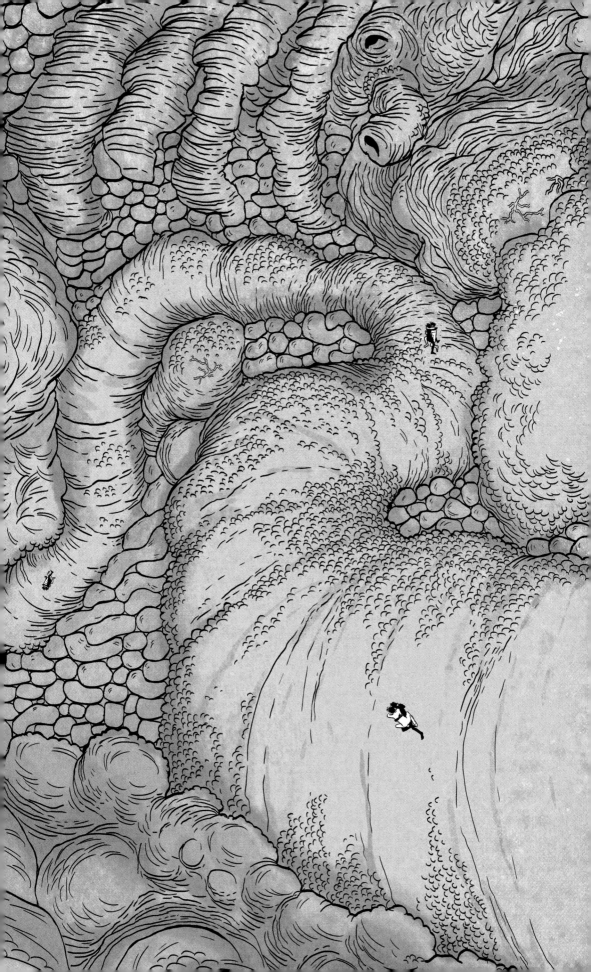

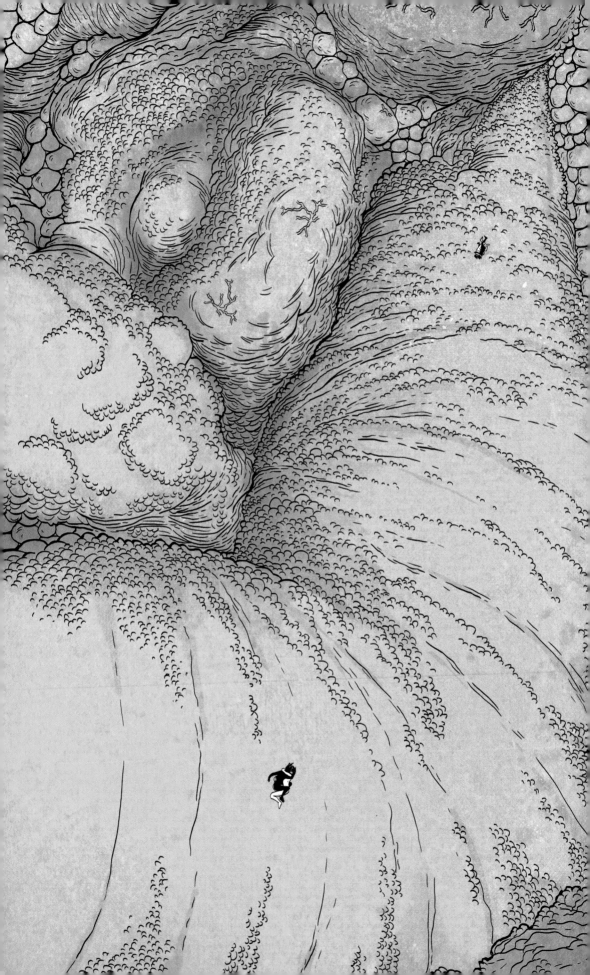

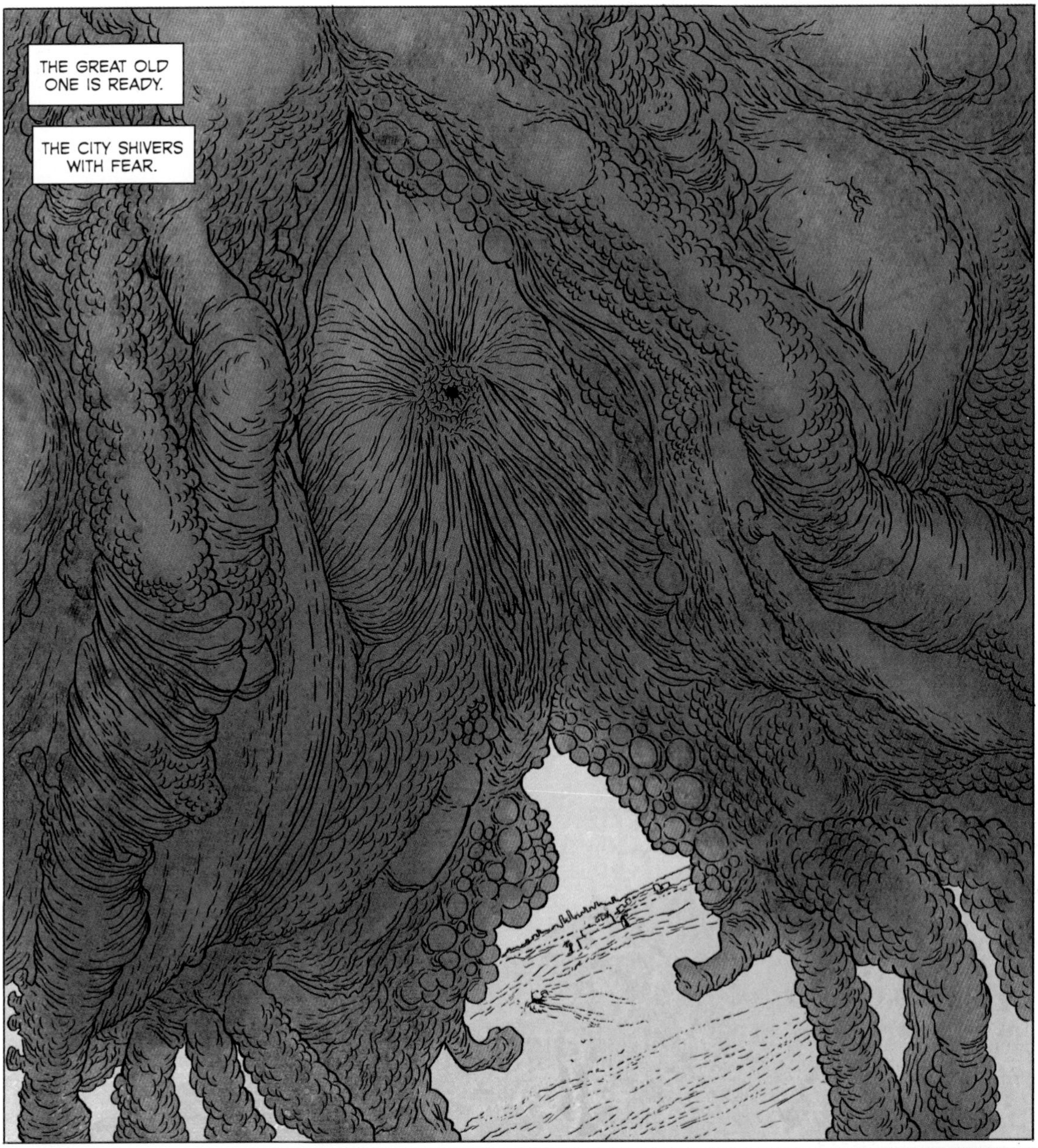
THE GREAT OLD ONE IS READY.
THE CITY SHIVERS WITH FEAR.

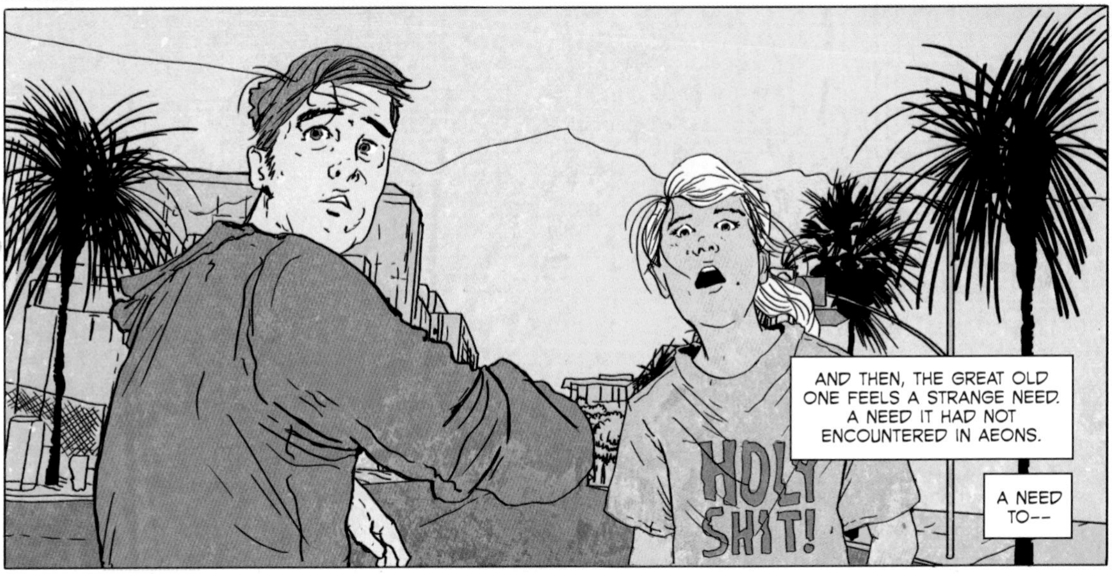
AND THEN, THE GREAT OLD ONE FEELS A STRANGE NEED. A NEED IT HAD NOT ENCOUNTERED IN AEONS.
A NEED TO--
HOLY SHIT!

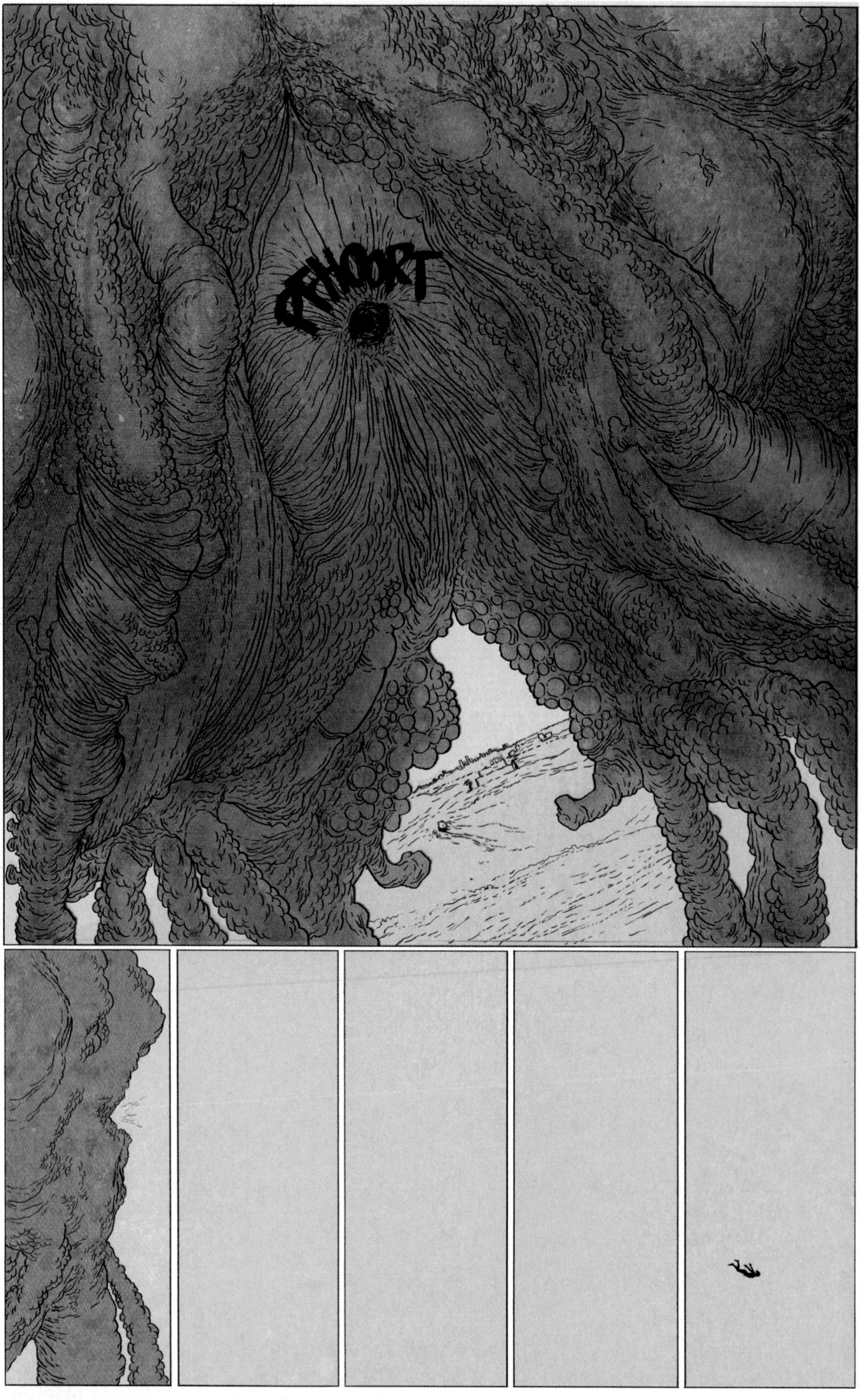

PFHOORT

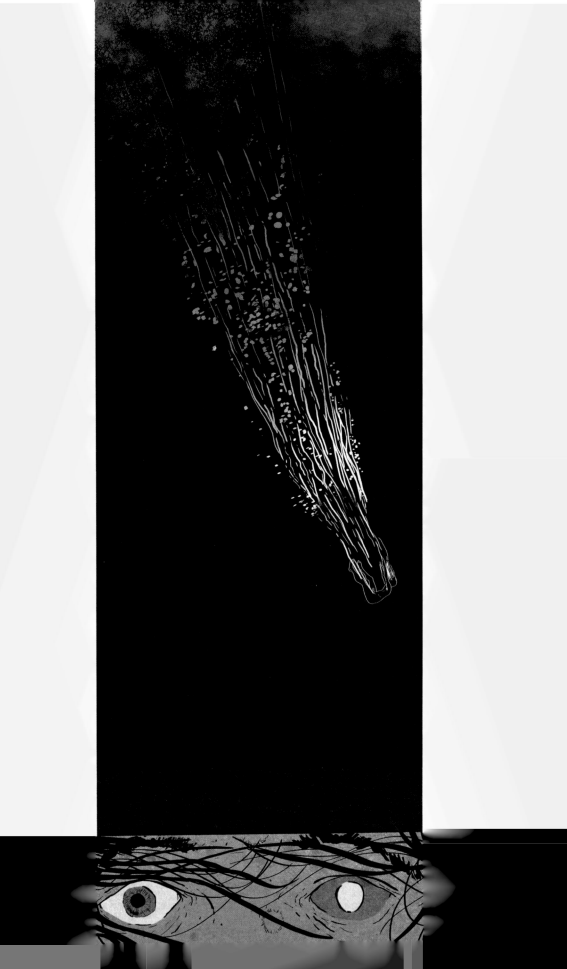

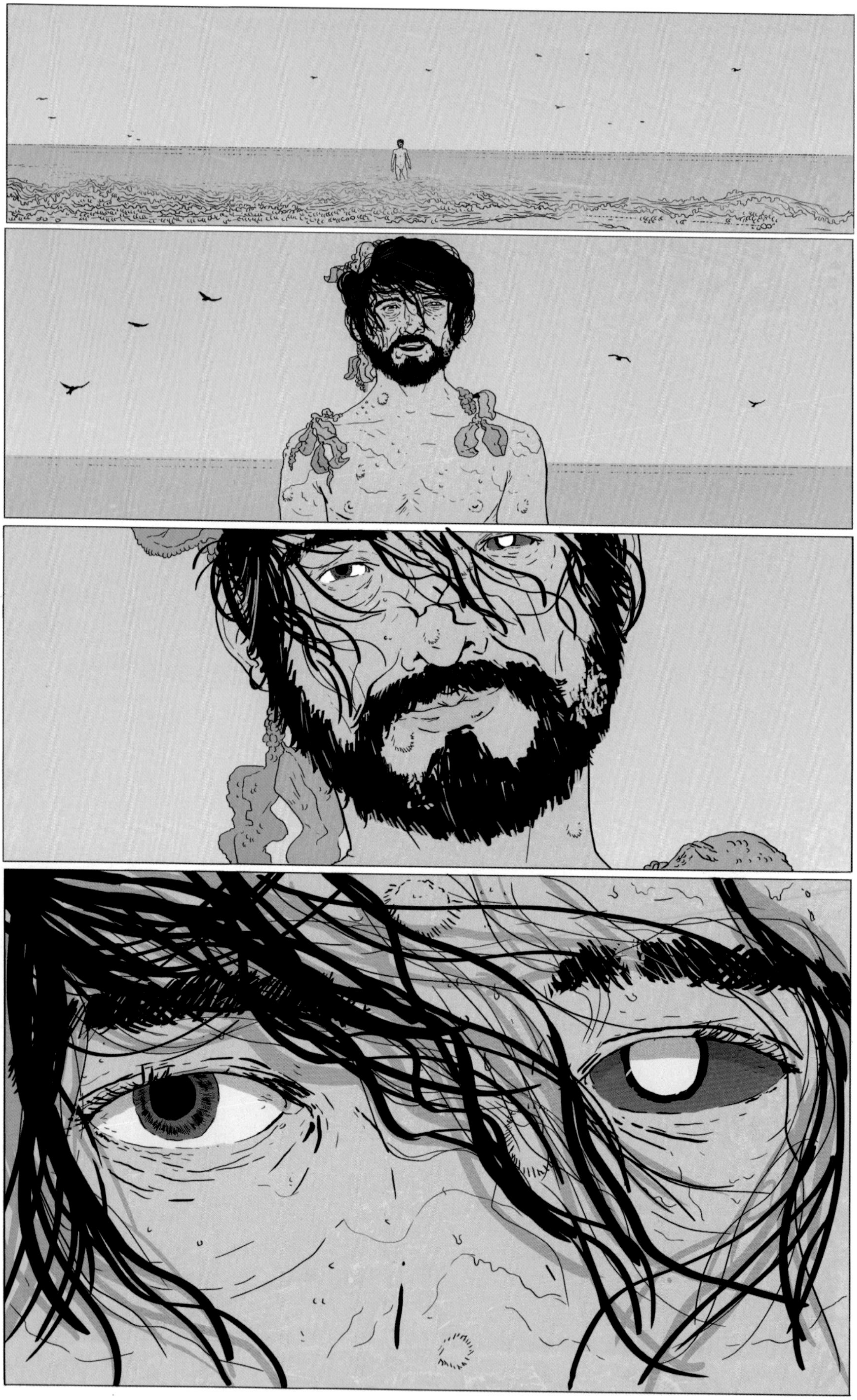

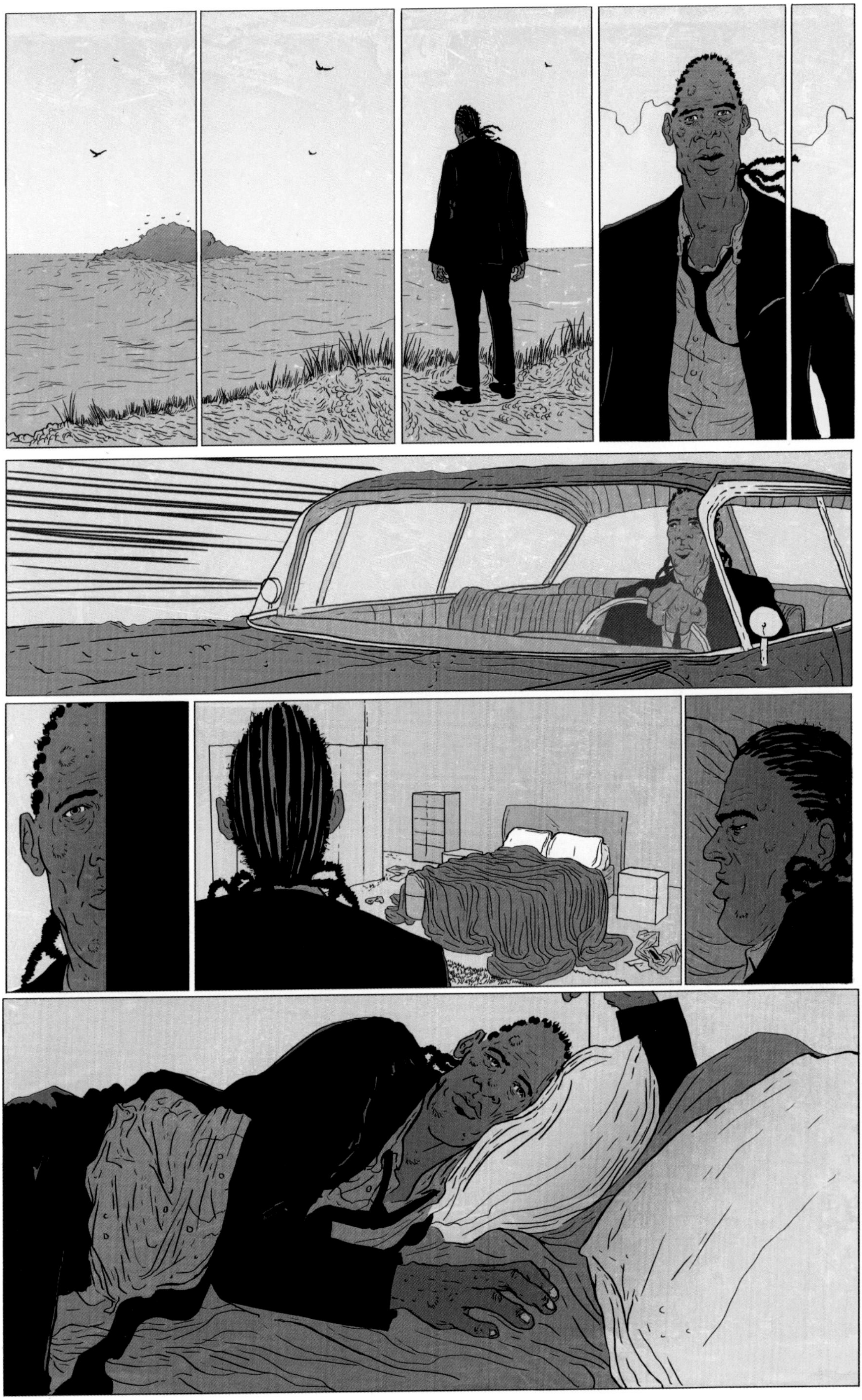

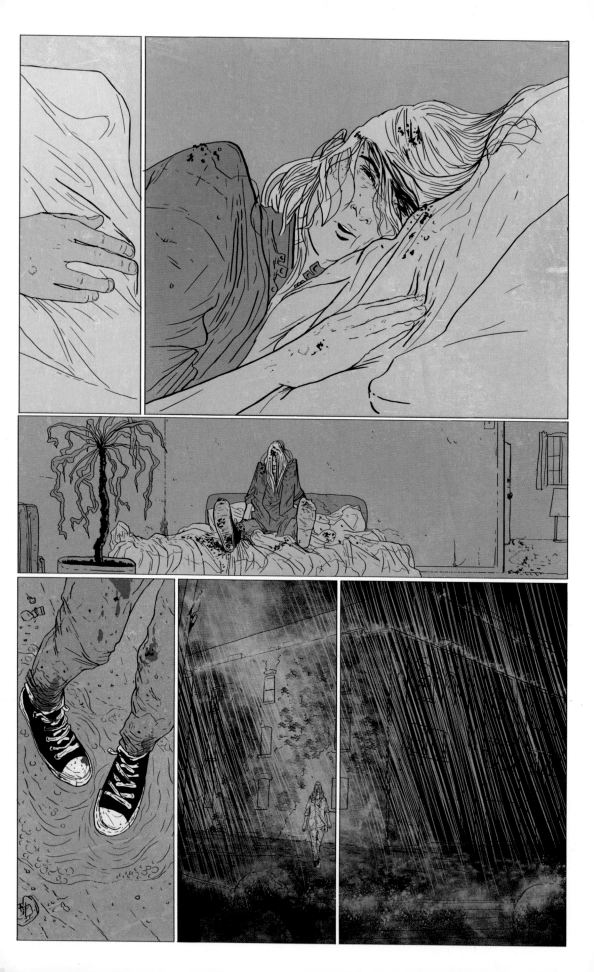

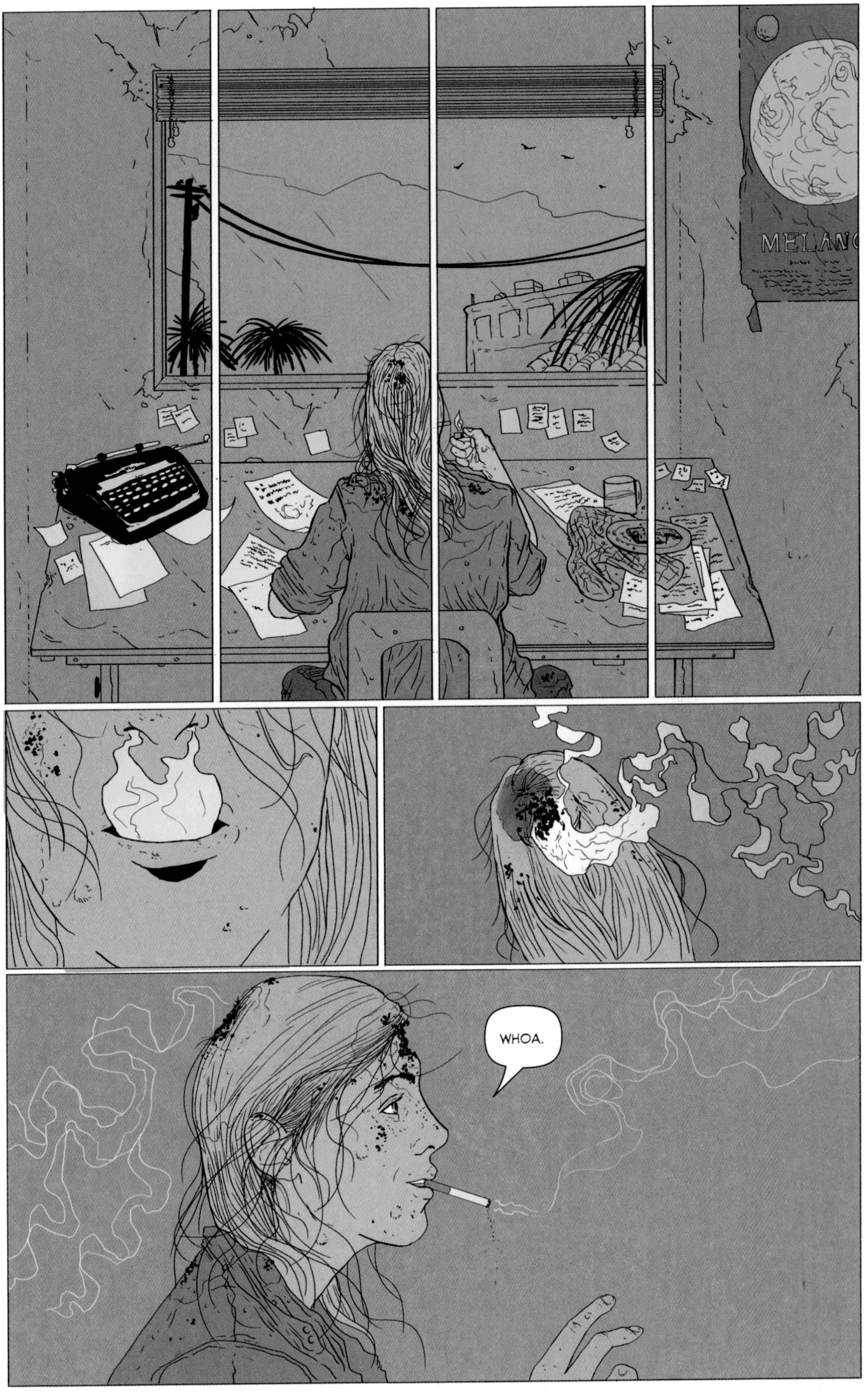
MELANC
WHOA.

THE PHONE IS
RINGING. IT'S NOT
YOU. IT'S THE
DEADLINES.

YOU ARE GONE.

SOMETIMES I WRITE YOU
A LETTER TO TELL YOU
EVERYTHING. THEN I SEND IT TO
YOUR EMAIL ADDRESS, HOPING
YOU CAN STILL SOMEHOW READ
IT. BECAUSE I LOVE YOU,
AND I ALWAYS WILL.

YOU ARE GONE THOUGH,
THE YOU I WANTED TO
BE WITH -- I FINALLY MADE
MY PEACE WITH THAT.

I MISSED HOME SO MUCH. I
THOUGHT YOUR FACE WAS HOME
ONCE. I THOUGHT IT WAS SOMETHING
INESCAPABLE AND TRAGIC AND
BEAUTIFUL, BECAUSE MY HOME CONFUSED
THE LITTLE BOY INSIDE ME INTO THINKING
THAT ANYTHING BEAUTIFUL WILL
INEVITABLY BREAK.

THERE'S ONE LAST
THING TO WRITE, AND I
AM INCREDIBLY AFRAID
TO WRITE IT, BUT I WILL,
BECAUSE IT IS WHAT
IS ALIVE IN ME.

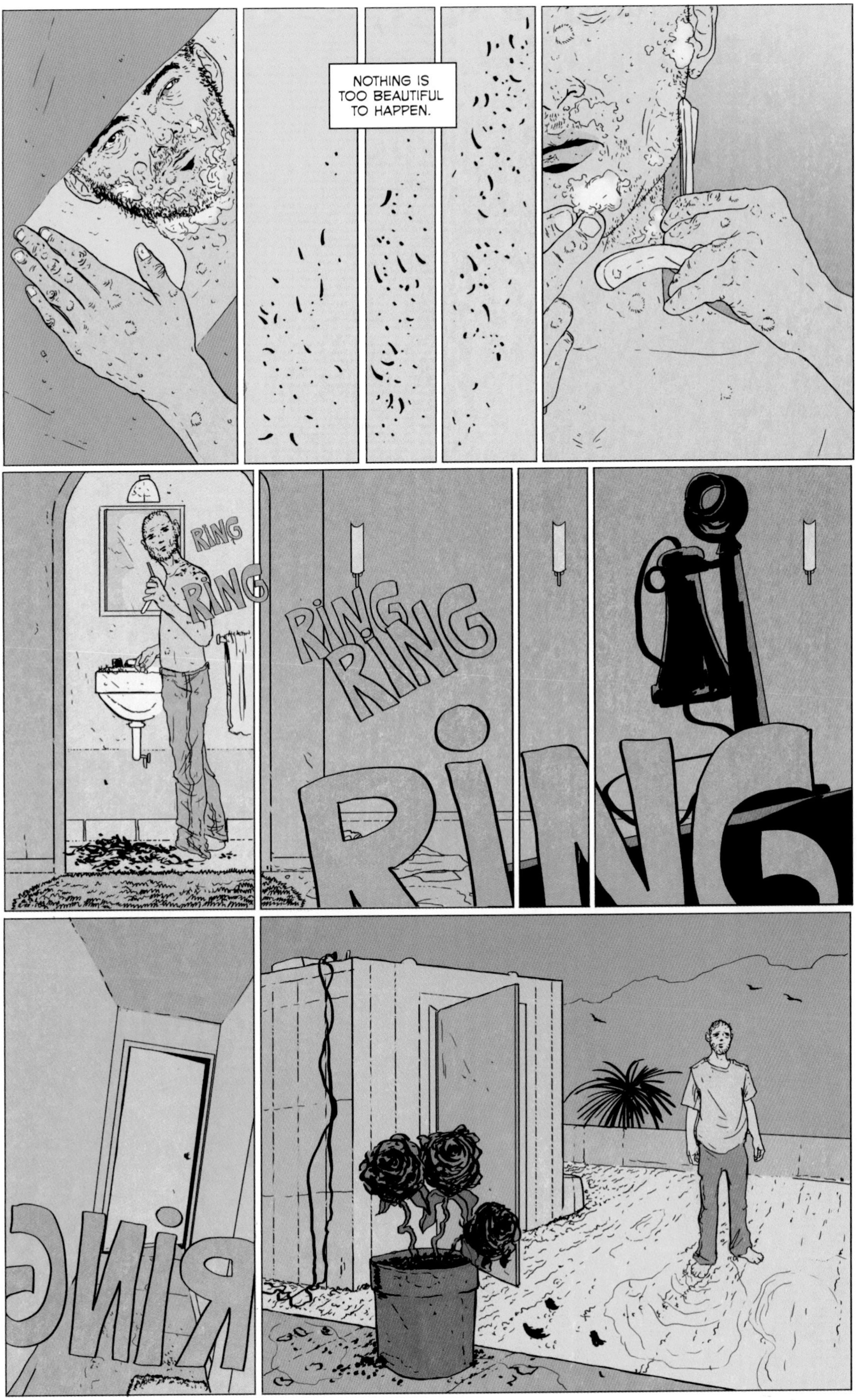
NOTHING IS TOO BEAUTIFUL TO HAPPEN.
RING
RING
RING
RING
RING
RING

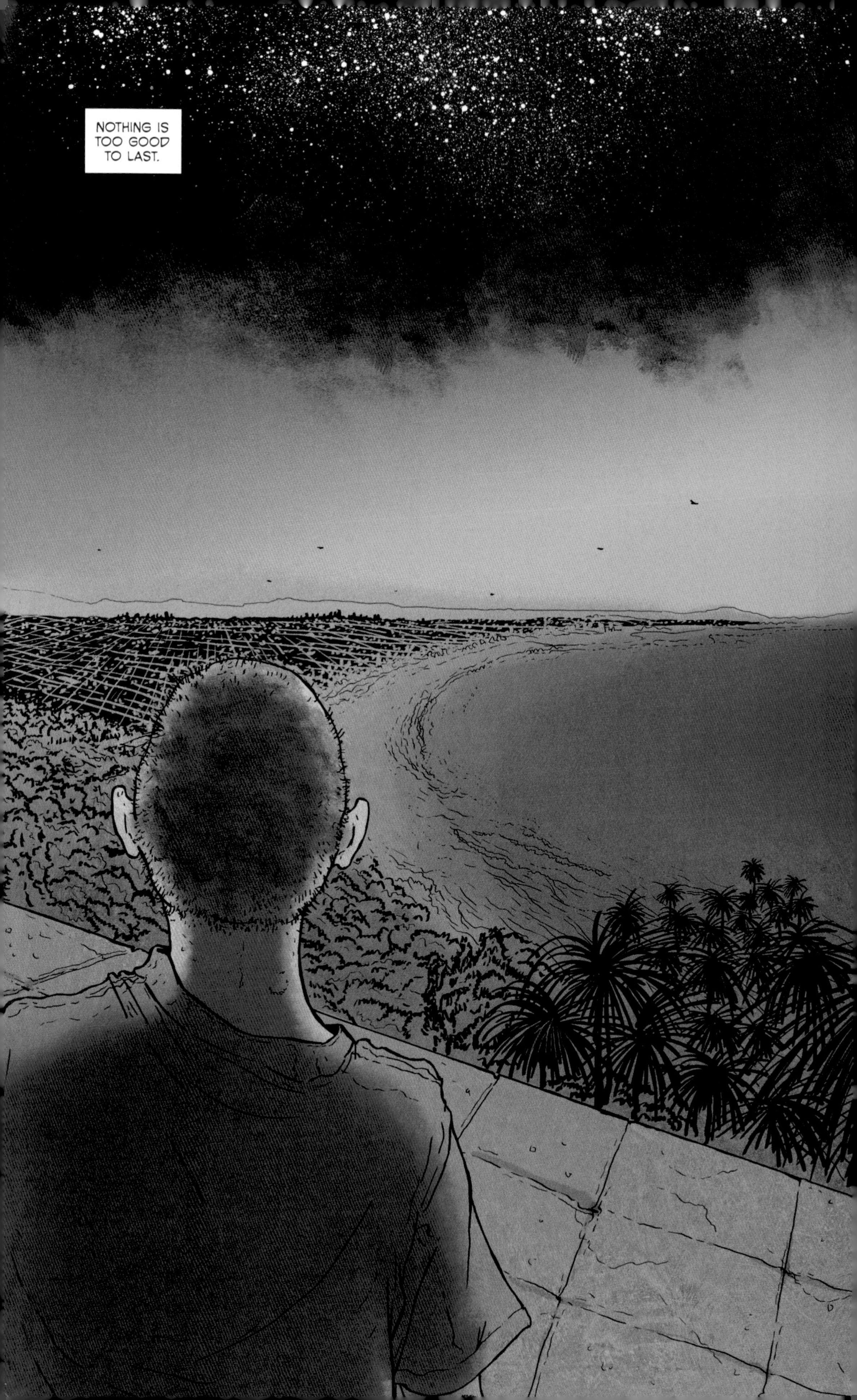
NOTHING IS TOO GOOD TO LAST.

EXTRAS

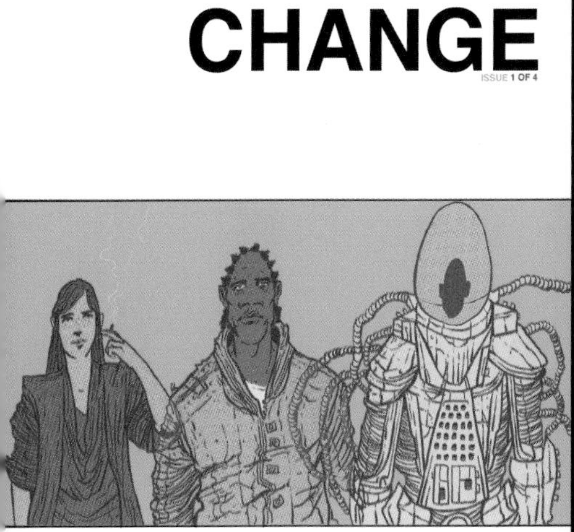
CHANGE
ISSUE 1 OF 4

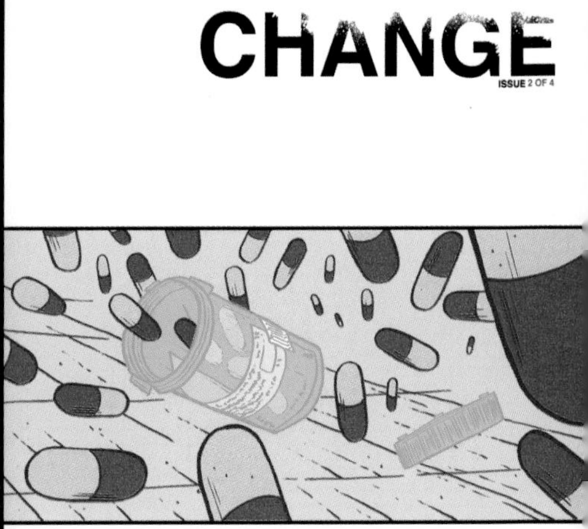
CHANGE
ISSUE 2 OF 4

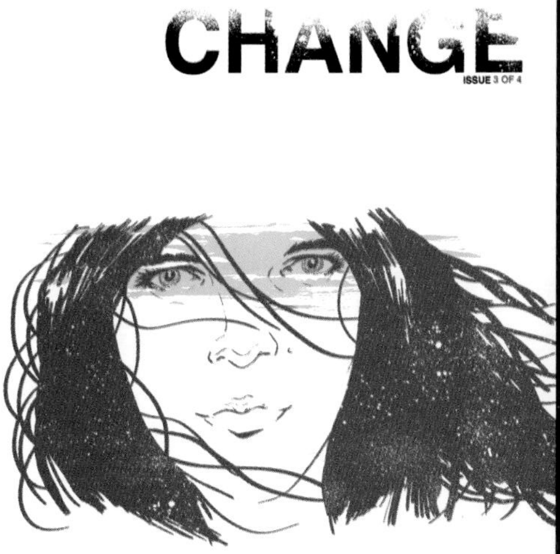
CHANGE
ISSUE 3 OF 4

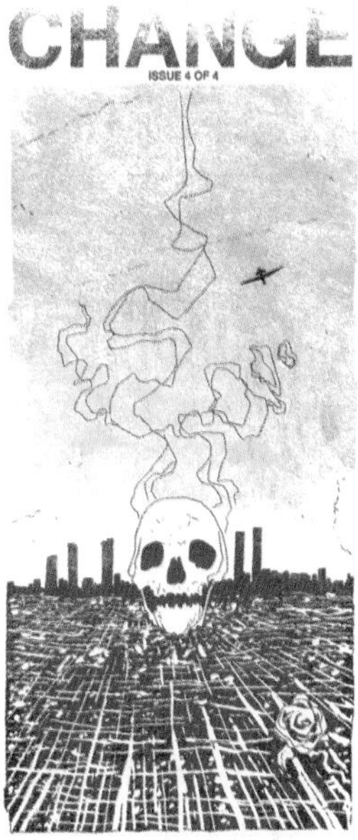
CHANGE
ISSUE 4 OF 4

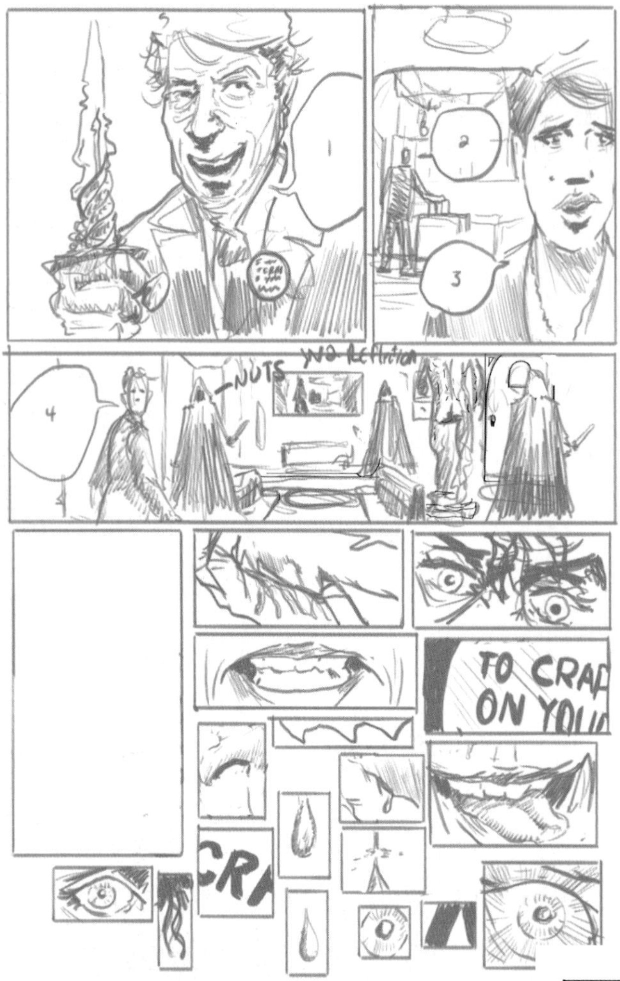
1
2
3
4
NUTS
w/o Reflection
TO CRAP
ON YOUR
CRA

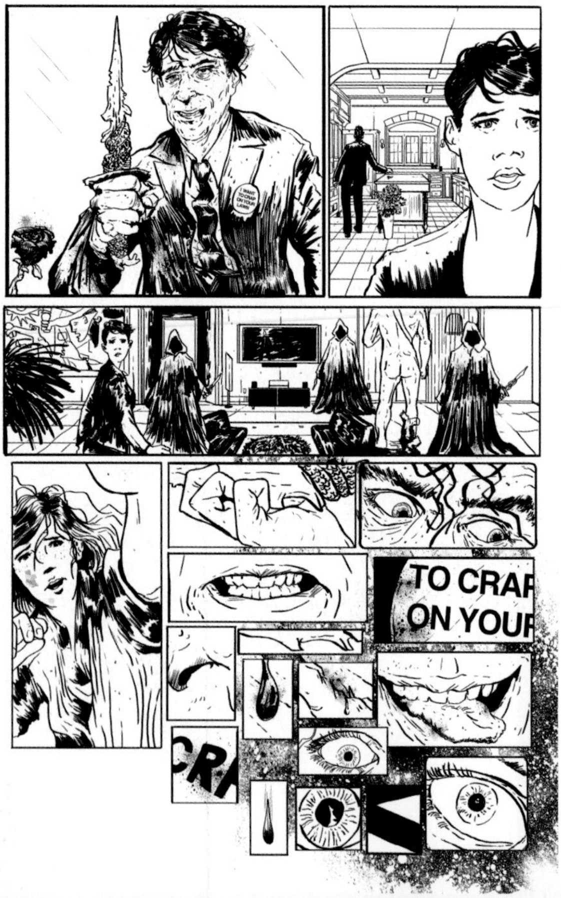
TO CRAP
ON YOUR
CRA

PAGE LAYOUTS

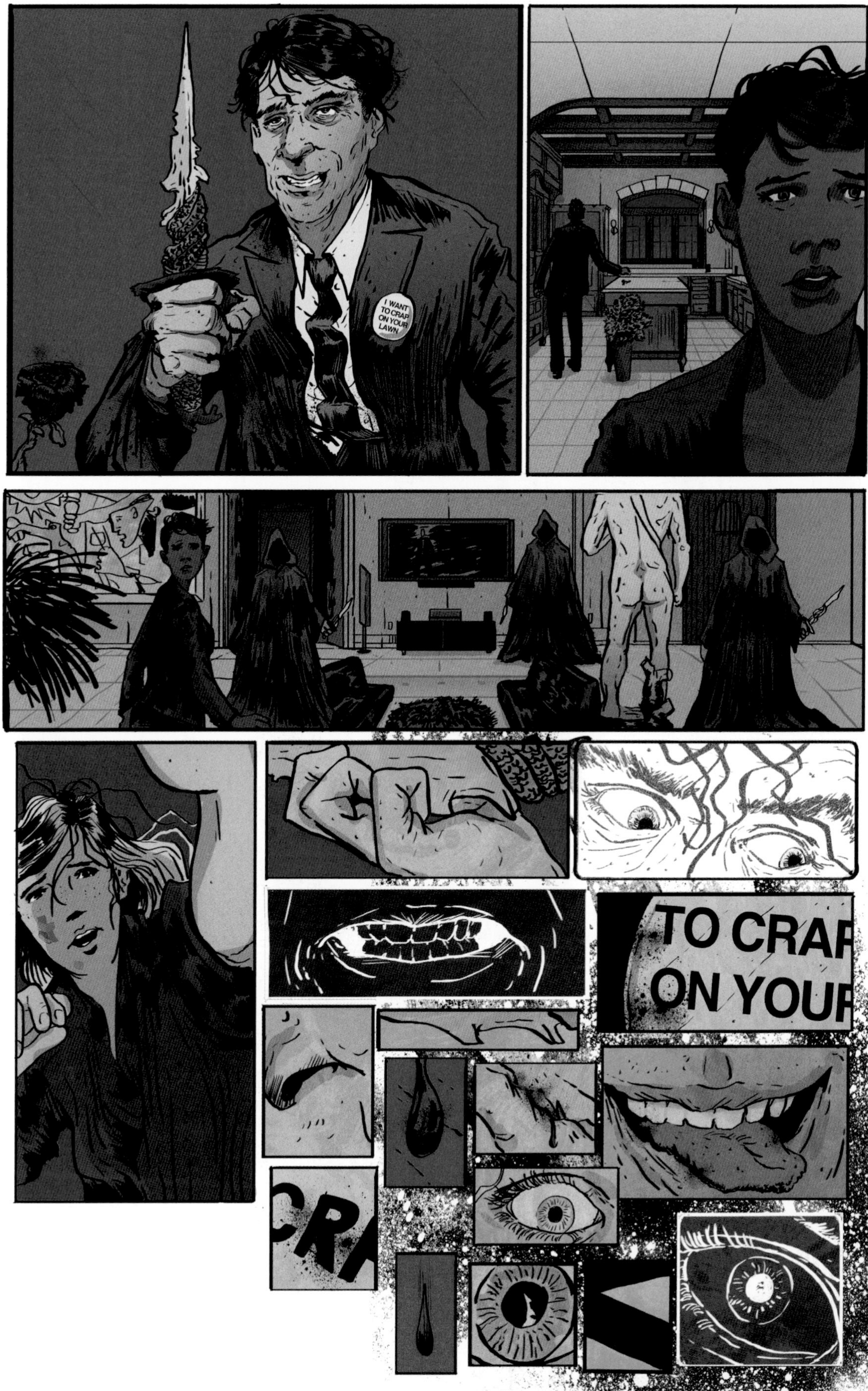
I WANT TO CRAP ON YOUR LAWN
TO CRA
ON YOUR
CR

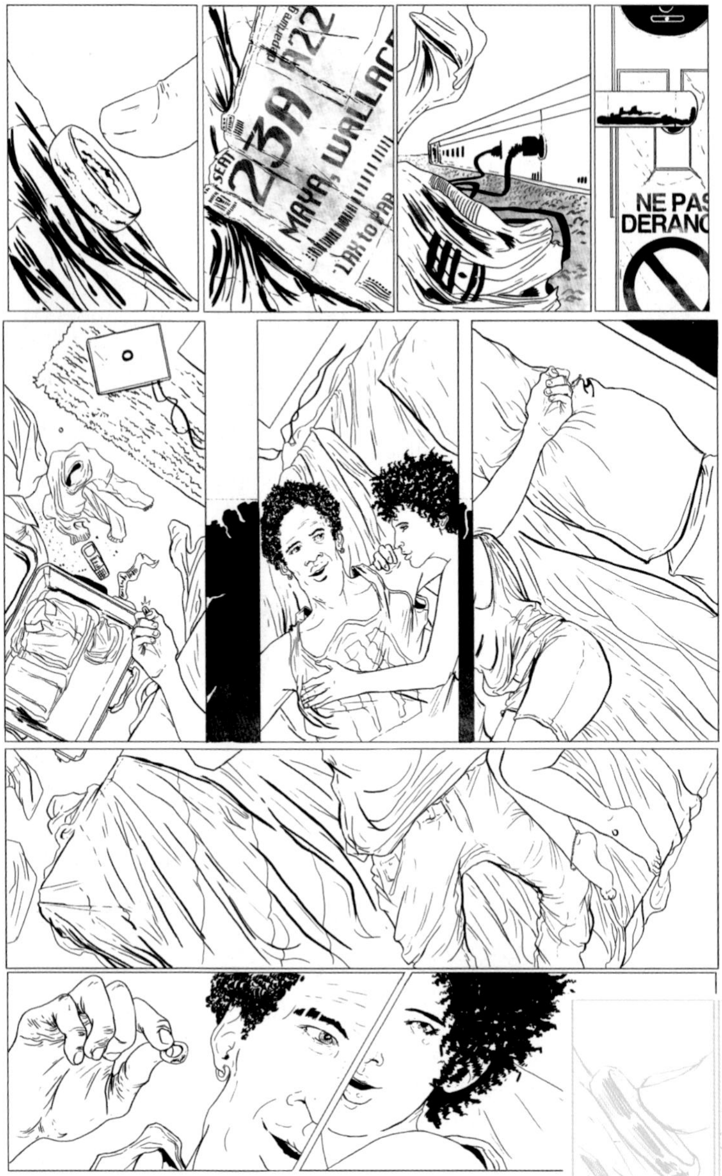
departure
SEAT
23A
A22
MAYA, WALLAC
LAX to PAR
NE PAS
DERAN

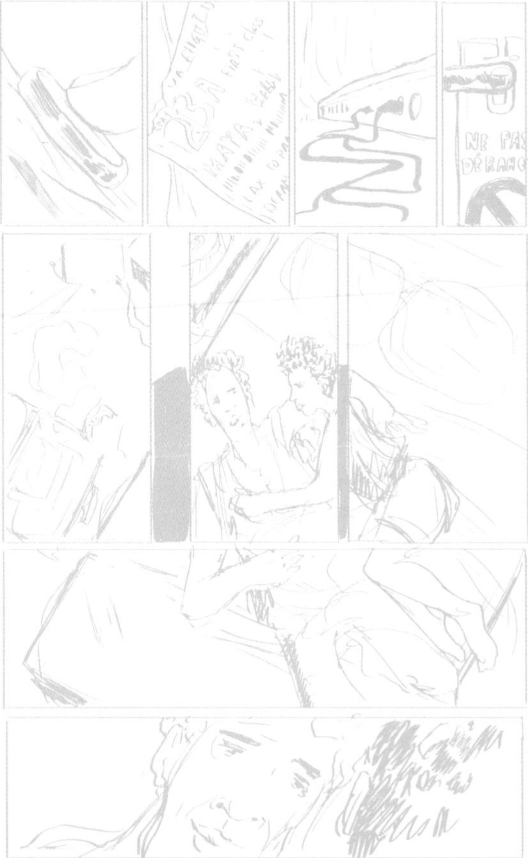

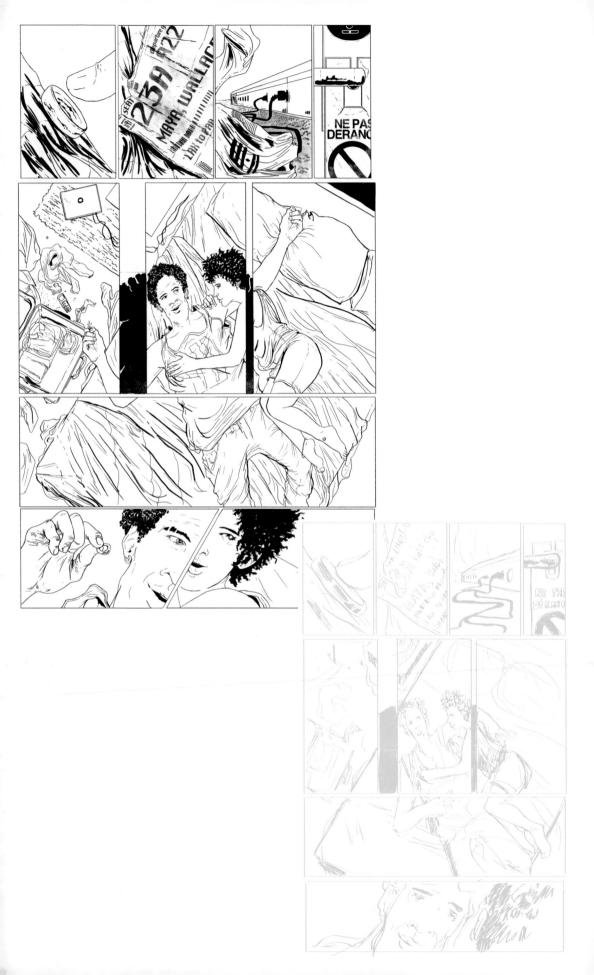

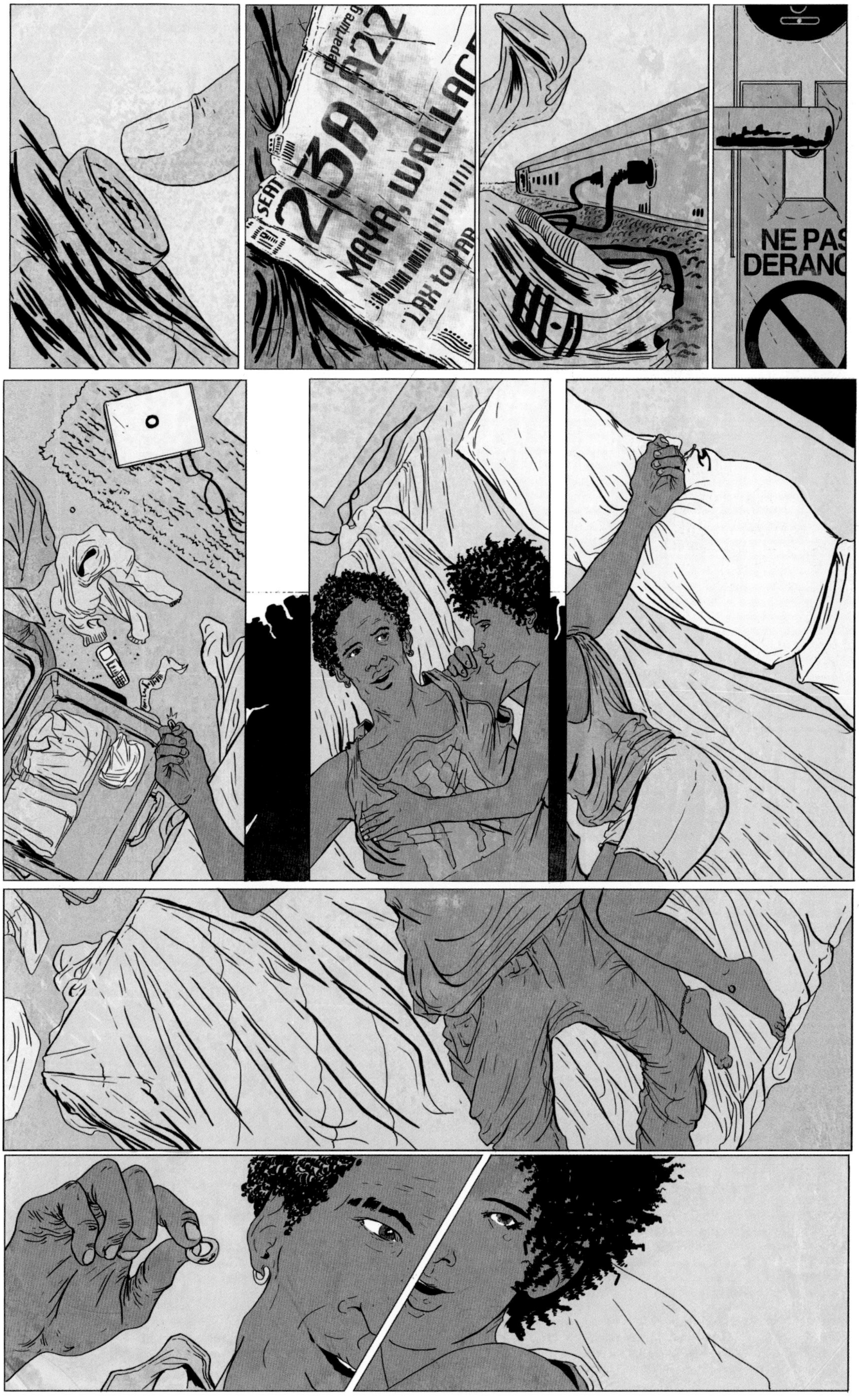

departure g
A22
SEAT
23A
MAYA, WALLAC
LAX to PAR
NE PAS
DERAN

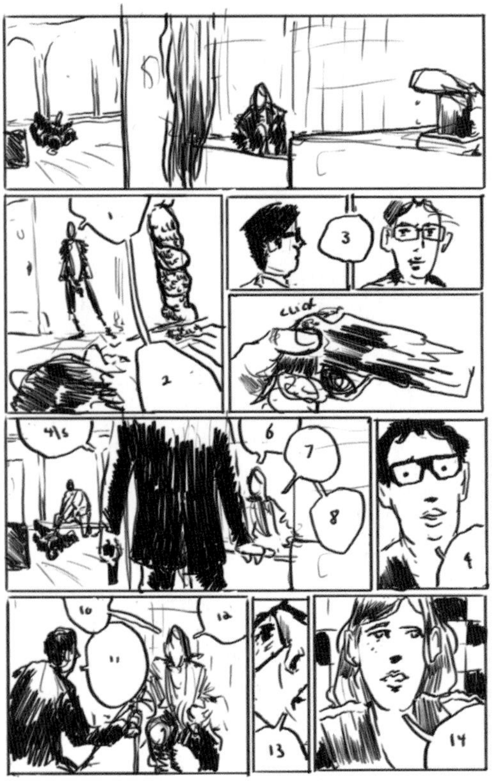
1
2
3
click
4/5
6
7
8
9
10
11
12
13
14

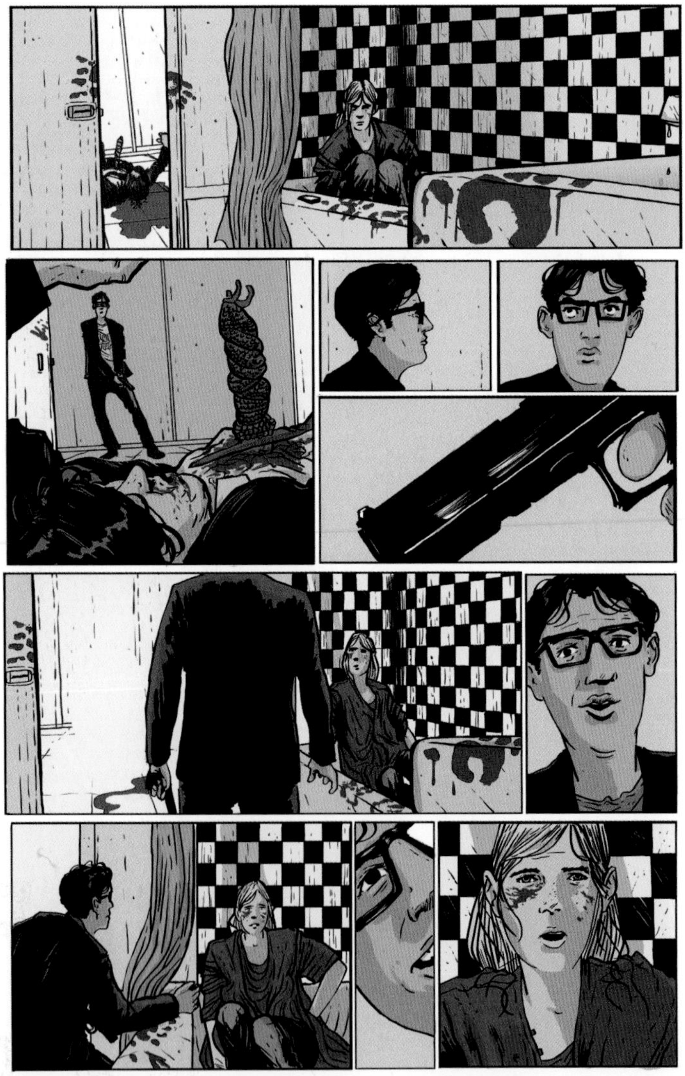

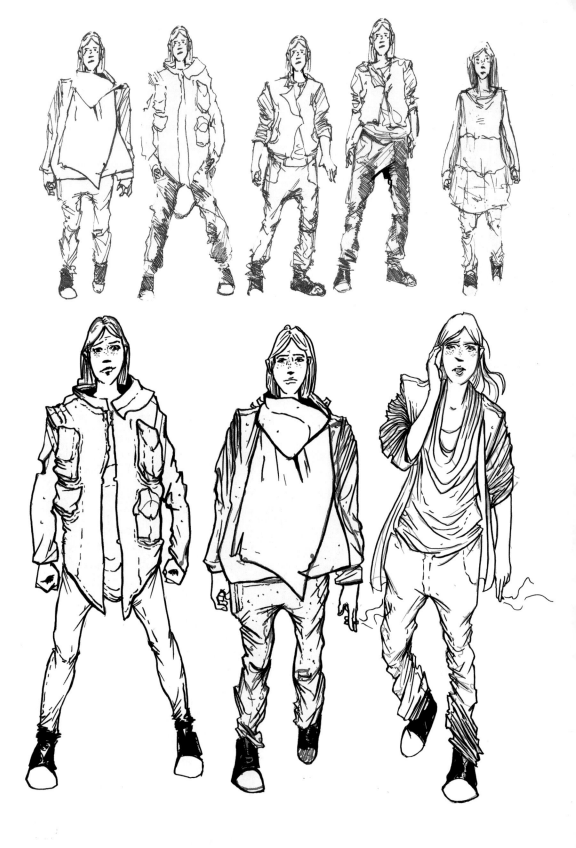

CHARACTER
SKETCHES

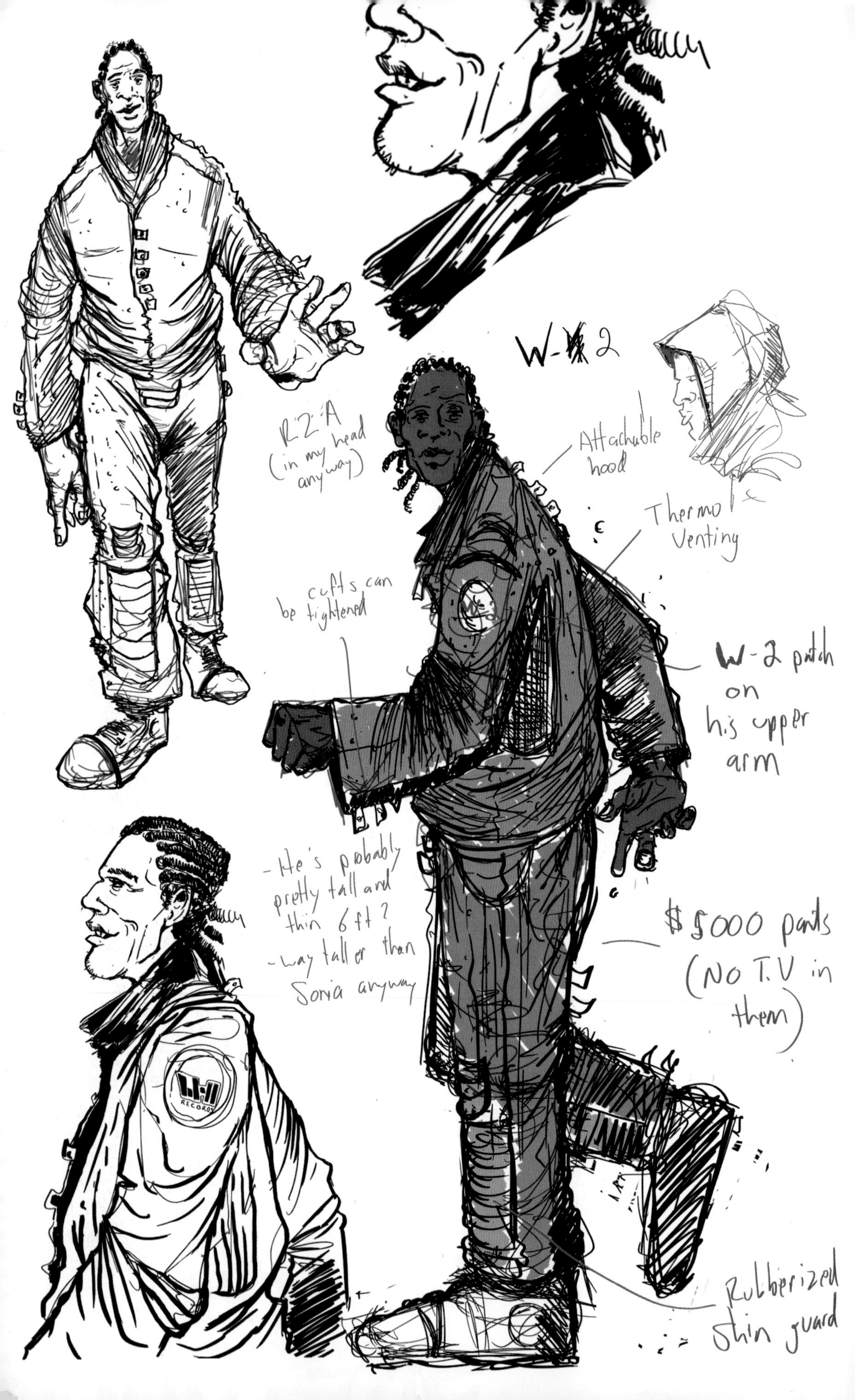

W-2
R2-A
(in my head anyway)
Attachable hood
Thermo Venting
cuffs can be tightened
W-2 patch on his upper arm
-He's probably pretty tall and thin 6 ft?
-way taller than Sonia anyway
$5000 pants (NO T.V in them)
RECORDS
Rubberized shin guard

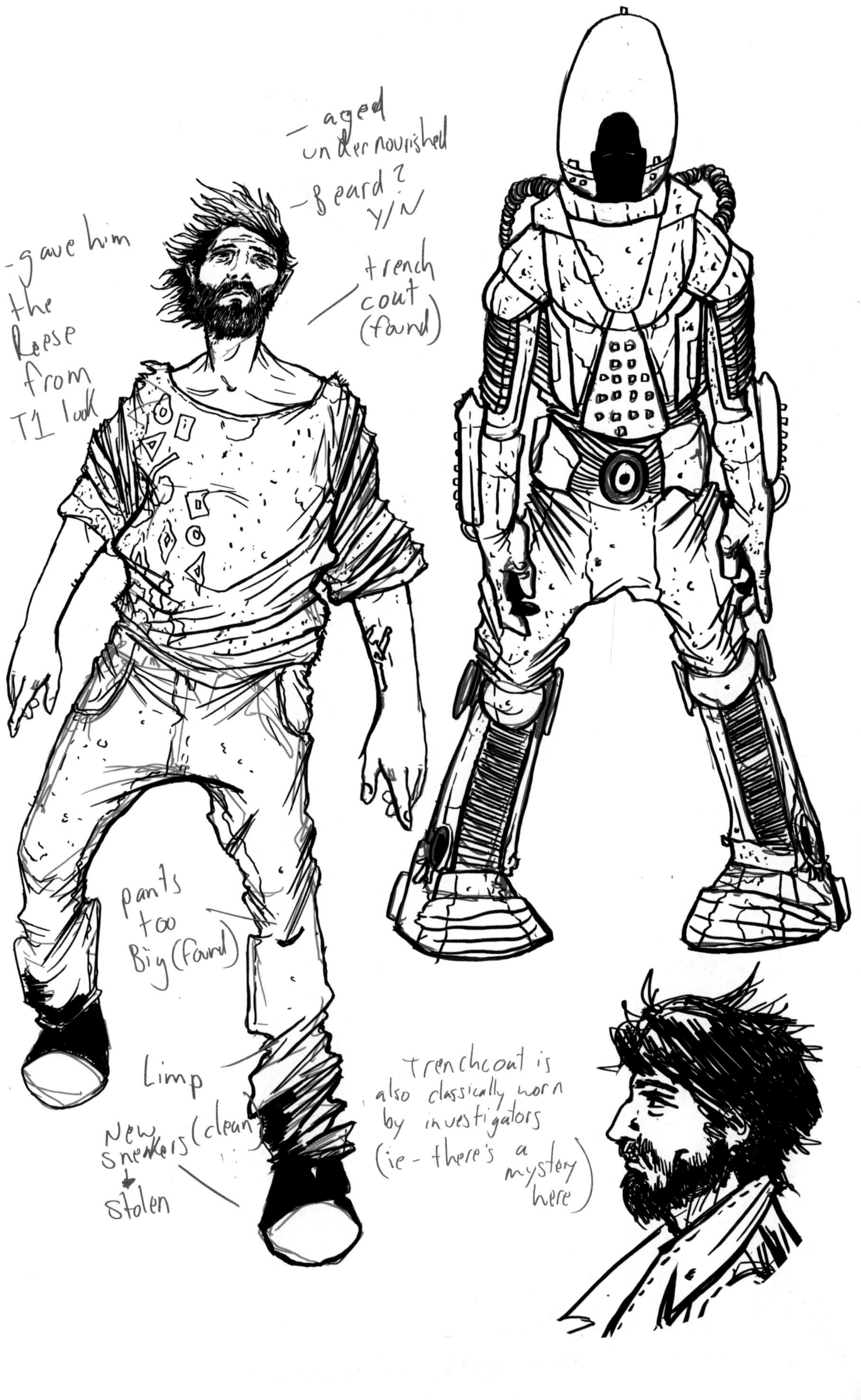

- aged
undernourished
- Beard ? Y/N
- gave him the Reese from T1 look
trench coat (found)
pants too Big (found)
Limp
New sneakers (clean) → stolen
Trenchcoat is also classically worn by investigators (ie - there's a mystery here)

CHANGE